COMPUTER-AIDED DATABASE DESIGN
The DATAID Project

COMPUTER-AIDED DATABASE DESIGN
The DATAID Project

Edited by

Antonio ALBANO
Università di Pisa
Italy

Valeria DE ANTONELLIS
Università di Milano
Italy

and

Antonio DI LEVA
Università di Torino
Italy

1985

NORTH-HOLLAND
AMSTERDAM • NEW YORK • OXFORD

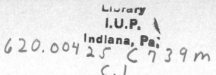
© Elsevier Science Publishers B.V., 1985

ISBN: 0 444 87735 5

Published by:
ELSEVIER SCIENCE PUBLISHERS B.V.
P.O. Box 1991
1000 BZ Amsterdam
The Netherlands

Sole distributors for the U.S.A. and Canada:
ELSEVIER SCIENCE PUBLISHING COMPANY, INC.
52 Vanderbilt Avenue
New York, N.Y. 10017
U.S.A.

PRINTED IN THE NETHERLANDS

PREFACE

At present, database is an important area of study in computer science. On the one hand, it is in itself an area of interest, having produced a large number of results on specific topics, like relational theory, data models, database system architectures, database programming languages, distributed databases, and physical file design. Secondly, it is an area where results of other areas of computer science, such as Programming Languages, Artificial Intelligence and Software Engineering, have been used to produce new interesting applications.

In the last few years, there has been a great interest in database design, where the goal is to combine results from knowledge representation schemas, software engineering, data semantics, relational theory and physical file design in order to define: a) a methodology to go from user requirements to the implementation of applications using DBMSs, through a sequence of structured steps; b) an environment of automated tools to assist the designer during the development process: documentation tools, graphical interfaces, mapping tools between specifications given at different levels of abstraction.

This book addresses both the aspects of database design, and presents a methodology, for centralized and distributed databases, together with a set of automated tools to support the design process. The book itself evolved from the experience of researchers from different Italian universities, industries and research institutions participating in a joint 5-year project, called DATAID, supported by the Italian National Research Council, within the nationwide Progetto Finalizzato Informatica research project.

The book follows a previous one, published two years ago: S. Ceri (ed.), Methodology and Tools for Database Design (North-Holland, Amsterdam, 1983). The latter was mainly concerned with the proposed methodology for centralized databases, although preliminary results regarding the tools under implementation were also included. This book, instead, is mainly dedicated to the description of tools in an advanced stage of implementation and contains the extension of the methodology to distributed databases. We have decided to publish these results because we believe that the DATAID project has achieved significant contributions to the database design field, and the two books contain specific solutions to issues of general interest.

The preparation of the book has covered a period between June and December 1984.

ACKNOWLEDGEMENTS

This book would not have been possible without the support and the encouragement from the direction of the Progetto Finalizzato Informatica, in the persons of Prof. Angelo Raffaele Meo and Dott. Paolo Bronzoni.

THE DATAID PROJECT

DATAID is a 5-year project financed by the Italian National Research Council within the Progetto Finalizzato Informatica. The project started in September 1979 with the participation of several working groups from both the academic and the industrial environments. The aim of the project is the development of a computer aided methodology for database design.

In 1980 a survey was carried out concerning existing methodologies and related tools, and the architecture of a manual methodology, called DATAID-1, was defined.

In 1981 a first version of the methodology was released, and the introduction of automated tools in the design process was considered.

In 1982 the functional specifications of a first set of tools for conceptual design have been produced. For the dissemination of the methodology, several workshops and a first course were held, for which a training manual was prepared. Experimentation of the methodology has been initiated in Local and Central Government applications.

In 1983 and 1984 the methodology has been revised and extended to include distributed database design. At the same time, prototypes of the tools have been developed.

At present, the DATAID working groups are

Universities:

Dipartimento di Elettronica, Politecnico di Milano

Dipartimento di Informatica, Università di Pisa

Dipartimento di Informatica, Università di Torino

Dipartimento di Informatica e Sistemistica, Università di Roma

Istituto di Cibernetica, Università di Milano

Research Centers of Italian National Research Council:

CIOC, Centro di Studio per l'Interazione Operatore-Calcolatore, Bologna

CNUCE, Centro per il Calcolo Elettronico, Pisa

IASI, Istituto di Analisi dei Sistemi ed Informatica, Roma

Industries:

CRAI, Consorzio Calabro per la Ricerca e le Applicazioni nel Settore dell'Informatica, Rende (Cosenza)

CSELT, Centro Studi e Laboratori Telecomunicazioni, Torino

DATABASE Informatica, SpA, Roma

ELEA, SpA, Olivetti Formazione e Consulenza, Firenze

IPACRI, SpA, Istituto per l'Automazione delle Casse di Risparmio Italiane, Roma

Systems & Management, SpA, Torino

Carlo Batini and Antonio Di Leva were coordinators of the project from 1979 to 1981, while the present coordinators of the project are Valeria De Antonellis and Antonio Di Leva.

A list of contributions in journals and of papers presented at conferences as well as technical reports written by project members, from 1979 to 1985, is given in Appendix. Requests for publications may be addressed to the authors.

CONTENTS

COMPUTER-AIDED DATABASE DESIGN: The DATAID Project
A. Albano, V. De Antonellis, and A. Di Leva (Editors)
© Elsevier Science Publishers B.V. (North-Holland), 1985

COMPUTER-AIDED DATABASE DESIGN: THE DATAID APPROACH

Antonio Albano
Dipartimento di Informatica, Università di Pisa
Corso Italia, 40 - 56100 Pisa

Valeria De Antonellis
Istituto di Cibernetica, Università di Milano
Via Viotti, 5 - 20133 Milano

Antonio Di Leva
Dipartimento di Informatica, Università di Torino
Via V. Caluso, 37 - 10125 Torino

The approach to the design of applications using centralized
and distributed databases adopted in the DATAID Project is
described, together with the role of the automated tools that
are to be integrated into a database development environment
to support the design methodology.

1. INTRODUCTION

The development of computer technology, and the reduction of its
costs, continuously increase the use of DBMSs to maintain the data
needed by the functions of an organization. In the early '70s, DBMSs
were used to support basic, independent and structured organizatio-
nal functions. The trend is now toward a global integration of
functions, with DBMSs used to support managers in decision making;
and in the future DBMSs will be integrated with expert systems to
build computerized information systems that will be more effective
for decision makers, and able to assist non-expert users in gaining
access to data and in interpreting them.

The growing use of DBMSs, the complexity of the new applications,
and the need to implement database applications that can be readily
adapted to changes in user requirements, has led to an increasing
demand for environments with an integrated set of automated tools to
support both the design and the maintenance of database
applications. The problem is similar to that of software engineering
and the following strategies have been suggested: a) the definition
of a design methodology composed of a set of structured steps in
which design decisions are considered one at a time to obtain a
satisfactory design; b) the definition of techniques to be used
during the design steps; c) the definition of tools for an automated
development support system. Database design techniques are required
basically for the following activities:

. Data Analysis, to help the users in organizing their information
  needs in a structured and stable way to support the evolution of
  the applications easily.

. Prototyping, to build an early version of the system to be
  implemented that exhibits the essential features of the future
  operational system, except for the resource requirements and
  performance. A prototype helps the users both to determine

whether or not the system in development matches their
requirements before the final implementation begins, and to
improve their perception of organization needs.

. Implementation, to convert the results of analysis and the
  prototype into an operative system with a satisfactory storage
  use and an efficient execution of applications.

The approach to the design of applications using a centralized or a
distributed database adopted in the DATAID Project is described,
together with an overview of the role of the automated tools under
development. Section 2 describes the aspects considered during the
database design process, the proposed abstraction mechanisms and the
diagrammatic representations used. Section 3 presents the DATAID
methodology, and Section 4 describes the automated tools.

2. WHAT TO MODEL AND HOW TO MODEL

Among researchers and practitioners there is general consensus about
the basic aspects that should be modeled during the database design
process:

. Concrete knowledge, that is, the entities of the observed
  system, their properties and relationships between them.

. Abstract knowledge, that is, the integrity constraints, which
  impose restrictions on the legal states of the model of the
  observed system.

. Procedural knowledge, that is, the basic operations that must be
  applied to the concrete knowledge so that the model evolves to
  reflect the changes in the observed system.

. Dynamics, that is, how the concrete and procedural knowledge can
  be used to model the permissible sequences of events in the
  organization's functions (or activities), and communication both
  among activities and activities and users.

The approaches to database design can differ about the methodology
adopted in data analysis, the abstraction mechanisms used to model
the above aspects, and the features of the language designed to
support the abstraction mechanisms during requirements specification
and conceptual design /6,7,8/. In the DATAID Project the following
alternatives have been investigated.

Concrete Knowledge

Two data models have been used: an Enriched Entity Relationship
Model (EERM) and a Semantic Data Model (SDM).

EERM provides the analyst with four abstraction mechanisms:
entities, relationships, attributes, and abstraction hierarchies
/9/. The differences between the EERM and the ER model introduced by
P.P. Chen /11/ are:

Abstraction hierarchies. The first type of hierarchy is the 'subset
relationship': an entity E_1 is a subset of the entity E_2 if every
occurrence of E_1 is an occurrence of E_2 as well. The second type of
hierarchy is the 'generalization': an entity E is a generalization

of the entities $E_1, \ldots, E_n$, if each occurrence of E is also an occurrence of at most one of the entities $E_1, \ldots, E_n$ (ISA exclusive hierarchy). The partition over the occurrences of E is established by the value of a property of E (underlying attribute). Both in subset relationships and in generalizations, attributes and relationships of the entity at the upper level of a hierarchy are inherited by the entities at the lower level, which may have additional attributes and relationships. Abstraction hierarchies are 'complete' if for each occurrence of the upper level entity there exists a corresponding occurrence of the entity immediately lower in level.

Aggregates. A set of attributes that can be referred to as a single property.

Repeating attributes. Attributes that can have more than one value.

Identifiers. An internal identifier is an attribute or a group of attributes that determine uniquely an entity; entities may also be identified through other entities associated with them (external identifiers).

The diagrammatic representation of the EERM abstraction mechanisms is shown in Table 1.

SDM provides the analyst with at least the following mechanisms:

Classification. The entities being modeled that share common properties are gathered into classes. The names of the classes denote the elements present in the database. The elements of a class are represented uniquely, that is, only one copy of each element is allowed.

Aggregation. The elements of classes are aggregates, i.e., they are abstractions having heterogeneous components and may have elements of other classes as components. Consequently, relationships among entities are represented by aggregations, rather than with a separate mechanism as in EERM.

Generalization. Classes themselves can be organized in a hierarchy through a partial order relationship, often referred to as the ISA hierarchy: classes in this relationship model entities that play different roles in the observed system, and may be described with a different level of detail. If A is a subclass of B, the following properties hold: a) the elements of A are in every state a subset of the elements of B; b) the elements of A inherit all the properties of the B elements.

Other features of a SDM are: a) it supports multi-valued attributes; b) it allows the definition of procedurally defined information, such as derived attributes or derived classes; c) it provides special syntax for common constraints, such as ranges for attributes, cardinality of relationships, identifying attributes, optional vs. required attributes, modifiable vs. constant attributes /6,14/.

The diagrammatic representation of the abstraction mechanisms is the same as that of EERM, with only this difference, that instead of naming a relationship in a diamond, in the case of SDM the names of the attributes used to model the relationship with the aggregation are shown.

CONCEPT	REPRESENTATION
ENTITY	
RELATIONSHIP (total/partial)	
RELATIONSHIP (1:1 / 1:n / n:m)	
ATTRIBUTE (total/partial)	
IDENTIFIER (internal/external)	
REPEATING ATTRIBUTE	
AGGREGATE	
GENERALIZATION HIERARCHY with underlying attribute: a	
SUBSET HIERARCHY	
COMPLETE HIERARCHY	

Table 1

Abstract Knowledge

General constraints, different from those for which a special
syntactic form is provided in the data models, can be stated in
natural language in EERM and in the conceptual language Galileo in
SDM /1/.

Procedural Knowledge

Several forms are provided to define special operations for
manipulating objects in semantically meaningful ways, and to specify
access requirements.

In the requirements collection and analysis phase the procedural
knowledge is described by Operations Glossary. For each operation
(transaction) the following aspects are specified: a natural
language description; operation type (read, insert, delete);
execution type (on-line, batch); frequency of execution; data
involved and their role (input, output, visited) /13/.

In the conceptual design phase, with the approach based on EERM,
operations can be defined at three levels of abstraction:
conceptual, navigational and executable. The goal of a conceptual
description is to specify the names and types of the data needed by
an operation to ensure that the operation view is consistent with
the conceptual schema. The goal of a navigational description is to
specify the data needed by an operation, together with: a) the
sequence in which tha data are accessed; b) the type of usage (read,
insert, delete); c) the quantitative information on data usage in a
period of interest (the number of times that an access step is
executed, and an estimate of the number of records accessed by each
such step).   Finally, the goal of an executable description is to
give an operational specification. For each level both a textual and
a diagrammatic representation is provided /4/.

With the approach based on SDM, the procedural knowledge is
described for three different purposes using the conceptual language
Galileo. First, to specify derived information, such as derived
attributes and derived classes. Second, to define domain-dependent
operations to manipulate objects in a semantically meaningful way.
The role of these operations is similar to those associated with
abstract data types. Third, to define procedures guaranteed to leave
the database in a consistent state (transactions), providing
moreover facilities for raising and handling exceptions /1/. A
version of Galileo has been defined to specify operational
requirements at different levels of abstraction in a non-executable
language including a construct to specify quantitative data during
the requirements collection and analysis phase /2/.

Dynamics

In the requirements collection and analysis phase, dynamics is
described by Events Glossary, which deals with the following
aspects: precedence relationships among events; data and operations
involved. For each event an Event Specification Form is filled to
give information on the related conditions and operations /13/.

In the conceptual design phase, dynamics is described by means of
Petri Nets or by processes /2,9/. Petri Nets are used with the

Condition-Event interpretation and they have been extended with definitional capabilities to deal with message passing among the functions to be automated. Processes are modeled in Galileo, which has been extended with a construct similar to 'scripts' of Taxis /2,3/.

3. THE DATAID METHODOLOGY

The aim of a database design methodology is to transform a user-oriented linguistic representation of the information needs of an organization into a DBMS-oriented description. This process is performed through several phases.

In the requirements collection and analysis phase, user requirements are translated into a requirements schema which is: user independent (that is, requirements are normalized according to established standards); and conceptual model independent (that is, no choice is made at this level regarding the structures of a model used to represent the information of interest). In the conceptual design phase, the requirements schema is formalized into a conceptual schema which is DBMS independent (in that, no choice is made at this level regarding the implementation structures). Finally, in the logical and physical design phases, the result is a DBMS dependent schema, that is, it is a DBMS processable schema.

The DATAID-1 methodology covers all these phases as illustrated in the following /10/. It assumes that the analysis of the organization, of its information flows, and the cost-benefit analysis have already been performed before the actual start of the database design process.

Inputs of the requirements collection and analysis phase are informal and heterogeneous descriptions of the observed system. Two classes of descriptions are considered: natural language sentences (derived from pre-existing documents, results of interviews or meetings, paper files); traditional/DBMS files. A recent extension of DATAID-1 deals with forms analysis as well /5/.

Output of the phase is a collection of glossaries describing data, operations, and events. To fill in the glossaries, natural language descriptions are filtered and rewritten in a restricted language; revised requirements are then classified into different sentence types (data, operations and events sentences). Intra-glossary and inter-glossaries checks concerning completeness and consistency are performed to prevent transmission and amplification of errors.

In the conceptual design phase a conceptual view is built for each environment of the organization (view modeling); these views are then integrated to form a global conceptual description of the database (view integration). The conceptual schema of an environment is the formalized representation of both the static and dynamic requiremants. As regards the conceptual model, we have adopted the EERM for data, constraints and operations modeling, and Petri Nets for functions modeling.

The design of local views is based on operations modeling. For each operation, an operation schema is built which describes the required data. The data schema is built progressively: when an operation schema is completed, data structures which have been introduced are aggregated with the previous partial data schema. This process is iterated for all the operations and, eventually, it produces the data schema. To start the aggregation process, we consider two alternative cases. In one case we use a skeleton schema: this happens when in the organization data are found naturally structured into entities, attributes and relationships. In the other case, an initial operation schema is built for the most relevant operation.

The organization functions are analyzed in terms of events, and are represented by Petri Nets graphs. These graphs show the causal dependencies/independencies between events (by means of structures of sequence, conflict and concurrency) and represent the way in which the functions to be automated must be executed.

In the views integration process, strategies (based on conflict analysis, merging, enrichment, and restructuring) are provided to deal with the problem deriving from the fact that objects (and their properties) which are common to different views have not been modeled in the same way (i.e. by means of the same name, classification structures, and integrity constraints structures) in the different schemata. After the integrated data schema has been constructed, integrated operation schemata are produced, and the events schemata are coordinated through communication links which represent message exchanges between functions.

The process of logical design maps from the conceptual schema to a logical schema of the DBMS chosen for the implementation. Two classes of DBMS are considered in the present version of the methodology: relational DBMSs and network (Codasyl-like) DBMSs.

The transformation process is based on two fundamental tasks:

.   Simplification of the global conceptual schema: data structures not directly translatable into the logical model (like generalization hierarchies and multiple relationships) are converted into simpler ones. This task produces a simplified schema which contains only entities and binary relationships.

.   Refinement of the simplified schema: a set of transformations on the simplified schema is applied (typically, partitioning of the entities and replication of attributes); performance measures are used in order to select, among different alternatives, the solution which optimizes the execution of the most important operations.

The aim of the physical design phase is to provide database designers with a complete framework of design decisions and to guide them through the design process to select the best physical design.

The physical design decisions for Codasyl-like databases are subdivided into three broad decision areas:

.   Access path support decisions: implementation strategies for entry point records (LOCATION MODE clause options) and sets (SET MODE clause options) are considered.

.   Placement strategy decisions: member records of a set are dispersed throughout the database area or clustered so that neighbouring member records tend to be stored in the vicinity.

.   Storage allocation decisions: database areas for storage of records, indexes and pointer array tables are selected; each area is subdivided into a number of pages and the page length is fixed.

The methodology is based on the evaluation of all possible record and set implementation strategies from the global processing point of view. This is accomplished in the following tasks:

.   Creation of record usage trees: accesses to a record are globally described as a tree where the leaf nodes are the different types of operations performed on the object record.

.   Storage allocation: heuristic rules are used for calculating record length, record allocation in areas, area and page sizes, and other physical parameters.

.   Evaluation of implementation strategies: starting from the relative costs and frequencies of the operations, implementation strategies are evaluated.

The main goal of the physical design for relational DBMSs is the selection of the secondary indexes of the relations of the schema; the choice of primary indexes (or keys) has already been made in the logical design phase.

The method is based on the following assumptions, that are quite realistic in the case of small/medium size DBMSs:

a) The indexes are structured as B^+-trees.
b) At most one index per relation can be used to access tuples in executing an operation.
c) Joins are performed according to the nested loops method.
d) The primary key cannot be updated and an index cannot be used to access tuples if it is currently modified.
e) The criteria used by the optimizer to evaluate execution costs are known.

The physical design is then consistent with the choices made by the optimizer and consists of four tasks:

.   Specification of database statistics: these data are obtained transforming the results of the logical design phase.

.   Cost evaluation: it provides a matrix giving the costs of all operations, each being executed when only one of all possible indexes is built on the relations.

.   Index comparison: indexes are compared and the less efficient are eliminated.

.   Generation of an efficient set of indexes: the final relational schema, in which all secondary indexes are determined, is constructed.

Classification of Methodologies and the DATAID Role

In the following we consider some classification criteria for methodologies and specify the role of the DATAID-1 methodology with respect to them. Methodologies can be classified according to several features.

A first classification distinguishes data-oriented methodologies which focus on properties of data (to enhance the stability of the design with respect to changes of the application), and function-oriented methodologies which focus on functions (to enhance the efficiency of the application execution). In recent years, however, methodologies are oriented so as to integrate both these approaches. As regards the DATAID-1 methodology, both data and functions are analyzed. Specifically, in designing a data schema we start from the data involved in each function.

A second classification distinguishes top-down approaches (in which the design process starts from the general constraints imposed by a skeleton schema), and bottom-up approaches (in which the design process starts from the examination of the detailed user needs). In practice, the development of a complete top-down design for the entire organization has proven to be too time-consuming and difficult. Nevertheless, an overall organization view must be developed and used to insure the consistency of the design. Thus, recent proposals suggest the use of both approaches in different phases of the methodology. In DATAID-1 we start from an overall view of the organization, of its environments, and of the functions to be automated. If possible, a skeleton schema is constructed. Then, single views are obtained by aggregating new knowledge in incremental way in respect to operations description. Finally, these views are integrated to obtain the global conceptual schema. In this sense, we have both global and modular design. Furthermore, to enhance the initial analysis of the organization, extensions involving the definition of interfaces toward information system design methodologies are being investigated.

A third classification distinguishes methodologies in which a conceptualization phase exists, and methodologies which directly provide a logical schema. In DATAID-1 conceptual design and logical design are distinguished. Conceptual modeling is performed by means of a DBMS independent data model.

Finally, a fourth classification distinguishes, according to the system architecture, methodologies oriented to centralized systems, and methodologies oriented to distributed systems. The extension of DATAID-1 to the distributed aspects has been performed and is described in this book. Specifically, the logical and physical phases have been extended to take into account horizontal and vertical fragmentation (logical design) and the allocation of fragments into the network nodes (physical design).

4. TOOLS FOR DATABASE DESIGN

The availability of a set of automated tools is an important feature of a design methodology, since many design activities are complex and time-consuming. In /12/ a survey of the state of the art for database design tools reports on the characteristics of 55 manual or automated tools. The aim of a tool is to support the designer in performing the following activities: schema specification and testing; detection of specification inconsistencies; proposal of scenarios which help in solving inconsistencies; maintenance and updating of the specifications.

Such activities can be classified into:

.   Documentation activities, whose aim is to build a representation of the design objects which can be retrieved and updated.

- Design activities, whose aim is to build a schema which satisfies user requirements.

According to this classification, in a tool we distinguish documentation functions (which aid in describing, maintaining, and analyzing design descriptions), and design functions (which aid in making choices related to the schema design).

Documentation functions allow communication among designers, and are particularly useful when many people are involved in the design. Further they allow the users to verify the design and to test its adequacy in respect to the initial requirements. The availability of such functions results in several advantages:

- The documentation quality is improved (descriptions are more precise and consistent).
- Capabilities of automatic information analysis are provided (analytic, synthetic, and cross-referencing reports are produced).
- The completeness of the documentation is enforced (input is guided via menu, forms, graphical symbols).

Design functions allow to check the consistency of a large amount of data and to guide the designer in performing design transformations. As regards the semantic checks: synonyms, homonyms, types consistency, constraints consistency, and redundancies are verified. To solve inconsistencies, scenarios are proposed when possible. As regards transformations, the designer is guided through the different phases of the design process (analysis, conceptualization, translation into logical/physical schema).

Automated Tools in the DATAID Project

Several automated tools have been developed within the project. In the following, we will give a brief description of INCOD-DTE, Dialogo, and ISIDE, which are presented in this volume. A preliminary description of these tools was given in /10/, where other tools were also included: NLDA, a tool with a natural language interface to support requirements analysis, and ISTDA, a tool for conceptual modeling of data and transactions based on a binary data model. Another tool under development is CATRA, to construct and verify glossaries during the requirements collection and analysis phase.

INCOD-DTE (Interactive Conceptual Design: Data, Transactions, Events) was developed at the Dipartimento di Informatica e Sistemistica - Università di Roma, and at the Istituto di Cibernetica - Università di Milano, with the collaboration of Database Informatica SpA - Roma. The tool provides an integrated environment for the definition of data, transactions, and events. Data are described using the EERM. Transactions are described at different levels of abstraction: conceptual, navigational, and executable. Events are modeled through Petri Nets, and are specified using events specification commands. INCOD-DTE can support the designer in the conceptualization of static and dynamic requirements, automatically checking the consistency of the process and simplifying the management of the documentation. It handles several types of metadata, interacts with the user in discovering conflicts, prompting possible solutions (scenarios) and guiding him through certain steps of the design activities. INCOD-DTE is now being extended with GINCOD, a graphical interface that can also be seen as a self-contained graphical editor for interactive design of conceptual schemas expressed in terms of diagrams. Placement of symbols and layout of diagrams can be controled by the designer (with classical graphic editing commands) or by the system.

Dialogo was developed at the Dipartimento di Informatica - Università di Pisa with the collaboration of Systems & Management SpA - Torino. Dialogo is an interactive system that allows the use of the conceptual language Galileo in the design of a conceptual schema, which is an operational design specification to be used as a prototype of the system to be implemented. This prototype is useful to test the conceptual schema on sample data to validate both the design and the requirements together with the users. The main characteristics of Dialogo are that the user interacts with the system using a single language to: edit the schema and operations definitions; ask the system for information about definitions; load sample data to test the behavior of the operations; define new functions to personalize the working environment. Dialogo is now being extended to manage also the phase of requirements collection and analysis in a unified environment.

INCOD-DTE and Dialogo can be seen as two complementary attempts to design effective tools for the conceptual design. In INCOD-DTE major emphasis is given to identifying specific design activities which can be charged to an automatic system; e.g. in order to increase the readability of the schema, several possible restructurings can be tried out: while it is the designer who must find the fragments of the schema to be restructured, the system can perform the transformation. In Dialogo the central effort is to provide a programming language to express data semantics, constraints, transactions, and dynamics naturally at the conceptual level. Although the systems are based on different data models, i.e., EERM and SDM, the facilities provided by INCOD-DTE can also be embedded in Dialogo, and, in fact, the conceptual design produced by INCOD-DTE can be considered as a first step toward an executable design specification formulated in Galileo.

The automated tools for the logical and physical design phases are under development as a joint project - the ISIDE (Integrated System for Implementation DEsign) project - by the Dipartimento di Informatica - Università di Torino, CIOC - Bologna, CSELT - Torino and CRAI - Cosenza. ISIDE is a collection of integrated tools that support the logical and physical design phases and give an evaluation of data manipulation operations considered in the conceptual phase. ISIDE has six modules:

The Dynamics Analyzer generates the quantitative parameters for the logical and physical design processes.

The Logical Designer (EASYMAP) maps from the conceptual design to a Codasyl or relational logical design. The mapping process is driven by the quantitative parameters that characterize the workload defined on the database.

The Relational Physical Designer (IDEA) and the Codasyl Physical Designer (EROS) refine the logical schema with the appropriate physical data structures statements provided by the target DBMS.

The Relational and Codasyl Performance Predictors (IDEA and EOS) help the designer in testing the adequacy of the design decisions. Giving a processing scenario (number and type of transactions simultaneously active on the DBMS at a given time), and the hardware configuration description, the predictors evaluate the expected response time for each transaction. This information can be used to check whether the design is likely to satisfy user efficiency requirements.

5. CONCLUSIONS

The approach adopted within the DATAID Project to computer aided design of applications using a centralized or a distributed database has been described. The main results of the project are: a) a design methodology which covers all phases of the database design process; b) interactive tools for conceptual data analysis and prototyping to reduce coding and maintenance costs; c) a collection of design techniques supported by automated tools. At the moment, the tools have not been integrated into a database development environment since the project aims first at experimenting their effectiveness separately. Once the tools have been validated, they will be integrated into an industrial prototype.

REFERENCES

/1/   Albano, A., L. Cardelli, and R. Orsini, Galileo: A Strongly Typed, Interactive Conceptual Language, ACM TODS (1985) (to appear).

/2/   Albano, A., and R. Orsini, A Software Engineering Approach to Database Design: the Galileo Project (in this volume).

/3/   Barron, J., Dialogue and Process Design for Interactive Information System Using TAXIS, Proc. ACM SIGOA Conf. on Office Information Systems (June 1982) 12-20.

/4/   Batini, C., M. Lenzerini, and M. Moscarini, Views Integration, in: Ceri, S. (ed), Methodology and Tools for Database Design (North-Holland, Amsterdam, 1983).

/5/   Batini, C., B.G. Demo, and A. Di Leva, A Methodology for Conceptual Design of Office Data Bases, Information Systems 9, 4 (1984).

/6/   Borgida, A., Features of Languages for Conceptual Information System Development, IEEE Software (1984) (to appear).

/7/   Brodie, M.L., J. Mylopoulos, and J.W. Schmidt (eds.), On Conceptual Modeling (Springer Verlag, New York, 1984).

/8/   Bubenko, J.A., Information Modeling in the Context of System Development, IFIP Congress 80 (North-Holland, Amsterdam, 1980) 395-411.

/9/   Bussolati, U., S. Ceri, V. De Antonellis, and B. Zonta, Views Conceptual Design, in: Ceri, S. (ed), Methodology and Tools for Database Design (North-Holland, Amsterdam, 1983).

/10/ Ceri, S. (ed), Methodology and Tools for Database Design (North-Holland, Amsterdam, 1983).

/11/ Chen, P.P., The Entity Relationship Model: Toward a Unified View of Data, ACM TODS 1,1 (1976) 9-36.

/12/ Chen, P.P., I. Chung, D. Perry, Survey of the State of the Art of Logical Database Design Tools, National Bureau of Standards, GCR 82-389 (1982).

/13/ De Antonellis, V., and B.G. Demo, Requirements Collection and Analysis, in: Ceri, S. (ed), Methodology and Tools for Database Design (North-Holland, Amsterdam, 1983).

/14/ King, R., and D. McLeod, Semantic Data Models, in: Yao S.B. (ed.), Principle of Database Design (Prentice-Hall, Englewood Cliffs, N.J.) (to appear).

PART I
TOOLS FOR DATABASE DESIGN

COMPUTER-AIDED DATABASE DESIGN: The DATAID Project
A. Albano, V. De Antonellis, and A. Di Leva (Editors)
© Elsevier Science Publishers B.V. (North-Holland), 1985

CHAPTER I

A TOOL FOR MODELING DYNAMICS IN CONCEPTUAL DESIGN

V. De Antonellis (*), B. Zonta (**)

(*)   Istituto di Cibernetica - Università degli Studi di Milano
      Via Viotti 5, 20133, Milano (Italy)
(**) Consiglio Nazionale delle Ricerche - Milano

The aim of our research is to model database procedures in
terms of events, and to execute the modeled procedures
against a database. From the modeling point of view, we
have developed a methodology and a tool for the computer-
-aided design of procedures, INCOD-E. The proposed methodology is briefly illustrated, the architecture of INCOD-E
is described, and a sample work session is shown.

1. INTRODUCTION

The development of a database application is concerned with the
identification and organization of facts relevant to an object
system in order to obtain a consistent and efficient representation
(of information) useful in supporting the activities, or functions,
which are to be automated in the system. Since the design of a
database application is generally a difficult and time-consuming
process, the adoption of a methodology can greatly reduce complexity
and improve quality, as well.

In current methodologies, great relevance is given to the conceptual
design phase, the aim of which is to provide a formal and DBMS
independent description of the system to be represented in the
database application /7,13,14,15,16,18,20/. In particular,
conceptual design consists in two processes: the acquisition and
organization of knowledge about the object system; the translation
of the organized knowledge into a predefined set of representation
structures, that is, into the so-called conceptual model.

Recent proposals distinguish four types of representation structures
in a conceptual model according to whether they describe: data
classes of the model; integrity constraints; operations on data
classes; or application dynamics. While several proposals exist for
the first three types /1,6,8,11,12/, only a few proposals are
concerned with the fourth /3,9,19,20/, though the relevance of
dynamics modeling has been recognized for some time in /14,15/, and
stressed in /13,16/.

Our research is devoted to investigating problems related to the
specification of dynamic properties of database applications /4/.
Specifically, we analyze behavioral aspects of the object system:
that is, the activities which are executed in it and to which the
operations to be automated belong. Such activities are formalized
into procedures, i.e., in a clear and unambiguous representation of
the way in which the activities to be automated must be executed. To
this purpose, operations and causal dependencies/independencies
between them are identified, and the related conditions are described. This representation, if expressed in a formal language,

highlights the design choices, allows the discovery of inadequacies and inconsistencies, and suggests alternatives. In the conceptual design, it allows one to check the completeness and consistency of the data and operations schemata (i.e., to test whether all the operations are defined in the operations schema, and whether all the data that are needed to execute the operations are adequately represented in the data schema). In the logical/physical design, it provides guidelines for choosing optimization parameters. Furthermore, such a formal representation, approved by experts and designers, can be made automatically executable. In this way, operations are executed according to their causality relationships. At the same time, track of the execution 'iter' is kept.

Other similar approaches differ from ours in various aspects /3,18,19,20/. In /3/, nets are used to express only the control flow of procedures, with knowledge about them expressed in production rules. In our approach, nets also express knowledge. This is a consequence of the adopted methodology, in which the description of the knowledge acquired on events is an integral part of the net building itself, from the first step to the last step. Unlike /18,19,20/, in which Petri Nets constitute only a starting point for peculiar modeling formalisms, our approach exploits the original Condition-Event interpretation of Petri Nets with both its syntactic and semantic capabilities and the related simulation rules.

In this paper, the concept of procedure is defined and the main features of procedures are described. The methodology proposed in /7/, to design procedures starting from an analysis of activities in terms of operations and conditions, is briefly illustrated. A tool for the computer-aided design of procedures, INCOD-E, is described as regards its architecture and functions, and a sample work session is shown.

2. OUR APPROACH TO DYNAMICS DESCRIPTION

By dynamics description we mean the definition of procedures against a database. The procedures defined in our approach are oriented to describe not so much the details of the operations of which they are constituted as the transformations produced in the context in which they are executed, the relationships between such operations, and the communication links between procedures.

We propose a causal model of procedure. A procedure is a set of operations and of precedence relationships between them. Precedence relationships are expressed by means of conditions which hold before (after) the execution of an operation. The causal model is based on the notion of event. An event is a change of conditions from those which hold before the execution of an operation (pre-conditions) to those which hold because of such an execution (post-conditions). In this sense, a procedure can be considered as a 'texture' of events which expresses their mutual dependencies/independencies.

Main features of procedures are the following.

a. The events of a procedure are related by structures of 'sequence', 'conflict', or 'concurrency'; that is, the involved operations are performed respectively one after the other, in alternative, or in parallel.

b. Procedures can interact between them according to communication protocols (synchronous or asynchronous); in fact, it is possible that a procedure needs information from another procedure, or a procedure starts another one. Communication is synchronous if a procedure sends a message to another one, and it cannot proceed until the other answers. Communication is asynchronous if a procedure sends a message to another one and can proceed without waiting for an answer. In this case, different procedures can go on concurrently.

c. Since not all the aspects of the activities can be automated, procedures can communicate with users; they, in turn, provide information which cannot be obtained automatically.

d. A procedure can have more instances activated either by the user or by some other procedure. Different instances of the same procedure can be in concurrent execution at any instant. The behavior of an instance depends on the occurrence of events, that is, on actual changes of conditions because of the execution of operations.

3. METHODOLOGICAL STEPS

In defining procedures, we proceed according to the following steps /10/:

a. First of all, we define as many work-schemas as there are departments whose activities are to be automated . For each schema, we single out these activities, taking into account how they are distributed-grouped according to offices, sectors, tasks and documents.

b. Each activity to be automated is then fragmented into the operations which make it up, according to the descriptions provided by operative people.

c. Each operation is given a short name, which is indicative of its nature and is as close as possible to the original one.

d. For each named operation, the conditions activating it are made explicit in order to point out the relationships of cooperation, mutual exclusion or compatibility existing between such conditions in respect to the operation in question. Thus, as many events are defined as there are operations, leaving their post-conditions implicit in the semantics of the respective operations. Events whose operations share the same pre-conditions are compacted into major units. Pre-defined structures, the so-called events-blocks, are then associated to the results of this step.

e. These events-blocks, which are given names, too, are composed according to rules which establish sequences, conflicts and concurrencies between them. Composition results in a texture of events which represents the way in which the activity to be automated must be executed, that is, the corresponding procedure. Note that more than one procedure may correspond to an activity; for example, when a part of the activity can be executed in parallel, or when it cannot be automatically connected to the others. The resulting procedures are given names evocative of the original activity.

f. Finally, the defined procedures are analyzed in order to recognize their communication points and to establish the corresponding links. This analysis is carried out starting from the procedures belonging to the same schema (department of the organization) up to those belonging to different ones.

The language used to describe activities in terms of events is restricted natural language. Lexicon is determined by the jargon of the particular organization/department/activity in question, and is regulated by glossaries containing definitions, synonyms, etc. Syntax is a production-like one, that is, for each events-block, <pre-conditions> : <operations>.

Petri Nets is the language introduced to represent procedures, starting from events-blocks /17/. The net interpretation here adopted is essentially the basic one, i.e., the C(ondition)-E(vent) interpretation, both in the structural and in the dynamical aspects. Specifically, transitions (graphically, bars) represent operations; places (graphically, circles) represent conditions; an arc from a (input) place to a transition defines a pre-condition of an operation, while an arc from a transition to a (output) place defines a post-condition. A marker in a place (graphically, a dot in a circle) indicates the holding of the corresponding condition. If all the input places of a transition are marked, and if no output place is marked, the transition is enabled, that is, it can fire; after this firing, the markers disappear from the input places and a marker appears in each of the output places of the transition. In our interpretation, the firing of a transition corresponds to the happening of an event, or in other words to a change of conditions because of the execution of an operation. Labels naming the defined procedure, its events, conditions, operations, are here associated to the corresponding elements of each net.

4. ARCHITECTURE OF INCOD-E

INCOD-E is a tool developed to aid the database designer in:

. modeling procedures, from the definition of events-blocks to the
  coordination of the procedures into a global schema;
. handling current documentation about the modeled procedures;
. keeping track of the whole design history.

At present, INCOD-E is being implemented on Tower-NCR under UNIX operating system (a previous version was on VAX 11-780). As DBMS the relational system INGRES has been chosen. The parser of the design language has been developed by using LEX, an automatic generator of scanners, and YACC, an automatic generator of parsers.

In this paper we describe the actual version of INCOD-E, of which a prototype exists with the following functions implemented: design by name, design by structure (limited to: create events, delete events, compose events), directory.

The graphical interface is being experimented on M20-Olivetti. In particular, an algorithm for the automatic layout of graphs starting from the description of procedures in the design language is being designed. Future efforts will be devoted to integrating this interface with the other functions of INCOD-E.

The functions of INCOD-E are given in Figure 1, and briefly described in the following. They are a little different with respect to the previous version /2/.

Design

The design function comprehends two operational modalities: acting on names and acting on structures.

As regards 'name', the available operations are: to give name to, that is, initialize, schemas or procedures, and to change existing names of schemas or procedures.

As regards 'structure', the available operations are of various types:

1. 'Create events' means to define an events-block by specifying:

   a. For each schema, the name of the procedure to which the events-block belongs.

   b. The name which identifies that particular events-block.

   c. Its pre-conditions coordinated, if more than one, by AND/OREX and hierarchized by parentheses. The pre-conditions are distinguished according whether they hold as a consequence of operations within the same procedure or outside that procedure (for example, time-reference, messages from other procedures or from the user). Conditions syntax is shown in Figure 2.

   Ex.   WHEN MSG positive-answer AND WHEN MSG loan-agreement-ready

   Ex.   IF check-customer.EXIST

   d. Its operations coordinated, if more than one, by AND/OREX, and hierarchized by parentheses. The name of each operation, which is expressed in the imperative form of a verb, must be unique within the same procedure. Operations syntax is shown in Figure 2. The creation of an operation generates automatically a post-condition for it, expressed by DONE plus the operation name.

   Ex.   prepare-loan-agreement AND prepare-money

   Ex.   DONE prepare-loan-agreement

   Ex.   DONE prepare-money

2. 'Re-create events' means to modify name/conditions/operations of an already defined events-block.

3. 'Delete events' means to delete an events-block and its name.

4. 'Compose events' means to combine already defined events-blocks in order to give rise to a procedure. Rules are applied which allow the merging of conditions with the same label and the connecting of IF-conditions to the corresponding operations through their DONE-conditions. The composition modes available to the designer are: sequence, conflict, and concurrency.

5. 'De-compose events' means to annull mergings and connections.

6. 'Delete procedure' means to delete a procedure and its name.

7. 'Coordinate procedures' means to define communication links from one procedure to another by specifying the sending operation and the receiving one.

8. 'De-coordinate procedures' means to annull communication links.

9. 'Delete schema' means to delete a schema and its name.

D o c u m e n t a t i o n

The documentation function allows the obtaining of design information at any level. In particular, information is obtained according to three modalities.

1. 'Directory' provides, according to the request, the name of the defined schemas, procedures, and events, and for the events the details of their conditions and operations.

2. 'Display' provides Petri Nets graphs of schemas, procedures, and events, with the possibility of moving up/down/left/right, of enlarging/shrinking, and of obtaining the hardcopy of the portion of the graph in the screen.

3. 'Print' provides hardcopies of Petri Nets graphs corresponding to schemas, procedures, and events.

5. AN EXAMPLE

In this section we present a work session in which procedures corresponding to banking activities are designed. Specifically, we consider the activities of a bank agency in which relations between customers and the bank are handled, and the activities of the central bank in which the customer registry is maintained. The following procedures will be designed:

NEW RELATION OPENING ⎫
                     ⎬ ──────────── of the schema AGENCY REGISTRY
PRINTING   ⎭

DEFINITIVE POSITION REGISTERING ──── of the schema CENTRAL REGISTRY

(In the sample, designer input is preceded by the character > . Characters *** comprehend comments.)

*** In the main menu, the option 'design' is selected; then, in the design menu 'name' is chosen in order to give name of schema - AGENCY REGISTRY - and give names of procedures for that schema - NEW RELATION OPENING and PRINTING. In order to define the events-blocks of the procedure NEW RELATION OPENING, in the design menu 'structure' is chosen, after which the following menu appears: ***

```
  design:structure

------------------------------------------------------------------

                    1   create events
                    2   re-create events
                    3   delete events
                    4   compose events
                    5   de-compose events
                    6   delete procedure
                    7   coordinate procedures
                    8   de-coordinate procedures
                    9   delete schema

------------------------------------------------------------------

  type number of your choice, then RETURN:>
```

*** After the option 'create events' and after entering the
appropriate names of schema and procedure, and a new name of
events-block - 'relation-request' -, a form appears: ***

```
  schema:     AGENCY REGISTRY
  procedure:  NEW RELATION OPENING
-------------------------------------------------------------------
  event name:    relation-request

  conditions:    >



  operations:    >



-------------------------------------------------------------------
  type conditions, operations, or type HELP for syntax,
  then RETURN:>
```

*** The form is filled up by the designer: ***

```
schema:    AGENCY REGISTRY
procedure: NEW RELATION OPENING
----------------------------------------------------------------
  event name:   relation-request

  conditions:   >WHEN MSG relation-request



  operations:   >check-customer



----------------------------------------------------------------
  type conditions, operations, or type HELP for syntax,
  then RETURN:>
```

*** If syntax is correct and the operation name is not already existing, the form is substituted in the screen by the corresponding net graph: ***

```
schema:    AGENCY REGISTRY
procedure: NEW RELATION OPENING
----------------------------------------------------------------
                            E1: relation-request
                        C1: WHEN MSG relation-request
   C1  ◯                O1: check-customer
                        C2: DONE check-customer
   O1  ↓

   C2  ◯

----------------------------------------------------------------
  RETURN for saving, type D for deleting, then RETURN:>
```

*** The system is now ready to accept the definition of a new events-block of the same procedure. The following event is defined by the designer: ***

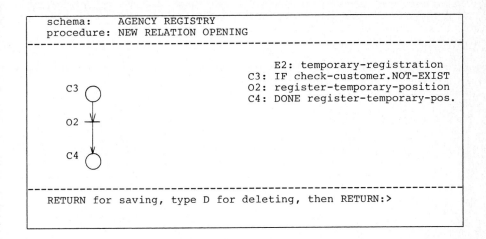

```
schema:    AGENCY REGISTRY
procedure: NEW RELATION OPENING
------------------------------------------------------------

                              E2: temporary-registration
                              C3: IF check-customer.NOT-EXIST
                              O2: register-temporary-position
                              C4: DONE register-temporary-pos.



------------------------------------------------------------

RETURN for saving, type D for deleting, then RETURN:>
```

*** Then, it is the turn of the event 'opened-relation', whose conditions are defined as: IF check-customer.EXIST OREX IF register-temporary-position.EXIST ***

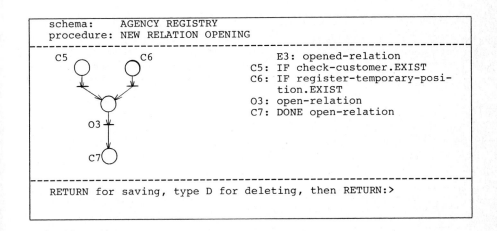

```
schema:    AGENCY REGISTRY
procedure: NEW RELATION OPENING
------------------------------------------------------------

                              E3: opened-relation
                              C5: IF check-customer.EXIST
                              C6: IF register-temporary-posi-
                                  tion.EXIST
                              O3: open-relation
                              C7: DONE open-relation



------------------------------------------------------------

RETURN for saving, type D for deleting, then RETURN:>
```

*** In order to combine the defined events, in the design menu the option 'compose events' is chosen. In applying the composition rules, the designer is aided by the system which selects possible application cases for him. In the example, one rule is applied in two steps, that is, the connection rule between a DONE-condition and the corresponding IF-conditions; specifically, first from DONE-condition C2 to IF-conditions C3 and C5, then from

DONE-condition C4 to IF-condition C6, with the following final
result in which composition arcs are traced in dotted lines: ***

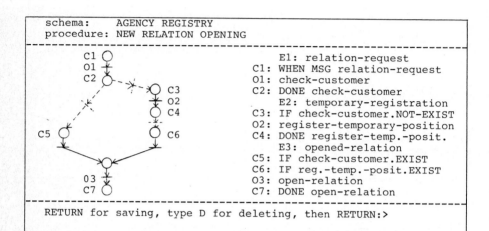

*** The procedure PRINTING of the same schema   consists in one
event only ***

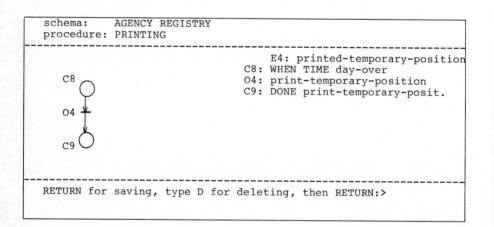

*** The procedure DEFINITIVE POSITION REGISTERING, of the schema
CENTRAL AGENCY, also consists in one event only: ***

```
  schema:     CENTRAL AGENCY
  procedure: DEFINITIVE POSITION REGISTERING
 -----------------------------------------------------------------
                                   E1 definitive-position
                                   C1 WHEN MSG temporary-position
                                   C2 WHEN MSG documents
    C1  ◯      ◯  C2              O1 register-definitive-position
             ╲  ╱                  C3 DONE register-definitive-pos.
              ╲╱
      O4  ⊻
              │
              │
      C3  ◯


 - - - - - - - - - - - - - - - - - - - - - - - - - - - - - - - -
  RETURN for saving, type D for deleting, then RETURN:>
```

*** Then the coordination of the defined procedures is performed in
the following way. For each procedure, first MSG conditions which
hold because of communication from another procedure are connected
with the corresponding operations in it; then, for each operation
which can be performed only after the execution of some operation of
another procedure, a MSG condition is defined, through which these
operations are causally connected. In our case, the analysis of the
conditions of the procedure DEFINITIVE POSITION REGISTERING shows
that the holding of C1 depends on the execution of the operation O2
in NEW RELATION OPENING. In order to represent this communication
link, an arc is traced from O2 to C1. From the analysis of the
operations of the procedure PRINTING, the designer realizes that the
operation O4 can be executed only after the execution of O2 in NEW
RELATION OPENING. A new condition C10 must be defined in PRINTING,
then the arc can be traced. (Coordination arcs are represented here
by dotted lines.) ***

With coordination, which is the final step in the definition of
procedures, the role of INCOD-E in modeling is exhausted. As regards
the actual execution of the defined procedures, two ways can be
followed: to translate the corresponding nets into a program written
in a programming language with constructs for defining and handling
processes /1,3/; to execute directly the corresponding nets,
possibly reducing, by means of net morphisms, redundant elements,
i.e. those whose existence comes uniquely from the adopted
construction methodology.

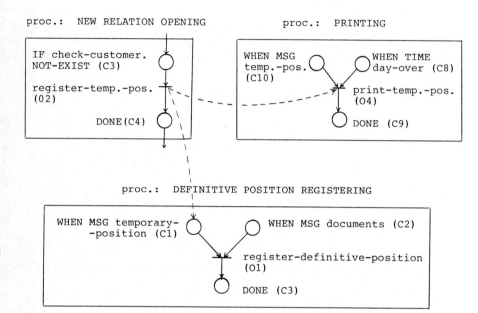

proc.:   NEW RELATION OPENING   proc.:   PRINTING

proc.:   DEFINITIVE POSITION REGISTERING

6. CONCLUSIONS

In this paper, we have presented INCOD-E, a tool which provides an interactive support environment for designing procedures against databases and automatically maintaining a complete history of the investigated design alternatives. Its implementation is in an experimental phase. The first objective is to implement all its funtions as they have been described in this paper. The long-range objective is to integrate these functions with the functions of INCOD-DT, the associated tool for the computer-aided design of data and transactions, implemented by the Dipartimento di Informatica e Sistemistica - Università di Roma and DataBase Informatica Spa /2/.

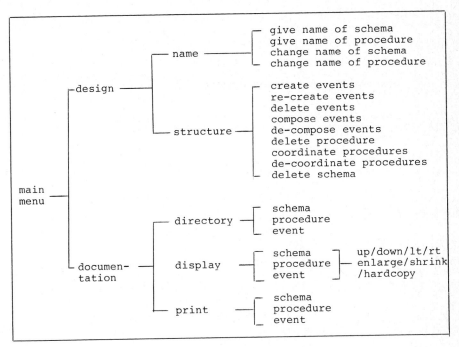

Fig. 1 INCOD-E functions

```
                        S y n t a x

condition : c-one / many
operation : o-one / many
c-one : WHEN MSG <message-name> /
        WHEN TIME <relat. operator> <date-var> /
                                                ⎧ DAYS ⎫        ⎧ <date-var>  ⎫
        WHEN INTERVAL<relat.operator><integer>  ⎨      ⎬ AFTER  ⎨             ⎬  /
                                                ⎩ MONTHS⎭       ⎩ <oper-name> ⎭

        IF <o-one>.<state-var>
o-one : name of the operation in the imperative form of verb
many : same level / different level
same level : c-one AND/OREX c-one, etc. /
             o-one AND/OREX o-one, etc.
different level : use embedded parentheses for different levels
                 ex. (a OREX b) AND (c OREX (d AND e))
```

Fig. 2 Conditions/Operations syntax

BIBLIOGRAPHY

/1/   Albano,A., Cardelli,L., Orsini,R., Galileo: A Strongly Typed,
       Interactive, Conceptual Language, to appear in ACM TODS (1985).

/2/   Atzeni,P.,   Batini,C.,   De   Antonellis,V.,   Lenzerini,M.,
       Villanelli,F., Zonta,B., A Computer-Aided Tool for Conceptual
       Design, Proc. IFIP WG 8.1 Working Conf. on Automated Tools for
       Information Systems Design and Development, New Orleans (1982)
       85-106.

/3/   Barron,J.L.,   Dialogue   Organization   and   Structure   for
       Interactive Information Systems, TR-CSRG-108, University of
       Toronto (1980).

/4/   Bertocchi,R., De Antonellis,V., Zonta,B., Concepts and
       Mechanisms for Handling Dynamics in Database Applications,
       Proc. 7th International Computing Symposium, ACM European
       Regional Conference, Nurnberg (1983) 367-381.

/5/   Bertocchi,R., De Antonellis,V., Zhang,X.W., An Interactive
       Events Handling System, Proc. 1th International Conf. on
       Computers and Applications, Peking (1984) 523-532.

/6/   Brodie,M., Silva,E., Active and Passive Component Modeling:
       ACM/PCM, in: Olle, T.W. et al. (eds.), Information System
       Design Methodologies: a Comparative Review (North Holland,
       Amsterdam, 1982) 41-91.

/7/   Ceri,S.(ed), Methodology and Tools for Database Design (North
       Holland, Amsterdam, 1983).

/8/   Chen,P.P., The Entity-Relationship Model: Toward a Unified View
       of Data, ACM TODS, 1.1 (1976).

/9/   De Antonellis,V., Degli Antoni,G., Mauri,G., Zonta,B.,
       Extending the Entity Relationship Approach to Take into Account
       Historical Aspects of Systems, in: Chen, P. (ed.), E-R Approach
       to Systems Analysis and Design (North Holland, Amsterdam, 1980)
       231-235.

/10/   De Antonellis,V., Zonta,B., Modeling Events in Database
       Applications Design, in Proc. 7th Int. Conf. on Very Large Data
       Bases, Cannes (1981) 23-31.

/11/   El-Masri,R., Wiederhold,G., Data Model Integration Using the
       Structural Model, Proc. ACM SIGMOD (1979).

/12/   Hammer,M., McLeod,D., Database Description with SDM: a Semantic
       Database Model, ACM TODS, 6 (1981).

/13/   ISO, TC97/SC5/WG3-81, Concepts and Terminology for the
       Conceptual Schema (1981).

/14/   Lum,V.Y., et al., New Orleans Database Design Workshop, IBM
       Report RJ2554-33154 (1978).

/15/   Navathe,S.B., et al., Information Modeling Tools for Database
       Design, Data Base Directions, Fort Lauderdale, Florida (1980).

/16/ Olle,T.W., Sol,H.G., Verrijn-Stuart,A.A. (eds.), Information Systems Design Methodologies: a Comparative Review (North Holland, Amsterdam, 1982).

/17/ Petri,C.A., Introduction to General Net Theory, in: Lecture Notes in Computer Sciences, 84, (Springer-Verlag, 1980) 1-19.

/18/ Rolland,C., Richard,C., The REMA Methodology for Information Systems Design and Management, in Olle,T.W., Sol,H.G., Verrijn-Stuart,A.A. (eds.), Information Systems Design Methodologies: a Comparative Review (North Holland, Amsterdam, 1982) 369-426.

/19/ Rolland,C., Database Dynamics, DATA BASE, 14.3 (1983).

/20/ Tardieu,H., Nanci,D., Pascot,D., Conception d'un Système d'Information (Les Editions de l'Organisation, Paris, 1980).

COMPUTER-AIDED DATABASE DESIGN: The DATAID Project
A. Albano, V. De Antonellis, and A. Di Leva (Editors)
© Elsevier Science Publishers B.V. (North-Holland), 1985

CHAPTER II

GINCOD: A GRAPHICAL TOOL FOR CONCEPTUAL
DESIGN OF DATA BASE APPLICATIONS

C. BATINI[(*)], E. NARDELLI[(*)], M. TALAMO[(**)], R. TAMASSIA[(*)]

(*) Dipartimento di Informatica e Sistemistica
Università di Roma "La Sapienza"
Via Buonarroti 12, 00185 Roma - Italy

(**) IASI - C.N.R.
Viale Manzoni 30, 00185 Roma - Italy

The general features of a graphical tool for conceptual design of data base applications are described. A set of primitives that aid the
designer to incrementally specify data of interest by means of an
Entity Relationship Diagram is shown. Symbols can be placed in the
diagram both by the user and by the system, that is able to produce
diagrams automatically, taking into account a set of aesthetics for
better readability.

1. INTRODUCTION

Conceptual design is a complex task, as pointed out in [15], and a lot of research
efforts have been made to simplify and make effective the involved activities.
One aspect of such research efforts has been the developement of conceptual representations of data sufficiently simple and understandable to be used as a common language between designer and user. Natural candidates for this are diagrammatic representations, whose effectiveness is thoroughly recognized. Diagrams are
indeed widely used in all phases of the information systems life cycle (see Table
1).

LIFE CYCLE PHASE	DIAGRAMMATIC REPRESENTATION
Feasibility study	PERT
Functional analisys	SADT [17], Data flow diagrams [13]
Conceptual data design	Entity Relationship diagrams [11]
Functional design	Jackson diagrams [14]
Logical data design	DBMS Models diagrams [19]

Table 1: Examples of Information Systems Diagrams.

Enrico Nardelli was supported by Enidata S.p.A.

Roberto Tamassia was supported by Data Base Informatica S.p.A.

While diagrams cannot represent all the semantics that is meaningful at conceptual level, they represent an effective tradeoff between formality and readability, and make the user more conscious of design decisions.

Several graphic editors for conceptual design have appeared in the last years
(see for instance [1], [10], [12], [21]). In such tools the placement of new
symbols and connections is usually under responsability of the designer; when
it is done by the system, naif algorithms are applied (see Figure 1).

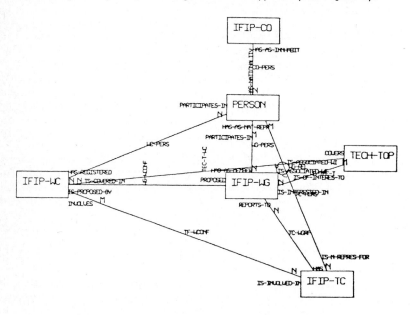

Fig. 1: Diagram produced by an existing graphic tool.

Recently, some interest has arisen in the literature and industrial products on
the development of graphic editors provided with an effective automatic layout
capability (see [16]).

In this paper we describe a graphic tool for conceptual design currently under
implementation at the University of Rome. The features of the tool are influenced
by the previous development of INCOD (INteractive COnceptual Design of Data,
Transactions and Events), a tool that provides an integrated environment for the
definition of data, transactions and events. Data are described using an extended
Entity Relationship (E-R) Model. Transactions are described at different levels
of abstraction, as the tool provides transaction definition commands at a conceptual level (describing the data involved), at a navigational level (describing
access paths) and at an executable level (testing a prototype implementation of

the data base). Events are modelled through Petri Nets. INCOD can support the designer in the conceptualization of static and dynamic requirements, providing design commands that allow interactive enrichement of data, transactions, events
descriptions, automatically checking the consistency of the process and simplifying the management of the corresponding documentation. It handles several types
of metadata, interacts with the user in discovering conflicts, prompting possible
solutions (scenarios) and guiding him through some steps of the design activities.
A detailed description of INCOD may be found in [2].

A natural extension of INCOD is a graphic interface that allows to perform several design activities concerning the data schema directly in terms of its E-R diagrammatic representation. The general architecture of the tool, hereafter called
GINCOD (Graphics INCOD), is shown in Figure 2.

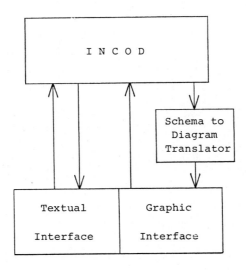

Figure 2: General architecture of GINCOD

The designer can interact with GINCOD either via the textual interface provided
by INCOD or via a graphic interface. When in textual mode, he issues commands and
fills forms. When in graphic   mode, he selects items on the screen by means of a
locator device. Also the documentation provided by GINCOD can be either textual
or graphical; in the latter case a translation is needed between the internal
schema representation used by INCOD and the graphic representation. To perform
such automatic generation of the diagrammatic representation, GINCOD makes use of

a novel layout algorithm, that takes into account a set of aesthetics typically adopted by human beings in drawing diagrams. In this paper we discuss the capabilities of the graphics interface and the schema-to-diagram translator.

The following section is concerned with diagrammatic conventions, user interface and types of interaction used in GINCOD. Section 3 describes the commands of the tool. Section 4 focuses on the automatic layout capability, and examines with some detail the associated topics.

2. GENERAL FEATURES OF GINCOD

The Data Model used by GINCOD is an extension of the Entity Relationship Model [11]. For the semantics of the model, see [2]. Symbols used in the diagrammatic representation are shown in Table 2 (attributes are optionally represented).

CONCEPT	SYMBOL
Entity	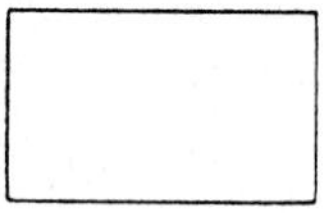 ▭
Relationship	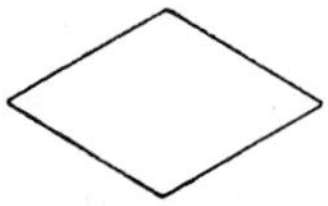 ◇
Attribute	 —○
Subset	 ↑
Generalization Hierarchy	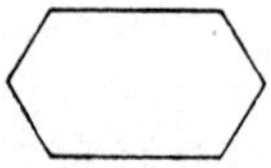 ⬡

Table 2: Symbols used in ER diagrams.

Only the core of the model is represented in E-R diagram; the rest of the model
is defined by means of forms. For instance, each entity form describes name and
synonyms of the entity, identifiers, attributes, the value set of each attribute,
and a textual description.

The screen of the graphic terminal is divided into two areas (see Figure 3): the
Drawing Area represents a window on the diagram; the Message Area the dialogue
between system and user. Logical input devices used in GINCOD are the keyboard,
for issuing commands, and a locator, for selecting items in the drawing area.

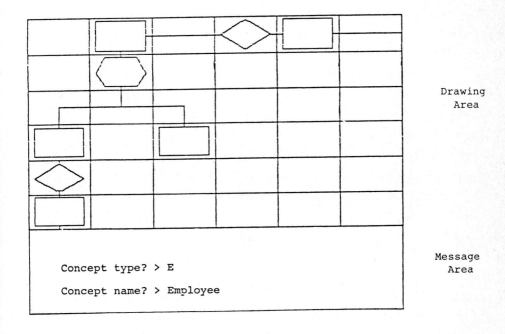

Drawing
Area

Message
Area

Concept type? > E

Concept name? > Employee

Figure 3: Graphic Interface.

Typical standars adopted in graphic   editors for placing symbols and connections
belong to two different classes:

1. The straight line standard, where connections between symbols are straight
lines.

2. The grid standard, where connections run along the lines of a rectangular grid,

in which the diagram is embedded. GINCOD adopts the grid standard, to have diagrams with high regularity and modularity. Connections run orizontally and vertically in the middle of grid cells (so that, except in case of crossings, each cell
contains at most one connection), and place symbols into arrays of grid cells,
whose perimeter grows with the number of connections (see Figure 4).

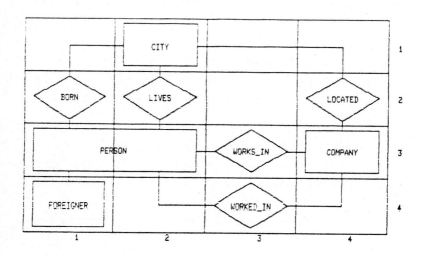

Figure 4: Example of E-R diagram on a grid.

Symbols placement is performed in GINCOD either in system driven mode (S-mode) or
in user driven mode (U-mode). We introduce these concepts by means of examples.
The CREATE command adds a new concept to the schema. In S-mode, the designer de-
clares the concept to be added plus its conceptual connections with the rest of
the schema, while the layout, i.e. placement of symbols and routing of connections
is responsibility of the system. Conversely, in U-mode, all the layout activities
are performed by the designer. As a second example, consider the INTEGRATE command,
that merges two previously defined schemas. In S-mode, the system produces the
new integrated diagram; in U-mode the user is asked to move symbols in order to
conform diagrams. Drawing the integrated schema in U-mode may result in a long
tedious task if the input schemas are of great size, while if one of the schemas
is small, the designer may find it convenient to build himself the new diagram.
The solution presently adopted in GINCOD is to associate an initial default mode

to each command; furthermore, if U-mode has been chosen, at each step of the execution the user may switch into S-mode to complete the task. Criteria respected by the system in S-mode are described in Section 4.

3. DESCRIPTION OF MODULES

The main components of GINCOD are three:

1. The DESIGN module provides primitives to perform design transformations. Such transformations may involve:

a. enrichement of the schema information content both by adding new concepts or integrating schemas (bottom-up primitives) and by refining previous concepts into more complex structures (top-down primitives).

b. restructuring of the schema in order to ensure some design quality (correctness, completeness, readability, minimality). Once the designer has identified the type of restructuring, the system performs the transformation and produces the new corresponding diagram.

2. The EDITING module performs graphic transformations that do not change the semantics of the schema, but only its graphic layout.

3. The DOCUMENTATION module retrieves graphic and textual information about existing schemas.

In the following we describe the commands available in the DESIGN and EDITING modules.

3.1 Design module

Commands available and related default modes are shown in Table 3.

COMMAND	MODE	
	U-mode	S-mode
Create	*	
Delete	*	
Expand		*
Integrate		*
Change		*

Table 3: Design Commands.

- CREATE: creates a concept (entity, relationship, attribute, subset, generalization hierarchy) without any references to its properties. In U-mode, the position of the symbol in the diagram must be provided with the locator; connections with other symbols are specified giving corner points of the path.

- DELETE: removes a concept from the schema together with all its connections. The concept can be referenced either by its name or by its position in the diagram.

- PROPERTIES: allows textual specification of concept properties by means of forms.

- EXPAND: is a top-down command that substitutes a concept in the schema with a new structure, that can be either chosen in a database of predefined expansions or interactively built by means of design commands. In the former case, the designer has to specify the type of expansion, and assign names to the new symbols. In the latter, a design session is started, during which only a subset of commands is available (CREATE, DELETE, SPACE). In both cases the designer has to specify how the new structure inherits the connections of the expanded concept: two possibilities are given:

1. select a concept of the new structure that inherits all connections;

2. declare endpoint concepts for all connections.

In S-mode, the diagram is automatically restructured in the neighbourhood of the new structure.

- INTEGRATE: integrates two schemas by merging concepts with the same name. The integration process is in principle a very complex one (see [4]). In the present version of GINCOD it is a responsability of the designer to make sure that all conflicts (e. g. synonyms, homonyms, type inconsistencies) are solved.

- CHANGE : is the restructuring command. In previous papers on INCOD (see especially [2] and [3]) we have shown examples of restructurings to achieve the completeness and minimality of the schema. Here we focus on readability. Two different types of readability can be considered:

1. conceptual readability, that concerns the structural properties of the schema, independently of its graphical description;

2. graphic readability, that concerns the layout of the diagram.

Graphic readability is handled by the editing command OPTIMIZE (see section 3.2): we show here an example of improvement of conceptual readability. Consider the schema fragment of Figure 5.a: since the pairs of relationships: A-C and B-C have the same meaning, and the same happens for pairs of relationships (A-D, B-D), (A-E, B-E), the diagram can be restructured by means of an abstraction process, into the one of Figure 5.b.

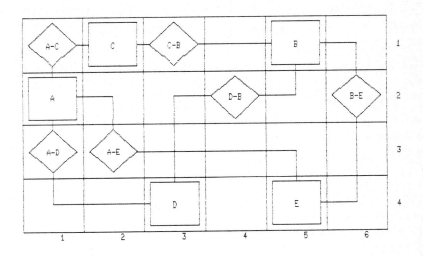

Figure 5a: Fragment of schema.

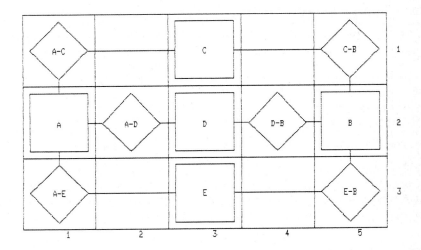

Figure 5b: Example of restructuring.

With the CHANGE command, the chosen substitution pattern is picked up from a data-base of transformations, and applied to the diagram.

3.2 Editing Module

- ZOOM: enlarges or shrinks the window on the diagram. The designer must specify the dimensions of the window that will be displayed into the drawing area. Since the drawing area contains a square array of grid cells, the parameter of this com-mand is the window side, in terms of grid cells. The new center of the window is kept as close as possible to the old one.

- SHIFT: translates the window over the diagram. The new center of the window is given with the locator device.

- SPACE: moves up, down, right, or left all the symbols lying on one side of a given line; this produces an empty strip of grid cells.

- OPTIMIZE: improves the graphic readability of the diagram, according to criteria described in section 4. The OPTIMIZE command can be conveniently issued after a sequence of commands performed in U-mode that may have lead to a tangled diagram. For example, the diagram of Figure 5.a can be graphically restructured as shown in Figure 6, in wich all crossing between connections have been removed, the total number of bends and the global lenght of connections have been minimized.

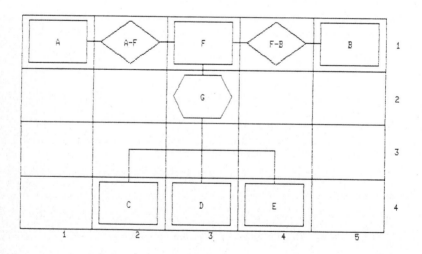

Figure 6: Graphic optimization of the diagram in Figure 5.a.

4. AUTOMATIC LAYOUT OF DIAGRAMS

A clear layout is a key issue for an effective use of diagrammatic representations. In section 3 we have shown different commands that invoke an automatic layout capability. We examine with some detail the problems involved in the automatic generation of aesthetically pleasing diagrams. Our considerations apply to a large class of diagrams used in the Information Systems Life cycle.

4.1 What makes a good diagram

The same abstract graph can be represented by many diagrams with different layouts; some diagrams, however, are better than the other ones in conveying clear information about the structure of the underlying graph. We refer to this capability as the readability of a diagram. Readability is concerned with three different aspects:

1. graphic features, that concern the shape of the diagram, independently of the meaning of symbols (e.g. crossings should be avoided in a tidy diagram).

2. semantic features of the model, that concern the meaning of symbols types used in the representation (e.g. the more abstract concept in a generalization hierarchy in the ER model should be placed above the less abstract ones).

3. semantic features of the diagram, that concern the meaning of the specific diagram (e.g. the most relevant concepts, if any, should be put in the middle of the diagram).

The first two factors can be expressed by means of general layout rules independent of the meaning of the diagram: we refer to such rules in the following as aesthetics. The third factor can be expressed by means of constraints on the layout, explicitly provided by the designer.

According to the above discussion, our approach to the automatic layout of diagrams is based on the following strategy.

1. Define a graphic standard according to the syntax of the diagrammatic representation.

2. Identify a set of aesthetics that closely approximate the notion of a graphically tidy diagram.

3. Add new aesthetics for semantic aspects that are derivable from the model.

4. Express semantic features of the diagram by means of constraints.

5. Design a layout algorithm based on the general aesthetics, that is able to take into account specific constraints, provided as additional input.

4.2 Aesthetics for Information System Diagrams

Two well-admitted aesthetics ([9] [13] [20]) valid independently of the graphic standard, are:

- Minimization of crossings between connections;

- Homogeneous density of symbols and connections.

When the grid standard is adopted, bends along connections should be avoided as much as possible, and the number of cells occupied by the diagram should be kept small. We have thus identified the following basic set of aesthetics for all diagrams drawn according to the grid standard.

A1. Minimization of the number of crossing between connections.

A2. Minimization of the number of bends along connections.

A3. Minimization of the global length of connections.

A4. Minimization of the area of the diagram.

The characteristics of the grid standard (that prevents connections and symbols from being drawn too closely) and aesthetics A3 and A4 (that avoid waste of space) make redundant the specification of an additional aesthetic for the homogeneous density. Note that aesthetic A3 and A4 refer to the discrete metrics induced by the grid.

The above aesthetics are not generally compatible: e.g. if we try to avoid crossings (aesthetic A1) both the number of bends and the length of connections might increase. Figure 7 shows two E-R diagrams that represent the same schema. Diagram 1 is optimal with respect to aesthetic A1, while diagram 2 is optimal with respect to A2, A3, and A4. It is easy to see that there is no diagram representing the previous schema that is optimal with respect to all the above aesthetics.
Our current approach to solve conflicts between aesthetics is to estabilish a priority among them. For instance, we consider A1, A2, A3 and A4 in decreasing order of importance. This choice is a consequence of the following considerations.

When the grid standard is adopted, a diagram can be viewed as an embedding of a graph in the grid. In this framework, the aesthetics we have identified refer to heterogeneous properties of grid-embeddings, as shown in Table 4. This fact suggests a hierarchic layout representation, where the above properties are successively considered (see figure 8).

The conceptual graph describes the diagram in terms of nodes and edges. The planar representation describes the topology of the embedding, that is the crossings between edges and the cycles contouring its faces (plane regions delimited by edges). The orthogonal representation is concerned with the shape of the embedding, without taking into account dimensions. The grid representation describes the embedding as a collection of horizontal and vertical segments; it is the skeleton of the final diagram. For a formal description of these representations see [6].

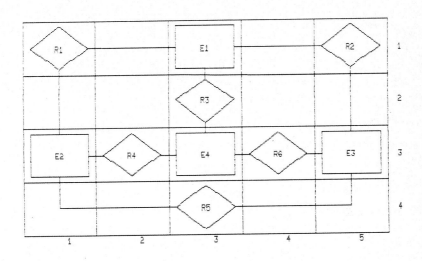

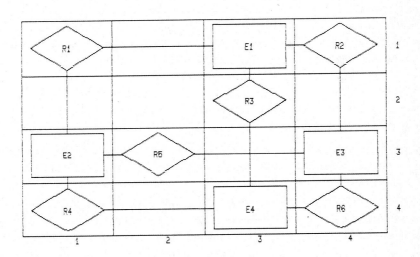

Fig. 7: Example of conflict between aesthetics.

AESTHETIC	PROPERTY
A1	TOPOLOGY
A2	SHAPE
A3,A4	METRIC

Table 4: Aesthetics and related properties of grid-embeddings.

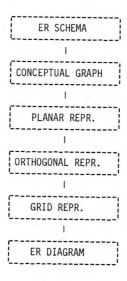

Fig. 8: Hierarchic layout representation for the grid standard.

The three representation levels are hierarchically related, and each level is a refinement of the previous one. If we estabilish the same hierarchy between the corresponding aesthetics, we obtain the following layout strategy.

1. First of all the topology of the embedding is specified, finding a planar representation for the conceptual graph with as few as possible crossings (aesthetic A1).

2. Then an orthogonal shape is given to the planar representation, building an orthogonal representation with the minimum number of bends (aesthetic A2).

3. Finally the grid-embedding is completed by assigning integer lenghts to segments, while keeping their sum as small as possible (aesthetics A3 and A4).

Concerning E-R diagrams, two aesthetics must be added in order to conveniently represent hierarchies.

A5. Verticality of hierarchic structures, i.e. the father of the hierarchy must be placed above its sons.

A6. Simmetry of sons in the hierarchy with respect to the vertical position of the father.

Useful types of constraints are:

C1. Symbols of the diagram representing concepts from a given set should be placed close together.

C2. A given symbol should be placed in the middle of the diagram.

For E-R diagrams, GINCOD adopts a layout algorithm described in [7] and [18], that presently respects aesthetics A1, A2, A3 and constraint C2 (an extension of the algorithm to take into account aesthetics A5, A6 is described in [8]).

The input to the algorithm is a description of an E-R schema. The output is a corresponding diagram, drawn according to the grid standard. Figure 9 shows the basic steps of the algorithm, together with an example.

Figure 10 shows two examples of diagrams produced by GINCOD.

5. CONCLUSIONS AND FUTURE RESEARCH

A running prototype of GINCOD has been implemented in Pascal; the prototype was developed at the Dipartimento di Informatica e Sistemistica - Università di Roma "La Sapienza",with the collaboration of Sarin SpA and Iris - Roma. Future improvements of GINCOD will concern:

1. Interactive design of transaction at conceptual and navigational level. At these levels transactions are described by means of an E-R diagram: their design can be performed extracting from the whole diagram concepts and paths involved in the transaction. An extension of the tool to graphic representations for events, i.e. Petri Nets, is presently under investigation at Istituto of Cibernetica, Università di Milano.

2. Extension to other phases of Information Systems development. An extension of the layout algorithm to Data Flow Diagrams is presented in [5].

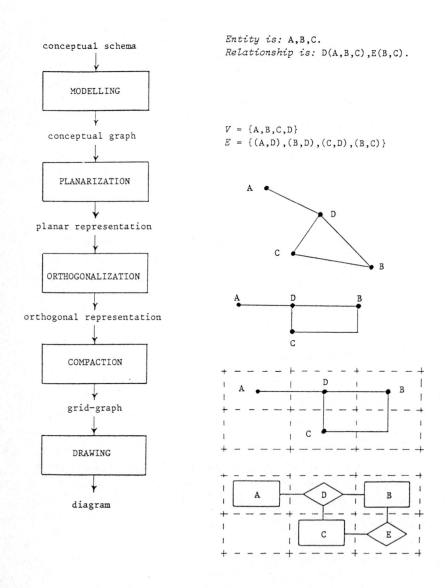

Figure 9: Steps of the layout algorithm

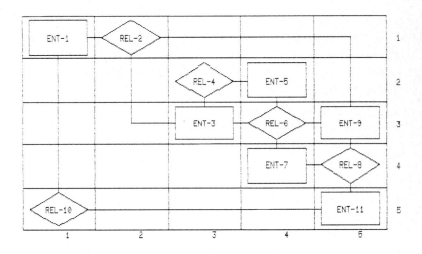

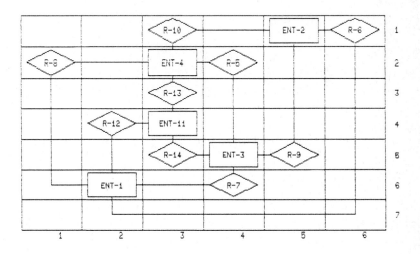

Figure 10: Diagrams automatically produced by GINCOD

REFERENCES

[1] Aschim, F., and Mostue, B.M., IFIP WG 8.1 Case Solved Using SYSDOC and SYSTEMATOR, in: Olle T. et al. (eds.), Information Systems Design Methodologies: a Comparative Review, Proc of the IFIP WG 8.1 Working Conference on Comparative Review of Information Systems Design Methodologies, Noordwijkerhout, The Nederlands, 1982, (North Holland, 1982) 15-40.

[2] Atzeni, P., Batini, C., Carboni, E., De Antonellis, V., Lenzerini, M., Villanelli, F., and Zonta, B., INCOD-DTE: A System for Interactive Conceptual Design of Data, Transactions and Events, in: Ceri S. (ed.), Methodology and Tools for Data Base Design, (North Holland, 1983) 205-228.

[3] Atzeni, P., Batini, C., Lenzerini, M., and Villanelli, F., INCOD: A System for Conceptual Design of Data and Transactions in the Entity-Relationship Model, in: Chen, P. (ed.), The Entity Relationship Approach to Information Modelling and Analysis, (The E-R Institute, 1981) 379-414.

[4] Batini, C., and Lenzerini, M., A Methodology for Data Schema Integration in the Entity-Relationship Model, IEEE Trans. on Software engineering, November 1984 (to appear).

[5] Batini, C., Nardelli, E.,and Tamassia, R., Automatic Layout of Data Flow Diagrams, Technical Report 11.84, Dipartimento di Informatica e Sistemistica Univ. of Rome, (1984).

[6] Batini, C., Nardelli, E., Talamo, M., and Tamassia, R., A Graph Theoretic Approach to Aesthetic Layout of Information Systems Diagrams, Proc. 10th Int. Workshop on Graphtheoretic Concepts in Computer Science, Berlin, (1984), to appear.

[7] Batini, C., Talamo, M,. and Tamassia, R., Computer Aided Layout of Entity Relationship Diagrams, The Journal of Systems and Software, 4 (1984) 163-173.

[8] Batini, C., Talamo, M., and Tamassia, R., Layout Algorithms for Sparse Diagrams, Proc. of the IASTED 2nd Int. Symp. on Applied Informatics, Innsbruck, Austria (1984) 88-91.

[9] Carpano, M., Automatic Display of Hierarchized Graphs for Computer Aided Decision Analysis, IEEE Trans. on Systems Man and Cybernetics, SMC-10 N°11 (1980) 705-715.

[10] Chan, E., and Lochowsky, F.H., A Graphical Data Base Design Aid Using the E-R Model, in Chen, P., (ed.), Entity-Relationship Approach to Systems Analysis and Design (North Holland, Amsterdam, 1980).

[11] Chen, P., The Entity Relationship Model: Toward a Unified View of Data, ACM

Trans. On Data Base Systems 1.1 (1976) 9-36.

[12] Graphics Interfaces V. 2.1 for PSA or SEM - User's Manual ISDOS Project, University of Michigan, ISDOS Ref. 82GI2-0400-0 (1982).

[13] Gane, C., Sarson, T., Structured System Analysis (Prentice Hall, 1979).

[14] Jackson, M., Principles of Program Design (Academic Press, 1975).

[15] Lum, V.Y., et al., 1978 New Orleans Data Base Design Workshop Report, IBM Res. Report RJ2554, and Proc. 5th Int. Conf. on Very Large Data Base, Rio De Janeiro (1979) 328-339.

[16] Reiner, D., Brodie, M., Brown, G., Chilenskas, M., Friedell, M., Kramlich, D., Lehman, J., and Rosenthal, R., A Data Base Design and Evaluation Workbench: Preliminary Report, Intl. Conf. on Systems Development and Requirements Specification, Gothenburg, Sweden (1984).

[17] Ross, D., and Shoman , K., Structured Analysis for requirements definition, IEEE Trans. on Software Engineering, SE-3 N°1 (1977).

[18] Tamassia, R., Batini, C., and Talamo, M., An Algorithm for Automatic Layout of Entity Relationship Diagrams, in: Davis C. et al. (eds.) Entity Relationship Approach to Software Engineering, Proc. 3rd Int. Conf. on Entity Relationship Approach, Anaheim, California (North Holland, 1983) 421-440.

[19] Tsichritzis, D., Lochowsky, F., Data Models (Prentice Hall, 1982).

[20] Warfield, J., Crossing Theory and Hierarchy Mapping, IEEE Trans. on Systems, Man and Cybernetics, SMC-7 N°7 (1977) 505-523.

[21] Zhang, Z., Mendelzon, A., A Graphical Query Language for Entity Relationship Data Bases, in: Davis C. et al. (eds.), Entity Relationship Approach to Software Engineering, Proc. 3rd Int. Conf. on Entity Relationship Approach, Anaheim, California (North Holland, 1983) 441-448.

COMPUTER-AIDED DATABASE DESIGN: The DATAID Project
A. Albano, V. De Antonellis, and A. Di Leva (Editors)
© Elsevier Science Publishers B.V. (North-Holland), 1985

CHAPTER III

A SOFTWARE ENGINEERING APPROACH TO
DATABASE DESIGN: THE Galileo PROJECT

Antonio Albano and Renzo Orsini

Dipartimento di Informatica, Università di Pisa
Corso Italia, 40 – 56100 Pisa, Italy

The current status of the Galileo Project is presented. The goal of the project is to implement an interactive integrated system to design and prototype database applications, with an approach based on recent trends in software engineering to the architecture of programming environment. The motivation, goals and results of the project will be described, with special emphasis on tools under development to support requirements specifications and conceptual design, integrated into a database designer's workbench called Dialogo. Dialogo will support in the future also appropriate tools for the logical and physical phases of the database design process.

1. INTRODUCTION

Several research projects are presently in progress to implement an integrated environment of tools to support the database design process [13], [25], [22], [26], [29]. A similar project is underway at the University of Pisa, with the following motivations and goals:

1) Programming languages of commercial DBMSs have the following basic limitations [24]: a) they support the abstraction mechanisms of traditional data models, considered nowadays too limited in their expressive power; b) the integration of the data model abstraction mechanisms into a programming language designed independently is unsatisfactory; c) it is not possible to deal with all the aspects of interactive information systems (e.g., dynamics, modularization, dialogs).

For these reasons, the first goal of the project was to define a programming language, called Galileo, to study the possiblities of integrating both the abstraction mechanisms of a modern programming language and those of semantic data models in the context of a strongly typed, interactive programming language [9]. A related research issue has been the investigation of appropriate techniques to implement such a language using the available technology.

2) There is a general consensus on the proper phases of the database design process and on the decisions to be made during those phases. This conventional approach is pictured in Figure 1, where it is shown that a common assumption is that, the design process produces a non executable specification of the application. This paradigm has a strong analogy with the conventional "software life cycle", which has been followed in the field of software engineering, and it presents the same drawbacks that have been pointed out by software designers [14]: a) the tools supporting the design process are of limited interest once the applications have been implemented. In particular, they can not be used to maintain the released information system, which has been implemented in a target language not contemplated during the design process; b) users have no means of ensuring that

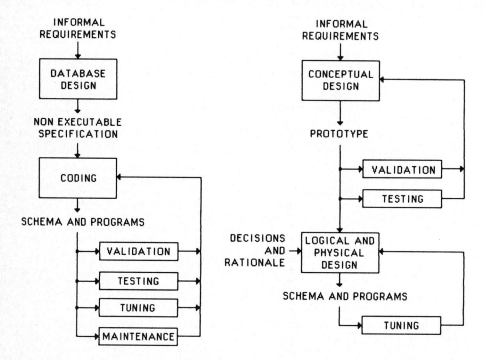

Fig.1 Conventional Paradigm   Fig.2 Operational Paradigm

the specified system matches their intent before a first release of the implementation is operational. This compounds the maintenance problem.

To overcome these difficulties a new approach to software development is gaining popularity among practitioners and academicians in the software engineering and information systems fields: an operational, or prototyping, approach to software development (Figure 2) [1], [19], [30], [32]. The basic assumption of this approach is that, during the design phase, computer specialists give an implementation independent, executable (operational) specification of the system to be implemented. The operational specification is a prototype, an early version of the system that exhibits the essential features of the future operational system, except for the resource requirements and performances. The first advantage of this approach is that users can experiment with the prototype to determine whether or not it matches their requirements. Such prototypes are expected to improve the users' perception of their needs, and so the resulting systems should be more responsive to those needs. A second advantage is that computerized tools can be designed to support the transformation of the prototype into an efficient, system dependent implementation. A third advantage is that the main result of the design phase, the prototype, is not discarded once the system is operational, but will be used to perform maintenance of the applications.

In our opinion, the operational approach is also relevant to the database field. The natural stage to introduce prototyping capabilities is at the conceptual level, by providing an executable, high level language to specify data, constraints, operations, and dialogs [3], [4], [25]. Investigations are required to define which features a language should have for these purposes and how to embed this tool in a system to support the database life cycle. We are presently interested in experimenting the use of the language Galileo for prototyping [8]. We do not claim that Galileo is the best language for this scope, because it is still a research topic to isolate the right language features. However, the language is sufficiently expressive and DBMS independent to be considered as a candidate to experiment.

3) The database life cycle requires an environment with an integrated set of tools to support both design and maintenance of applications. The problem is similar to that of software engineering where the following strategies are suggested: a) the definition of a software development methodology; b) the definition of a high level language supporting the methodology; c) the definition of automated tools for a development support system.

Accordingly, we are engaged in a project to design and implement a database designer's workbench, where the language Galileo, used for prototyping, supports the DATAID database design methodology [4], [8].

In the remainder of the paper, we present an overview of the results of the Galileo Project: the conceptual language Galileo, the language Galileo/R to specify user requirements, and in the conclusions we comment upon the tools under implementation and our future plans.

2. THE LANGUAGE Galileo

We assume that the goal of the conceptual design is the implementation of a working prototype that exhibits the essential features of the final product. Therefore a great deal of attention has been given to the design of a high level programming language that supports adequate abstraction mechanisms for database applications. The language should also allow the definition and test of the prototype in a small fraction of the time required to make the same prototype with languages available in commercial DBMSs. The main features of Galileo are:

• It is an expression language: each construct is applied to values to return a value.

• It is an interactive language: the system repeatedly prompts for inputs and reports the results of computations; this interaction is said to happen at the top level of evaluation. At the top level one can evaluate expressions or perform declarations. This feature, which is not present in other conceptual languages, allows the interactive use of Galileo without a separate query language.

• It is higher order, in that functions are denotable and expressible values of the language. Therefore, a function can be embedded in data structures, for instance to model derived properties of entities, passed as parameter and returned as value.

• Every denotable value of the language possesses a type. A type describes a set of values with the same "structure", that is values sharing common characteristics, together with the primitive operators which can be applied to these values. Besides predefined types, type constructors exist to define new types, from predefined or previously defined types. They are: tuple, sequence, discriminated union, array, function and abstract types. There are two constructors for abstract types: one is used to define a new type together with the operations available (the structure of an abstract type is hidden from the user of the type, but is available while defining the operations); the other constructor is used to define a new type which inherits the primitive operations of the representation type. In defining abstract types, it is possible to restrict the set of possible values with assertions.

● Every Galileo expression has a type. In general, any expression has a type that can be statically determined, so that every type violation can be detected by textual inspection (static type checking). Although any statically detectable error could also be detected at run-time, the language has been designed to be statically type checkable for the following basic reasons: firstly, programs can be safely executed disregarding any information about types; secondly, the language offers considerable benefits in testing and debugging applications, since the type-checker detects a large class of common programming errors without the need of executing programs, while error checking at run-time could be detected only by providing test data that cause the error to be raised. In fact, static type checking is considered an example of consistency checking extremely useful to detect frequent semantic errors. For database applications the above benefits are certainly valuable, but static type checking does not prevent dynamic testing for assertion enforcement. However, the type-checker is still useful to provide information to the translator to produce specialized testing code.

● The type system supports the notion of type hierarchy; if a type T is a subtype of a type T', then a value of T can be used as argument of any operation defined for values of T', but not vice versa because the subtype relation is a partial order. Type hierarchy is important to incorporate the generalization abstraction mechanism of semantic data models into a strongly typed programming language [5].

● A control mechanism is provided for failures and their handling.

● A database is described with the abstraction mechanisms of semantic data models. Classes are the mechanism to represent a database by means of sequences of modifiable, interrelated objects, which are the computer representation of certain facts of entities of the world that is being modeled. Class elements possess an abstract type and are the only values which can be destroyed. Predefined assertions on classes are provided and, if not otherwise specified, the operators for including or eliminating elements of a class are automatically defined.

● Modularization is another abstraction mechanism supported by the language to partition data and operations into interrelated modules. Therefore, a complex schema can be structured into smaller units. For instance, a unit may model a user view or a description of the schema produced by a stepwise refinement methodology [6].

● A process mechanism is provided to model user activities and dialogs with the system as long term transactions, which can proceed in parallel and interact by message passing [10].

● A form oriented interface is provided to input or to display database objects.

A detailed description of the language appears in [9], its definition in [7], its semantics has been given using a denotational approach in [20], while a comparison of Galileo with other languages appears in [12], [16]. Since the focus of the Galileo Project is the Galileo language, the next section presents the main features of the language by an example of session with the system.

2.1 Interacting with Galileo.

Galileo is an interactive language. Once the system is loaded, it prompts the user with the string 'E:'. The user types phrases, which can be expressions, top-level declarations or commands, and the system prints back a result in the case of an expression, and an acknowledgment in the other cases. Presently, there is no provision in the Galileo system for editing and storing programs or definitions given during a session, though the user can save the current state at any time with the command 'save', and restore it later in the same or a following session with the command 'restore'. For this reason Galileo schemas are usually prepared in text files and then loaded and tested interactively. The use of a multi-window editor like Emacs is very useful in this approach: one window may contain the Galileo system, and other windows contain Galileo definitions which can be modified (whitout having to exit Galileo) and reloaded when needed, or they can even be directly pasted from the text window in the Galileo window. The next paragraphs show an example of session with the system. The transcript of the interaction is shown enclosed in solid lines.

Expressions

E: 3*2+7;

   13 : int

E: it+1;

   14 : int

The previous phrases are numerical expressions. The system's answer to an expression is the printing of the expression's value and type. The variable 'it' is always bound to the value of the last expression evaluated, and is not affected by declarations or by computations which for some reasons fail to terminate.

Declarations

E: **use** x := 2*3;

> x = 6 : int

E: **use** y := 10 **and** z := x;

> y = 10 : int
| z = 6 : int

The phrase '**use** x:=e' is an example of top-level declaration: it binds the identifier 'x' to the value of 'e' in the global environment. From this moment, unless 'x' should be redefined, every occurrence of 'x' will be substituted by the associated value. A set of bindings can be introduced with the multiple declaration 'D_1 **and** D_2': this extends the global environment with the bindings of 'D_1' and of 'D_2', which are evaluated separately (identifiers defined in 'D_1' cannot be used in 'D_2').

```
E: use x := 3
=  and b := true
=  and s := "This is a string"
=  ext y := x+3;

>  x = 3 : int
|  b = true : bool
|  s = "This is a string" : string
|  y = 6 : int

E: use v := derived x+y;

>  v = - : derived int

E: v;

   9 : int
```

Predefined types are 'int', 'bool', with the only values 'true' and 'false', and 'string', with character strings as values. Note that it is not necessary to specify the type of a new identifier because it is automatically inferred by the system.

'**ext**' is another environment operator. It differs from 'and' in that, in the expression 'D_1 **ext** D_2', 'D_2' is evaluated in the current environment extended with the bindings of 'D_1'. If an identifier is defined both in 'D_1' and 'D_2', then its value in the resulting environment will be that evaluated in 'D_2'.

'A := **derived** E' returns an environment where the only binding is between 'A' and a "virtual" value, obtained by evaluating 'E' every time 'A' is being evaluated.

```
E: use rec Factorial (x : int) : int :=
=               if x = 0 then 1 else x * Factorial (x-1);

> Factorial = fun : int -> int

E: use x := 10
=    in Factorial (x);

   3628800 : int
```

The environment operator '**rec** D' permits recursive definitions, while the expression '**use** D **in** E' gives the value of 'E' evaluated in the current environment extended with the bindings of 'D' (local declarations). The global environment remains unchanged.

A function is defined with the list of formal parameters with their type, the result's type and the expression which gives the function's body. If the result's type is missing, then it is assumed equal to 'null', the type with the only value 'nil'. Note that the system does not print the function's value, but just its type.

The value and type of an identifier, or the type of a function, in the global environment, can be known by giving its name:

E: x;

　3 : int

E: Factorial;

　fun : int -> int

Concrete types

E: **use** Paul := (Name := "Paul" **and** Surname := "Smith");

> Paul = (Name := "Paul" and Surname := "Smith") : (Name : string and Surname : string)

E: Surname **of** Paul;

　"Smith" : string

E: **use** Paul **in** Surname;

　"Smith" : string

E: **use type** Date := (Day: int **and** Month: int **and** Year: int);

> type Date = (Day: int and Month: int and Year: int)

'Paul' is defined as an environment with two identifiers : 'Surname' and 'Name', associated to the values "Smith" and "Paul". Environments such as 'Paul', which do not contain type definitions, are expressible values called "tuples", and are similar to "records" of other languages. To get the value associated to a tuple's identifier, the operator '**of**' exists, and it is equivalent to the construct '**use** Tuple **in** Identifier'. A tuple's type is a set of pairs (identifier, type of associated value).

The user can give a name to a type with the environment operator '**type** D'. This name is an abbreviation which stands for the associated type. For instance, the types 'Date' and '(Day: int **and** Month: int **and** Year: int)' are the same type.

Abstract types

```
E: use type Month <=> int assert with "Illegal Month" this within (1,12)
= with newMonth (M : int) : Month := mkMonth (M)
= and NextMonth (M : Month) : Month :=
=         use ThisMonth := repMonth (M)
=            in if ThisMonth < 12 then mkMonth (ThisMonth + 1) else mkMonth (1)
= and EqMonth (M : Month, N : Month) : bool := repMonth (M) = repMonth (N);

> newType Month = -
| NewMonth = fun : int -> Month
| NextMonth = fun : Month -> Month
| EqMonth = fun : Month, Month -> bool
```

The operator 'type T <=> T' assert B with D' is used to construct a new type 'T', which is different from any other type (including its representation type 'T''), together with the operators of the new type, defined in 'D'. Only within 'D' one can use the automatically declared functions 'mkT' and 'repT', which map between a type and its representation. The assertion 'B' is a static integrity constraint which is dynamically controlled. It is a boolean expression which is evaluated every time a new value of type 'T' is constructed. If the evaluation returns 'false', the operation fails with the message specified in the assertion. A type definition may contain several assertions with different messages. The identifier 'this' used in an assertion is bound to the value of the representation type. If the representation type is a tuple type, then it is possible to put assertions on attributes, after the attribute's type specification. Note that the system does not print the representation type of the new type, but just its name.

```
E: use type Date <-> (Day : int assert this within (1,31)
=               and Month : int assert this within (1,12)
=               and Year : int assert this within (1983, 2000))
=           assert with "Illegal Date"
=           use this
=           in Day ≤ (if Month = 2
=                       then if Year mod 4 = 0 then 29 else 28
=                       else if Month=4 Or Month=6 Or Month=9 Or Month=11
=                           then 30 else 31)

> newType Date = -
| mkDate = fun : (Day : int and Month : int and Year : int ) -> Date
| repDate = fun : Date -> (Day : int and Month : int and Year : int )
```

The operator '<->' is an abbreviation of the general syntax of '<=>' [7], [9]. The representation type of a type defined by '<->' must be concrete. Another property of this operator is that the new type inherits all the operators predefined on the representation type. The operators maintain their name, but this overloading is statically resolved by the type-checker, by analysing the type of their operands. In addition, the functions 'mkT' and 'repT' are exported, and it is possible to restrict the set of the inherited operators.

The possibility of defining abstract data types is an important characteristic of Galileo: it allows the definition of application–specific data types and operators. In this way, the set of controls which can be made on programs increases, without the need of programming them in the applications. Before giving the description of the mechanism to model data bases, another important feature of abstract types will be shown: The possibility of defining abstract tuples with *default, derived,* and *optional* components.

```
E: use Today := var mkDate (Day := 19 and Month := 9 and Year := 1984);

> Today = var – : var Date

E: use type Person <->
=       (Age := derived use this in (Year of at Today – Year of BirthDate)
=        and BirthDate : Date
=        and Citizenship : default "Italian"
=        and Name : string
=        and Phone : optional int assert this within (100000,999999) );

> newType Person = –
|  mkPerson = fun : (Age: default int and BirthDate: Date and Citizenship: string
|                   and Name: string and Phone: int) –> Person
|  repPerson = fun : Person –>
|              (Age: default int and BirthDate: Date and Citizenship: string
|               and Name: string and Phone: int)

E: use Smith := mkPerson (Name := "Henry Smith"
=                    and BirthDate :=
=                        mkDate(Year := 1945 and Month := 3 and Day := 1 ));

> Smith : Person
```

A default attribute can be omitted in a tuple passed to the 'mkT' function. In such a case, the attribute will assume the value specified in the type definition. A derived attribute must not be present in a tuple passed to the 'mkT' function. The attribute's value will be generated automatically by the system: If it is defined with an expression, the value will be assigned at construction time; when it is defined as 'derived', the value will be computed every time the attribute is selected. An optional attribute can be omitted in a tuple passed to the 'mkT' function. If so, it assumes automatically the value '<unbound>'.

In the next section the mechanisms to define and use a data base will be shown. For brevity, we will omit the printing of the functions 'mkT' and 'repT' and the inherited operators for an abstract type 'T' defined with '<->'.

Classes

Classes in Galileo are used to model real world entities using the abstraction mechanisms of semantic data models. A class can be *base* or *subclass*. Subclasses, which will be described later, are used to model specialization hierarchies. A class possesses a name and an elements type, unique in the environment. The name of a class denotes a sequence of values, which are the elements of the class present in the data base. The elements type of a class is an abstract tuple type, so elements of different classes have different types, even if they have the same representation. Let us consider the situation described by the following diagram:

```
E: use
= rec type PhoneNumber <-> int assert this within (100000,999999)
= and type SixDigits <-> int assert this within (100000,999999)
= and Students class
=     Student <->
=       (BirthDate : Date
=        and Citizenship : default "Italian"
=        and ExamsGiven : derived all Exams with GivenBy = this
=        and Name : string
=        and StudentNumber : SixDigits
=        and Phone : optional PhoneNumber);
=       key (StudentNumber)
= and Exams class
=     Exam <->
=       (GivenBy : Student
=        and Course : string
=        and Date : Date
=        and Grade : int assert this within(1,100)
=        and Honor : <Yes or No>
=        and StudentNumber := derived StudentNumber of GivenBy of this)
=       key (GivenBy, Course)
=       assert with "IllegalHonor"
=            if Honor of this is Yes then Grade of this = 100 else true;

>  newType PhoneNumber = -
|  newType SixDigits = -
|  class Students = - : seq Student
|  newType Student = -
|  class Exams = - : seq Exam
|  newType Exam = -

E: mkStudent (StudentNumber := mkSixDigits (222222)
=             and BirthDate := mkDate (Year := 1963 and Month := 5 and Day := 10)
=             and Name := "Paul Smith");

   - : Student
```

```
E: mkEsam (GivenBy := get Students with StudentNumber = mkSixDlgits (222222)
=              and Course := "CS3"
=              and Date := mkDate (Year := 1983 and Month := 5 and Day := 10)
=              and Grade := 89
=              and Honor := <No>);

  - : Exam
```

The environment operator **'class'** defines a class name and its elements type, together with the assertions to be controlled when a new element is created. A class definition introduces the following set of bindings (we will refer to the class 'Students' of the above example):

a) 'Student' is bound to a new tuple type. The attributes of such a type can take values which are elements of other classes, to model the aggregation mechanism of semantic data models. 'ExamsGiven' of 'Student' is a derived property which models a multivalued partial association between 'Students' and 'Exams', which is the inverse of the total associaton described by 'GivenBy' in 'Exams'.

b) 'Students' is bound to a modifiable sequence, initially empty.

c) The identifiers 'mkStudent' and 'repStudent' are bound to two primitives functions similar to those of the abstract type mechanism. The only difference is that the values created with 'mkStudent' are also automatically inserted in the class 'Students'.

```
E: use AStudent := get Students with StudentNumber = mkSixDigits (222222);

> AStudent = - : Student

E: Name of it;

  "Paul Smith" : string

E: for Exams of AStudent do Grade;

  [89] : seq int

E: remove all Exams with StudentNumber of GivenBy = StudentNumber of AStudent;

  nil : null

E: remove [AStudent];

  nil : null

E: get Students with StudentNumber = mkSixDlglts (222222);

  Failure : get
```

E: Name **of** AStudent;

   Failure : killed

Since a class name denotes a sequence of values, all the operators on sequences can be applied to classes. The operator **'get** Q **with** B' returns the only element of the sequence 'Q' which satisfies the condition 'B', otherwise it fails with the name 'get'. To remove an element from a class, the operator **'remove'** exists:

• **remove** S_1, S_2, ..., S_n

'S_i' are expressions which denote sequences of elements of classes. All the elements of the sequences are removed from the corresponding class and from all subclasses in which they appear, but only if they are not used as a value of a non-derived attribute of some other class element. Otherwise, the operator fails.

Failures

Each top-level expression is considered as a **transaction:** if it fails, its effects are undone. Failures can be generated implicitly by the predefined operations, as well as generated explicitly by the programmer using the expressions **'failwith** "String"' and **'fail'**, **which is equivalent to 'failwith** "fail"'. A failure is always identified by a name and can be trapped in two alternative ways: a general one, which traps any kind of failure; a selective one, which traps failures with certain names. Let us show an example of the first kind:

E: **use** Mary :=
=   mkStudent (Name := "Mary Smith"
=   **and** StudentNumber := mkSixDigits (222222)
=   **and** BirthDate := mkDate(Year := 1963 **and** Month := 5 **and** Day := 10));

> Mary : Student

E: mkExam (**GivenBy** := Mary
=   **and** Course "CS3"
=   **and** Date := mkDate (Year := 1983 **and** Month := 5 **and** Day := 10)
=   **and** Grade := 100
=   **and** Honor := <No>);

  – : Exam

E: **remove** [Mary];

  Failure : remove

E: **remove** [Mary] **if_fails remove** ExamsGiven **of** Mary, [Mary];

  nil : null

If the evaluation of 'E$_1$' in the expression 'E$_1$ if_fails E$_2$' fails, then the value of the entire expression is that of 'E$_2$', which is evaluated as if the evaluation of 'E$_1$' did not take place. In other words, the effects of 'E$_1$' are undone before the evaluation of 'E$_2$'. 'E$_1$' and 'E$_2$' must be of the same type. In this way the failures control permits the trial of alternative actions.

Subclasses

The subclass mechanism allows the user to operate on the same data organized as generalization hierarchies. Basically, a subclass contains those elements of one or more other classes (the superclasses), which inherit all the properties of the superclass elements, and can have, in addition, new properties, mirroring the fact that in the real world entities can have multiple roles. A subclass can be defined in three ways: as *subset*, *partition* or *restriction*. For simplicity we will describe only the case of a subset class with an unique superclass.

Let 'A''' a class with elements of type 'T''', and 'A' a subclass of 'A''', with elements of type 'T'. The following integrity constraints must hold:

1)Structural constraint.

If 'A' is subclass of 'A''', then 'T' is a subtype of 'T''', and so it inherits all the properties, operators, and assertions of 'T'''

The subtype's notion can be applied to all the Galileo's types [5]. It has been introduced to model the generalization mechanism in a language with static type-checking. In fact, the generalization requires that all the objects of a subclass be also objects of the superclass in any aspect. Since in Galileo the types of the classes are all different, this property can be modelled only if we allow an object to have more than one type, maintaining, in the same time, the "safety" of the type system. If an expression has type 'T', then it can be statically determined that its evaluation does not produce errors due to an illegal use of types, and, if it terminates, it produces a value of type 'T'. For concrete types, the subtype relation is inferred by standard rules, and need not to be declared by the programmer, while for the new types (and so for the class elements type too), one must explicitly declare that a type 'T' is subtype of another type, which are the attributes possessed only by 'T', as shown in the following example.

2)Extensional constraint.

This rule specifies which elements of a class are contained also in the subclass. While the structural constraint is the same for all kinds of subclasses, this constraint differs according to the kind of subclass. For subset classes, it is:

if 'x' is an element of 'A', and 'A' is defined as 'A subset of A''', then 'x' is an element of 'A'''.

```
E: use GraduateStudents subset of Student class
=         GraduateStudent <-> (is Student
=                         and Thesis : string);

> class GraduateStudents = - : seq GraduateStudent
| newType GraduateStudent = -
```

The following example shows some operators on subclasses.

```
E: mkStudent (StudentNumber := mkSixDigits (222222)
=             and BirthDate := mkDate (Year := 1963 and Month := 5 and Day := 10)
=             and Name := "Mary Smith")

  - : Student

E: mkGraduateStudent
=     (StudentNumber := mkSixDigits (222222)
=      and BirthDate := mkDate (Year := 1963 and Month := 5 and Day := 10)
=      and Name := "Mary Smith"
=      and Thesis := "Data Bases");

  Failure : key
```

% The previous expression fails because of a Student with number 222222 is already present in the class %

```
E: mkGraduateStudent
=     (StudentNumber := mkSixDigits (222222)
=      and BirthDate := mkDate (Year := 1963 and Month := 5 and Day := 10)
=      and Name := "Mary Smith"
=      and Thesis := "Data Bases")
= if_fails use Mary := get Students with StudentNumber = mkSixDigits (222222)
=          in inGraduateStudent (Mary, Mary and Thesis := "Data Bases");

  - : GraduateStudent

E: use Mary := get Students with StudentNumber = mkSixDigits (222222)
=    in Thesis of Mary likein GraduateStudents;

  "Data Bases" : string

E: remove all GraduateStudent with StudentNumber = mkSixDigits (222222);

  nil : null
```

When a new element is inserted in a subclass, it also becomes an element of the superclass, provided that the integrity constraints are not violated. The operator 'inSubclassType' inserts an object of a class in one of its subclasses; the object remains the "same", possibly enriched with new properties. The predicate **'alsoin'** is used to test if an object of a class also exists in one of its subclasses, while the operator **'likein'** "transforms" an element of a class in an element of a subclass (and so with its own properties).

Data Persistence

All the definitions given in the global environment persist between the user's sessions. The Galileo system also provides commands to initialize the global environment or to hide some identifiers. The idea of treating the persistence of values without resorting to particular data types has been proposed in [2], [11].

Data Modularization

To structure complex data base descriptions, which may require a large number of definitions, Galileo offers the possibility of breaking the schema in a set of meaningful units, called *modules*. This is a notable improvement over the traditional way of defining schemas, which forces the programmer to put all the definitions in the same textual unit, the schema, making it difficult to have a global, structured view of the system. The mechanism used in Galileo to structure definitions is the *environment*, which allows the introduction of *subenvironments* in the global one, and to define new environments starting from other ones. This possibility has been shown useful in several ways [6]:

- An environment contains the definitions of a data base, together with the applicable operations over the data. A user has access to this environment with the command **'enter** EnvironmentName', making it the current environment, and evaluating in it any Galileo expression. Since a subenvironment is a value in the global environment, it is a permanent object, and any modification is made persistent by the system.

- An environment can be defined extending another one with new definitions. In this way, for instance, some environments will contain only general data, which may be used by people which do not want, or cannot, see all the details of the schema. By combining this mechanism with that of subclasses, one can organize the schema of a data base with several levels of refinement.

- An environment can be defined by hiding some definitions of another environment.

2.2 Modelling concurrent activities in Galileo

An activity is a dynamic entity, with the following characteristics: a) it is described by a set of actions on the data base which have a long or very long duration; b) it can proceed in parallel with other activities, interacting with them by message passing; c) it can be in a suspended state, waiting for a reply to a message. Galileo has been extended with constructs to model activities and their interactions with an approach similar to that adopted in TAXIS [10], [15]. The abstraction mechanism used is the *process*, a construct typical of languages for concurrent programming. The model of cooperation among the processes is the "local environment model", in which the processes interact only through message passing. The principal characteristics of the proposal are:

- A process is a denotable value whose structure is described by its type.

- Processes are dynamic entities. In this way we can model the beginning of an activity with the creation and activation of a process.

● To keep track of all the active processes of a certain time, there exists the mechanism of process classes. A process class has characteristics similar to those of data classes.

● Processes can communicate both synchronously and asynchronously, so that, for instance, a process can wait a reply to one of its messages or proceed independently.

● Through a transaction mechanism mutual exclusion is provided for having access to the date base objects. Non serialized forms of synchronization can be obtained by programming them explicitly with the process mechanism. In this way, one can take into account concurrency only during the definition of the activities, while one can ignore it during the definition of the objects of the data base. The synchronization of accesses to other resources is provided by encapsulating the resource in a process which manages it.

● To enforce the local environment model of cooperation, access to data base objects can be made only inside transactions. In addition, to avoid improper sharing, processes and message parameters cannot be data base objects or modifiable values.

The example in Figure 3 models a semplified version of the activity of the loan of books by students, where 'Books' is a class with attributes 'CallNumber' of type 'BookNumber', 'Title' and 'Authors' of type 'string', and 'LoanedTo' of type 'var optional Student'. A book can be given on loan to a student for ten days, with at the most three renewals of the loan. After the due date is expired, students are solicited every three days. Initially, the process controls if the book is already on loan. If not, it loans the book and starts an alarm process which will "ring" after ten days. Then, it starts waiting on one of three events: a) the ring of the alarm, which causes it to send a notice and to reset the alarm for the next sending; b) the arrival of a renewal, which is accepted only within the limits, and causes the restart of the initial conditions; c) the student giving back the book, which causes the process to make the book available again and to terminate.

The definition of a process type introduces in the current environment the following bindings (with reference to the above example):

a) The identifier 'Loan' is associated to a new process type.

b) The identifier 'newLoan' is associated to a function which creates and activates processes of type 'Loan'.

In a process definition there are two parts: the definitions of the parameters of the creation operations, and the expression which describes the computation executed by the process once it has been activated (process body). Besides the usual Galileo expressions, a process body can contain also:

● Expressions, like 'newAlarm', to create and activate new processes.

```
type Lend process (BookToLoan: BookNumber and Borrower: SixDigits)
is use CanBorrow := var false
   in (transaction
        (use TheBook := get Books with CallNumber = BookToLoan
                         if_fails failwith "Book unknown"
        and TheStudent := get Students with StudentNumber = Borrower
                         if_fails failwith "Student unknown"
        in if at LoanedTo of TheBook is bound
            then (send AlreadyOnLoan() to mycreator; CanBorrow <- false)
            else (LoanedTo of TheBook <- TheStudent; CanBorrow <- true));
      if Not at CanBorrow
      then nil
      else (use NumberOfSolicitations := var 0
            and DueDate := var AddDays(ToDay(),10);
            ext Alarm := var newAlarm (ExpireTime := at DueDate)
            and Returned := var false
            and Renewals := var 0
            in while Not at Returned do
               alternative
                 receive TimeOut() from (at Alarm)
                     in (SendNotice (Borrower,BookToLoan);
                         DueDate <- AddDays(ToDay(),3);
                         Alarm <- newAlarm (ExpireTime := at DueDate);
                         NumberOfSolicitations <- at NumberOfSolicitations+1)
                 or receive Renewal() from (mycreator)
                     in if at Renewals = 3
                        then send NoMoreRenewals() to mycreator
                        else (NumberOfSolicitations <- 0;
                              Renewals <- at Renewals + 1;
                              send Terminate() to at Alarm;
                              DueDate <- AddDays(ToDay(),10);
                              Alarm<- newAlarm(ExpireTime:=at DueDate))
                 or receive BookReturned() from (mycreator)
                     in (Returned <- true;
                         transaction
                         (LoanedTo of
                            get Books with CallNumber = BookToLoan
                         <- <unbound>) ) ) )
```

Fig. 3 Definition of Lend Process

- Expressions to exchange messages with other processes ('**send**' and '**receive**'). They allow asynchronous communication among processes: the sender, after the message has been sent, can proceed with the computation independently from the fact that the receiver is waiting or not on its message. Since a process involved in a message's exchange does not care if its partner is a human or another process, the '**send**' and '**receive**' primitives are also used to model dialogs with the user.

- Expressions to wait on several possible incoming messages ('**alternative**'). The selection of the communication partner is a non-deterministic one, if more than one message has to be processed. Once a branch of the construct has been selected, the evaluation of the alternative expression terminates.

- Expressions which guarantee mutual exclusion on the data base (**'transaction'**). In the previous example, the operations on the property 'OnLoan' of the book requested are enclosed in this construct, to avoid interferences from other 'Loan' processes running in parallel.

3. Galileo/R: A LANGUAGE FOR THE SPECIFICATION OF THE USER'S REQUIREMENTS.

The user's requirements analysis phase in database design produces a formal, but not necessarily executable, specification of the expected behavior of the system. The language used must be capable of expressing all the information that will be needed in the successive phases of the design: data, constraints, operations, activities, dialogs, quantitative parameters, and performance requirements. The result must be a coherent and accurate description, which can be used by different categories of people: the users, which approve the specification; the designers, which implement the system; the experts which are in charge of the maintainance and evolution of the system. A requirements' specification is used to impose "constraints" on the possible implementations of the system, without anticipating project choices. During the design of Galileo/R we used the following guidelines:

- The language should allow the analyst to describe requirements with different degrees of detail and precision, from an almost natural language description to an almost executable description given in Galileo. Specifications that are initially incomplete ultimately become precise through formal definition, refining and detailing.

- The language should be expressive, that is with a natural and concise notation for expressing database applications. A "natural" notation means that the language should support a set of abstraction mechanisms that reflect the concepts associated with the problem at hand, and so it makes it easy to model them. For instance, entities, their properties, relationships among entities, and constraints should be modeled using the abstraction mechanisms of semantic data models, which have been shown to be of great help in modeling complex databases at conceptual level.

- The language should support the same abstraction mechanisms that are used for the conceptual design. This choice riduces the number of notions to master during the design process and allows the analyst to move easily from one level of description to another one.

- The language should be used by experts, but the system supporting the language should provide, for the analyst and non experts, graphical notations and interactive interfaces to input or display high level descriptions of the requirements. The important assumption is that simple descriptions should be given easily, but the more a user becomes familiar with the capabilities of the system's tools and with the problem to solve, the more he should be able to give a detailed description of the requirements, eventually in Galileo. In other words, requirements' specification and conceptual design should not appear as two isolated worlds, but simply two different levels of description that, in simple cases, can be transformed one into another once the user becomes more expert. Of course, the less detailed the specification, the less possibilities there are to execute it.

Among other approaches that advocate the use of semantic modeling in requirements specification, we note the work reported in [17], [18], [23], [27], [29], [31].

3.1 Modeling in Galileo/R

Let us discuss briefly the basic features of Galileo/R, since a complete description of the language is outside the scope of this paper. The examples show the documentation produced by the system, while the specifications are given using a graphical interface, which it is not shown for brevity. Graphics is provided for different purposes: a) to input specifications by means of forms, a command language based on menus and a "mouse" as a pointing device; b) to input a gross description of specifications using diagrams, to be detailed later on; and c) to produce reports based on a diagrammatic representation of data, operations, and activities. Galileo/R offers four kinds of specification units: data type, class, operation and activity.

A data type is defined with the same mechanisms provided in Galileo, so there are simple types, structured types and abstract types.

A class, or a subclass, is the same concept of Galileo, but there are more facts that can be described when a class is used to specify requirements. Figure 4 is a description of the class Student, giving information about students for an hypothetical university. Besides the structure of the class elements and assertions, other attributes can be specified to give: quantitative parameters on the cardinality of the class and associations; natural language description of the class, attributes and associations; the attribute of another class element that describes the inverse of an association; the name of the operations used to insert, delete, update or retrieve a class element, together with an estimate of the number of elements affected. Another difference from a class description given in Galileo is that here it is not required to give a complete definition since from the beginning: the description can be completed gradually, in a way that depends on the kind of checks that the user expects the system to make on the definitions.

```
Students class
      description « Facts about students of interest in this application »
      user RegistrationOffice
      cardinality min = 200 max = 3000 avg = 1500
      inserted by EnrollStudent
      referenced by TakeOutBook
      updated by ANewExam quantity 1 using Exams
      Student <->
          (BirthDate : Date
           and Citizenship : default "Italian"
           and Name : string
           and StudentNumber : SixDigits
           and Phone : optional PhoneNumber
                   description « çampus phone number with format ddd-dddd »
           and Exams : association invert Exams on GivenBy
                               cardinality min = 0 max = 20 avg = 10
          and BooksBorrowed : association derived all Books with LoanedTo = this
          assert « a student cannot give an exam more than once »
          keys (StudentNumber)
```

Fig. 4 Specification of Student Class

An operation is the description of how classes can be manipulated to create or eliminate elements. The example in Figure 5 provides a flavor of the underlying ideas. The operations can be described at two levels of detail:

- Initially, the analyst can specify only the type of parameters and result, the classes and associations used, the modality (insert, update, retrieve or delete), an estimate of the number of class elements affected, and the activities that use the operation.

- At the second level of details, the analyst describes the meaning of the operations in two possible ways: by means of pre-(post-) conditions and exceptions, and by means of an algorithmic specification. In the first case, the pre-condition defines the state of classes affected by the operation, before its execution; the post-condition describes the final state when the operation terminates; the exception is a description of the possible exceptional cases. In the second way, the analyst expresses the meaning of the operation procedurally in Galileo. This choice is in contrast with the position that a requirements' specification should not suggest a solution to the implementator. However, practical considerations suggest that an operational specification is often an useful alternative to a complex declarative specification, specially when it is given in an high-level language, such as Galileo, with the intention to describe only the effect of the operation. When both the specifications are used, the user is responsible to ensure that the supplied pre- (post-) conditions are compatible with the operational specifications.

```
TakeOutBook :=
      operation ( AStudentNumber : SixDigits, ACallNumber : BookNumber )
      description « To give a book on loan to a student »
      user Librarian
      used in activity Loan
      pre-condition
         description « A student exists with the specified StudentNumber, a book exists
                        with the specified CallNumber, and the book is not on loan »
         (exactly 1 Students with StudentNumber = AStudentNumber
          And exactly 1 Books with CallNumber = ACallNumber
          And LoanedTo of (get Books with CallNumber = ACallNumber) is unbound)
      post-condition
         (LoanedTo of (get Books with CallNumber = ACallNumber) =
          (get Students with StudentNumber = AStudentNumber))
      exceptions
         if Not exactly 1 Students with StudentNumber = AStudentNumber
            then failwith "Student Unknown"
         if Not exactly 1 Books with CallNumber = ACallNumber
            then failwith "Book Unknown"
         if LoanedTo of (get Books with CallNumber = ACallNumber) is bound
            then failwith "Book on loan"
      class-used
         retrieves Students quantity 1 using StudentNumber
         retrieves Books quantity 1 using CallNumber
         updates Books quantity 1 using LoanedTo
      association-used
         modifies LoanedTo from Books to Students
```

Fig. 5 Specification of TakeOutBook Operation

An activity is the description of how data and operations are used to implement organization's tasks, using the process mechanism of Galileo. As for operations, an activity can be described at two levels of detail:

• Initially, the analyst can specify only the type of parameters, the classes used, the operations employed, the messages exchanged, and an estimate of the frequency of occurrence.

• At the second level of details, the analyst describes, in natural language or formally in Galileo, the meaning of the activity using the control structures for processes shown in the previous section.

An example is shown in Figure 6.

```
activity Loan (AStudentNumber : SixDigits, ACallNumber : BookNumber)
description « this is the requirements specification of the process described
                previously in Galileo »
modality on-line
priority low
happens 50 times-per day
invokes Alarm
employes TakeOutBook
references Students Books
messages
      send Terminate to Alarm
      send AlreadyOnLoan to mycreator
      send NoMoreRenewals to mycreator
      receive TimeOut from Alarm
      receive Renewal from mycreator
      receive BookReturned from mycreator
process
      if « the book is not available »
      then send AlreadyOnLoan to mycreator
      else (TakeOutBook (AStudentNumber, ACallNumber);
               « activate Alarm for loan duration »;
            use Returned := var false
            in while Not at Returned do
                  alternative
                  receive TimeOut() from Alarm
                        in « send a solicitation to the student and restart Alarm »
                  or receive Renewal() from mycreator
                        in « if he has not yet done three renewals,
                              accept it and reset Alarm »
                  or receive BookReturned() from mycreator
                        in (Returned <- true;
                            « make book available ») )
```

Fig. 6 Specification of Loan Activity

The requirements' specification is examined to detect errors or to produce reports. Two kinds of checks can be invoked: a) cross-checks based on the fact that the specifications are redundant, and so it is possible to detect omissions, e.g., a class X is **'referenced by'** an operation Y, and Y does not include a statement involving X; b) static analysis of Galileo expressions used in definitions of classes, operations, and activities, once the specifications include all type definitions.

4. CONCLUSIONS

An overview of the Galileo Project at University of Pisa has been presented. The project is finalized to the implementation of an experimental database designer's workbench for graphics workstations, called Dialogo, based upon an operational approach. The implementation of the workbench is in progress on a Sun Workstation and on a Vax 11/780, both running UNIX™ Berkely 4.2. The implementation is carried out in Pascal in cooperation with Systems & Management S.p.A., and our efforts are presently on the implementation of Galileo. The following tools are in the testing stage: a) an interactive compiler for Galileo. In the present implementation, the management of persistent data has not yet been included, but two functions, save and restore, are provided to save and restore the current state of a working session on a specified file; b) a syntax driven editor of Galileo programs. The editor and the compiler are presently two independent tools; c) an integrated syntax driven editor and interpreter, implemented at Systems & Management S.p.A.. The implementation reflects the kind of architecture we have in mind for the final system, but it does not make use of graphics [21].

The following tools are not yet operational: a) a graphical editor for requirement specification and analysis in Galileo/R; b) the metadatabase to collect information on projects in progress; c) a form oriented interface to input and display objects of a database described in Galileo. Since the graphics workstation has been acquired only recently, the graphical interfaces will be one of our main concerns for the near future, together with the integration of tools for producing and testing prototypes in Galileo. Next, the inclusion of tools to collect, analyze, and document requirements' specification will be considered. Finally, mapping tools, from the prototype in Galileo to specific DBMS languages, will be implemented.

REFERENCES

[1]   Alavi, M., "An Assessment of the Prototyping Approach to Information Systems Development," Communications of the ACM 27 (1981) 556-563.

[2]   Albano, A., M.E. Occhiuto, and R. Orsini, "A Uniform Management of Persistent and Complex Data in Programming Languages," in: Atkinson, M. P. (ed.), Infotech State of the Art Report on Database, Series 9, No. 4, (Pergamon Infotech, 1981) 321-344.

[3]   Albano, A., and R. Orsini, "An Interactive Integrated System to Design and Use Data Bases," Proc. Workshop on Data Abstraction, Data Bases and Conceptual Modelling, ACM SIGMOD Special Issue 11 (1981) 91-93.

[4]   Albano, A., and R. Orsini, "Dialogo: An Interactive Environment for Conceptual Design in Galileo," in: Ceri, S. (ed.), Methodology and Tools for Database Design (North Holland, Amsterdam, 1983) 229-253.

[5]   Albano, A., "Type Hierarchies and Semantic Data Models," ACM Sigplan '83: Symposium on Programming Language Issues in Software Systems,   San Francisco, (1983) 178-186.

[6]   Albano, A., M. Capaccioli, M.E. Occhiuto, and R. Orsini, "A Modularization

Mechanism for Conceptual Modeling," Proc. 9th Intl. Conf. on VLDB, Florence, Italy (1983) 232–240.

[7] Albano, A., M. Capaccioli, and R. Orsini, "La definizione del Galileo (Versione 83/6)," Rapporto Tecnico Collana DATAID N. 20 (Giugno 1983).

[8] Albano, A., and R. Orsini, "A Prototyping Approach to Database Applications Development," IEEE Database Engineering (1984) (to appear).

[9] Albano, A., L. Cardelli, and R. Orsini, "Galileo: A Strongly Typed, Interactive Conceptual Language," ACM TODS (1985) (to appear).

[10] Albano, A., F. Baiardi, D. Castelli, R. Orsini, and R. Santerini, "Il Trattamento della Dinamica in Galileo," Rapporto Tecnico Collana DATAID N. 22 (Febbraio 1984).

[11] Atkinson, M. P., P. J. Bailey, K. J. Chisholm, W. P. Cockshott, and R. Morrison, "An Approach to Persistent Programming," The Computer Journal 26, (1983) 360–365.

[12] Atkinson, M. P., P. J. Bailey, K. J. Chisholm, W. P. Cockshott, and R. Morrison, "Progress with Persistent Programming," Technical Report, University of Pennsylvania, Department of Computer and Information Science, School of Engineering and Applied Science D2, Philadelphia, New Jersey (1984).

[13] Atzeni, P., C. Batini, V. De Antonellis, M. Lenzerini, F. Villanelli, and B. Zonta, "A Computer Aided Tool for Conceptual Database Design," in: H. J. Schneider and A. Wasserman (eds.), Automated Tools for Information System Design, (North Holland, Amsterdam, 1982) 85–106.

[14] Balzer, R., T.E. Cheatham, and C. Green, "Software Technology in the 1990's: Using a New Paradigm," Computer (1983) 39–45.

[15] Barron, J., "Dialogue and Process Design for Interactive Information System using TAXIS," Proc. ACM SIGOA Conf. on Office Information Systems (June 1982) 12–20.

[16] Borgida, A., "Features of Languages for Conceptual Information System Development," IEEE Software (1984) (to appear).

[17] Brodie, M. L., and D. Ridjanovic, "On the Design and Specification of Database Transactions," in: Brodie, M. L., J. Mylopoulos, and J. W. Schmidt (eds.), On Conceptual Modeling (Springer Verlag, New-York, 1984) 277–306.

[18] Bubenko, J. A., "Information Modeling in the Context of System Development," IFIP Congress 80 (North-Holland, Amsterdam, 1980) 395–411.

[19] Budde, R., K. Kuhlenkamp, L. Mathiassen, and H. Zullighoven (eds), "Approaches to Prototyping" (Springer—Verlag, Berlin, 1984).

[20] Capaccioli, M., "La Semantica Denotazionale del Galileo," Rapporto Tecnico Collana DATAID N. 23 (Febbraio 1984).

[21] Capaccioli, M., and M.E. Occhiuto, "A Workbench for Conceptual Design in Galileo," (in this volume).

[22] Ceri, S. (ed.), "Methodology and Tools for Database Design" (North-Holland, Amsterdam, 1983).

[23] Greenspan, S. J., and J. Mylopoulos, "Capturing More World Knowledge in the Requirements Specifications," Proc. of the Sixth International Conf. on Software Engineering, Tokyo, Japan (1982) 225-234.

[24] Kent, W., "Limitations of Record-Based Information Models," ACM TODS 4 (1979) 107-131.

[25] O'Brien, P. D., "An Integrated Interactive Design Environment for TAXIS," Proc. SOFTAIR: A Conference on Systems Development Tools, Techniques, and Alternatives, Arlington, VA, (July 1983) 298-306.

[26] Reiner, D., M. Brodie, G. Brown, M.Chilenskas, M. Friedell, D. Kramlich, J. Lehman, and R. Rosenthal, "A Database Design and Evaluation Workbench: Preliminary Report," Intl. Conf. on Systems Development and Requirement Specification, Gothenburg, Sweden (August 1984) 28-30.

[27] Roussopoulos, N., "CSDL: A Conceptual Schema Definition Language for the Design of Data Base Applications," IEEE Trans. on Software Engineering 5 (1979) 481-496.

[28] Solvberg, A., "A Contribution to the Definition of Concepts for Expressing Users' Information Systems Requirements," in: Chen, P.P. (ed.), Entity-Relationship Approach to System Analysis and Design (North Holland, Amsterdam, 1980) 359-380.

[29] Teorey, T.J., and R. Cobb, "Functional Specification for a Database Design and Evaluation Workbench," Working Paper 82 DE 1.15, Information Systems Research Group, Graduate School of Business Administration, University of Michigan (1982).

[30] Wasserman, A., "The Role of Prototypes in the User Software Engineering (USE) Methodology," in: Hartson, H.R. (ed.) Directions in Human-Computer Interaction (Ablex Publishing Co., 1984).

[31] Yeh, R. T., and P. Zave, "Specifying Software Requirements," Proc. of the IEEE 68 (1980) 1077-1085.

[32] Zave, P., "The Operational Versus the Conventional Approach to Software Development," Communications of the ACM 27 (1984) 104-118.

COMPUTER-AIDED DATABASE DESIGN: The DATAID Project
A. Albano, V. De Antonellis, and A. Di Leva (Editors)
© Elsevier Science Publishers B.V. (North-Holland), 1985

CHAPTER IV

A WORKBENCH FOR CONCEPTUAL DESIGN IN Galileo

Maurizio Capaccioli and Maria Eugenia Occhiuto

Systems & Management S.p.A.
Research and Development Division
Vicolo S.Pierino, 4
56100 Pisa, Italy

An interactive environment for conceptual design is
described. Firstly, it is based on a high level programming
language, Galileo, that allows a uniform description of all
the aspects of a data base that are relevant to the conceptual level: data, constraints, operations and schema structuring. Secondly, it is an integrated environment, providing
in a unique context facilities for conceptual schema
development and validation: schema editing, static semantic
analysis, query and update of the database. Finally, it
provides a high degree of interactivity to allow an incremental development of applications. The implications of
these features on conceptual design are discussed and examples are given to provide evidence of the usefulness of the
approach.

1. INTRODUCTION

In recent years a general agreement has been reached about the division of the
data base design process into four phases: requirements collection and analysis,
conceptual design, logical design and physical design [10, 14, 16, 22]. Several
methodologies and tools supporting the various phases have been proposed and are
currently under development, and the need of a working environment supporting
all the design phases has been expressed [21].

This paper addresses the conceptual phase of data base design. Specifically, we
present an environment which supports the conceptual design, to define and test
prototypes.

Several proposals of environments to support the conceptual design exist in
literature [10, 18, 20]. Some limits of these proposals, as outlined in [5], are
the following:

a) usually, the tools address the various phases of the database design but once
   the database has been implemented they are no longer useful and the maintenance of the data base application is to be done on its code.

b) the conceptual design is not always specified in an executable formalism,
   hence there is no way to verify the correctness of the specification at the
   conceptual level.

An approach which is receiving a large consensus as a method to solve the general problem of software development and maintenance [7] is based on the user
validation of prototypes before of the implementation stage. According to this
approach, we propose an environment in which an executable formalism is used to

define a conceptual schema. The implementation independent executable specification is a prototype of the data base and can be used to test the conceptual design with sample data to validate both the design and the requirements with the user.

Features of the proposed environment are:

(1) Uniformity.
    In place of a traditional data definition language (ddl), with a data manipulation language (dml) to be embedded in a host programming language, the environment provides a unique high level programming language, Galileo, intentionally designed to meet the needs of the conceptual design. The language includes features to describe all the aspects relevant to the conceptual level: data, constraints, operations and schema structuring. As a consequence schema definition, queries and applications are all programs in a high level language.

(2) Integration.
    There is a unique context in which all the environment facilities are provided. This avoids the need of frequent changes of context and results in a uniform user interface and in a faster and more efficient application development.

(3) Incrementality.
    Because of the complexity of data base design, an important requirement is that the data base must be incrementally designed and tested. From a conceptual point of view, this means that the designer divides the project in parts whose definitions proceed independently, at different levels of detail. From a functional point of view, this means that the environment tools can process not only complete schema definition, but also parts of them or definitions that are not completely specified. For example, the type checker analyses function definitions in which only the types of arguments and result are specified, while the body is omitted. In this case the type checker verifies that such functions are correctly applied.

(4) Extensibility.
    The environment is intentionally designed to be easily enriched with new facilities, without affecting the existing ones.

(5) Ease of use.
    A friendly interface is provided both for querying and for designing. In addition, the generative approach for editing schema definitions, queries and applicative programs, based on a syntax directed editor, spares the user from useless syntactic details while writing a program.

(6) Granularity.
    Each tool supports one simple, well defined facility, or a small set of related ones.

Because of the simplicity in which it is possible to move from one tool to another and the incrementality of the tools, the resulting environment has a high degree of interactivity. The user is allowed to decide which phase to carry out and which intermediate result to obtain according to the context and the necessity of the moment. While a part of the conceptual schema is developed only up to the type checking phase, another can be evaluated and a subset of functions of the schema tested. For example, the user can start specifying the definition of entity classes, perform static checks on them, insert some element and also try some simple query. Successively he can define new entity classes to refine and complete the schema definition.

An environment for conceptual design in Galileo with the above features is presented. As far as we know the only proposal of a data base design environment including prototyping at the conceptual level is that of the TAXIED system [17]. TAXIED is based on the conceptual language TAXIS [15]. For a comparison of Galileo and TAXIS see [9]. Another difference between the two environment is the kind of interaction provided and the overall architecture of the systems.

In the next section a brief overview of the language is given. Section 3 describes the facilities of the environment, Section 4 describes the kind of interaction that is given by the environment and Section 5 briefly describes the architecture of the environment.

2. THE CONCEPTUAL LANGUAGE Galileo

A complete description of Galileo is beyond the scope of this paper. The motivations and a presentation of the features are reported in [6] and in the previous chapter of this book. Some features of the language that appear in the remainder of the paper are briefly presented in this section, and the implications on conceptual design are discussed.

(1) Galileo is an interactive language: the user writes expressions, said "top level expressions", that are immediately processed by the system that reports the result of the computation. The top level expressions can be either a definition of the conceptual schema or part of it, a database query or update. In this way Galileo allows an interactive, incremental definition of the conceptual schema and the user interactions.

(2) Galileo has a modularization mechanism, called "environment". Each environment describes the relevant aspects of a certain area of the data base, while the global environment results from the composition of all of them. The incremental definition gives the possibility to design and test the project related to a certain area before considering the next one. For a discussion of the use of environments as a modularization mechanism see [2]. For example, the expression:

use
R;

is used to extend the current global environment with the environment denoted by R. Also, the expression:

enter
R;

is used to "enter" the environment denoted by R and work in it; the expression "quit" allows to return to the global environment (top-level).

(3) Galileo is a strongly typed language. Every type violation can be detected by textual inspection (static semantic analysis). Types are provided to model the structure of the data base. Static semantic analysis allows to check that identifiers are initialized before use and operations are applied to objects of the correct type. In addition, abstract data types are used to define the operations that can be applied to values of a certain type. The last is an important aspect, especially for the user defined operations, which embed integrity checks. One of the main results is faster evaluation, because static semantic analysis can be carried out before execution. Another important aspect is the possibility to check separately the various aspects of the correctness of a project. There are three different types of checks that can be executed on a program at different times: syntactic, static and dynamic checks. Errors of the first category are prevented when the syntax directed editor is used.

(4) Galileo is an expression oriented language. Every expression has a type and denotes a value. This is important because it gives meaning to the application of the tools to portions of expressions, other than top-level expressions. For example, in the following expression ("||" means "else if"):

```
          if B1
              then E1
          || B2
              then E2
          else E3
```

every Bi or Ei, or the entire expression, possesses a type and a value when it is given a context, i.e., the current environment. The interpreter or the static semantic analyser can be applied to any of the previous expressions (Bi or Ei or the entire expression) and return the corresponding value or type.

(5) The language supports the notion of type hierarchies [3]. The subtype relation is a partial order defined among types. The important property of this relation is that, if a type T is a subtype of a type T', then a value of type T can be used as an argument of any operation defined on values of type T' (not vice versa). This property suggests a programming methodology based on stepwise refinements, as proposed in [15]. The project begins with the definition of the most general types. The successive steps produce, from a definition at a given level of generality, a more specialized definition because the types are specializations (subtypes) of the previous types. This is obtained, at every step, by adding details that are typical of the specialized types. Following this methodology, large projects can be incrementally designed and tested. The functions designed and tested at a given level of generality can be directly used for the data defined later in the software development process.

Another important result of type hierarchies is to provide an effective way to fit the notion of IS_A hierarchy, as presented in the area of semantic networks, in a strongly typed language. Sets of real world entities are described by means of classes, whose elements always have an abstract data type. The relation "subclass" is defined among classes. This relation has two important properties based, respectively, on static and dynamic aspects. If A and A' are two classes, whose types of the elements are, respectively, T, T' and A is a subclass of A', then:

- T is a subtype of T' (static constraint).

- if a is an element of A then a is also an element of A' (dynamic constraint).

The incremental definition and testing of the schema is provided, as far as the language features are concerned, by the possibility to decompose large software projects into small, manageable units, whose definition proceeds at different levels of detail.

3. ENVIRONMENT FACILITIES

A previous implementation of the language Galileo provides a kind of interaction which strictly resembles that of traditional interactive systems [4]: the user writes with a text editor a top level expression which is immediately and completly processed by the system. All kinds of checks previously described and execution are performed in a stiff order (syntactic and static analysis and then execution).

In the environment here presented all top level expressions relative to the data base definitions, queries and updates are available, if not explicitly deleted, for reelaborations as many times as needed. Furthermore the stiff order of processing of a top level expression is eliminated: it is the user that decides which elaboration to perform (editing, syntactyc and static analysis and execution) on any available expression, not necessarily at top level, using one of the following environment facilities:

(1) Editing.
     Purpose of editing is to write a new top level expression or modify an old one. Syntactical correctness is forced by the system, which supports two editing modes.

     – Generative mode.
       A syntax directed editor is used, which is guided by the syntactic structure of the language. The grammar of Galileo is embodied in a collection of templates predefined for all the language constructs. Top level expressions are created top down: the user inserts new operators at a cursor position within the skeleton of previously entered templates. The inserted operator is selected in a set of legal operators according to Galileo syntax.

     – Analitic mode.
       As an alternative to the syntax directed editor, a text editor can be used. Entering the analitic mode the user types the expression using usual text editor commands. The syntactic correctness of the expression is checked by a parser when editing is finished.

     In both cases, to improve readability, a pretty printing for the language constructs is provided.

(2) Static semantic analysis.
     Static semantic analysis allows static checks of schema definition, queries and applicative programs to take place.

(3) Evaluation.
     Any Galileo expression can be evaluated and the system will print the result. This facility can be used to initialize the data base, to insert sample data, to query the data base, or occasionally to compute any type of calculus.

(4) Debugging.
     The possibility of evaluating portions of expressions is already an elementary form of debugging. In addition the debugging mode makes possible to follow the intermediate steps of the computation, printing their results while showing the (sub-)expressions that are being evaluated. Consider, for example, the Galileo operators that construct sequences of elements. In the debugging "step by step" mode their evaluation gives an element at a time, waiting for user requests before continuing. At any moment it is possible to set "breakpoints", to inspect identifier values or the list of the active functions, or to continue the current evaluation.

(5) Compiling.
     For a more efficient execution, a compiling facility is provided to translate a program into machine code.

(6) Schema querying.
     Queries are allowed not only about data but also about metadata, that is definitions of data and operators accessible in the current environment. For example, it is possible to know which classes are accessible in a given environment, in which definitions appear a certain attribute, which relations (associations) exist among classes, and so on.

(7) Aided querying.
     A user friendly interface is provided to help casual user in formulating
     queries.

(8) Saving and restoring.
     At any moment the state of the session can be saved to be restored later
     on.   This includes saving and restoring also of data thus obtaining data
     persistence.

At present the available facilities are generative editing, evaluation, debugging, saving and restoring. A parser necessary for analitic editing is completed
but not yet integrated with the other tools.

4. USER INTERACTION

In this section examples will be given to show how the user interacts with the
environment, with respect to generative editing, evaluation and debugging. The
examples, which are intentionally simple, are concerned with the definition of a
database of departments and employees of a firm.

At present, the screen layout is the following:

```
 _____
|                                                         |
|    program text                                         |
|                                                         |
|                                                         |
|                                                         |
|    _____        |
|    input                        error messages          |
|    _____        |
|    tool dependent                                       |
|_____|
```

The screen is divided into three areas, each of them has a cursor which is shown
in reverse.   In the following, reverse areas are surrounded by a rectangle. A
command language is provided to utilize all the environment facilities.

The upper portion of the screen is reserved for the program text.   It contains
the current top-level expression, that is, the top-level expression one is
currently interested in. Inside it, a current expression is pointed out by the
cursor. Moving the cursor, any expression can become the current expression. The
current expression is usually an implicit argument for the issued command.   The
program text is shown by a pretty printer that follows the rules of well-writing
of the Galileo constructs.

The middle portion of the screen is a single line. The left part is used by the
tools to get strings of characters from the user. The right part is used by the
tools to send messages of various kind to the user.

The lower portion of the screen is used by the tools mainly to show their own
results. In particular, it is used by the interpreter to present the evaluation
result and by the syntax directed editor to show the list of available operators
in a certain context. The evaluation result is shown by a pretty printer that
follows the same rules of well-writing of the language.

Interactive editing

The user constructs and manipulates Galileo expressions, which are always syntactically correct. As already mentioned, expressions are written top down inserting templates, corresponding to Galileo operators, and filling the "holes" in the templates with other templates. The "holes" are expressions not yet specified, denoted by names enclosed in angular brackets and correspond to Galileo syntactic cathegories.

When the user starts defining a new data base there are no top level expressions previously defined and the screen layout is the following:

```
 _____
/                                                                \
|                                                                |
|   ┌──────────────────────┐                                     |
|   │ <TopLevelExpression> │ ;                                   |
|   └──────────────────────┘                                     |
|                                                                |
|   _____ |
|                                                                |
|   define_environment      enter_environment      expression    |
|                                                                |
_____/
```

At this level, the user can define a new environment, enter an existing one or construct any expression. These are the only alternatives for the syntactic category TopLevelExpression, i.e., the only ways to specify it. To define the classes Departments and Employees, the user has to choose the first one. This causes the substitution of the syntactic cathegory TopLevelExpression with the template relative to the use operator and produces the following screen layout:

```
 _____
/                                                                \
|                                                                |
|   use                                                          |
|       ┌───────────────────────────┐                            |
|       │ <Environment_Expression>  │ ;                          |
|       └───────────────────────────┘                            |
|                                                                |
|   _____ |
|                                                                |
|   and       as          at      binding    class               |
|   drop      emptyenv    ext     first      application         |
|   get       identifier  if      of         rec                 |
|   rename    sub_array   take    type       usein               |
|   with                                                         |
|                                                                |
_____/
```

In fact to define an environment the "use" operator is required. Since this operator must be followed by an expression denoting an environment, the operators potentially denoting an environment are listed. We choose "rec", and the screen becomes:

```
    use
        rec │<Binding>│ ;


    _____

    binding              class              type
```

The "rec" alternative has been used to give a list of mutually dependent definitions. In fact, the classes Employees and Departments are supposed to be defined
one in terms of the other. Now we proceed with the definition of the first
class, hence we point to the word "class", obtaining the following screen:

```
    use
        rec │<Identifier>│ class
                    <AbstractTupleType>
                    <ClassAssertions>
        and <Binding> ;

    _____

    identifier
```

The structure of a class definition is displayed, and the editor moves the program cursor onto "<Identifier>" (class name). Another "Binding" is presented for
a successive use. It is important to note that, moving the cursor on the program
text, the order in which the various parts are expanded can be changed as
wished. The user types the name in the middle window.

```
    use
        rec │<Identifier>│class
                    <AbstractTupleType>
                    <ClassAssertions> ;
        and <Binding> ;

    _____
    > Employees
    _____
    identifier
```

Given the class name, the editor asks for the type of the elements of the class.

```
use
    rec Employees class
         ⟨AbstractTupleType⟩
         ⟨ClassAssertions⟩ ;
    and ⟨Binding⟩ ;
    _____

    _____
    abbreviated_form          abstract_tuple_type
```

The editor shows that, in addition to the normal way to define an abstract tuple type, the abbreviated form can be used. Let us choose the second.

```
use
    Employees class
         ⟨Identifier⟩ ⟨SubTypeRelation⟩ ⟨->
             (⟨RepresentationType⟩)
         ⟨AssertionList⟩
         ⟨ImportClause⟩
         ⟨ClassAssertions⟩
    and ⟨Binding⟩ ;
    _____

    _____
    identifier
```

At this point it is possible to specify the name of the type of the elements of the class, the subtype relation, if any, the representation type and the list of the assertions. After the definition of this class and the class Departments, the screen is:

```
use
    rec Employees class
            Employee  <->
                (Name : string
                 and BirthDate : Date
                 and Salary : var int
                 and Dept := derived get Departments
                                            with
                                            this isin Staff)
            key (Name)
    and Departments class
            Department  <->
                (Name : string
                 and Manager : Employee
                 and Budget : var int
                 and Staff : var seq Employee)
                 assert Budget > 0;
```

The type Date is a system predefined type. Insuring the syntactical correctness, the syntax directed editor encourages the naive user in writing programs.

Evaluation

Another basic feature is the evaluation of the edited expressions. Since any Galileo construct is an expression, evaluation applies both to the data base definition, resulting in the initialization of the values (basically, classes and functions), and to the creation of new objects, resulting in their insertion in the respective classes, and to the query, resulting in performing the query. In any case, the pretty printer shows the result.

We now turn to our example, evaluating the previously edited definition. This can be done simply issuing the evaluation command when the entire definition is the current expression.

```
use
     rec Employees class
             Employee  <->
                 (Name : string
                  and BirthDate : Date
                  and Salary : var int
                  and Dept := derived get Departments
                                          with
                                            this isin Staff)
             key (Name)
     and Departments class
             Department  <->
                 (Name : string
                  and Manager : Employee
                  and Budget : var int
                  and Staff : var seq Employee)
                  assert  Budget > 0;
```

```
(Employees := [-]
 and mkEmployee := function
 and repEmployee := function
 and Departments := [-]
 and mkDepartment := function
 and repDepartment := function)
```

The result of the evaluation, shown in the lower portion of the screen, is an
environment containing the two (empty) classes Employees and Departments, and
four functions: mkEmployee and mkDepartment to insert new elements in the
respective classes, repEmployee and repDepartment to obtain the representation
of an employee or a department.

Element insertion

The next is an example of element insertion in the Employees class. Let us suppose that the following expression has been edited: to evaluate it, it is enough
to move the program cursor on it.

```
mkEmployee (Name := 'Sibille Ellis'
           and BirthDate := mkDate (Day := 15
                                    and Month := 6
                                    and Year := 1953)
           and Salary := 1000);
```

_____

```
(Name := 'Sibille Ellis'
  and BirthDate := (Day := 15
                    and Month := 6
                    and Year := 1953)
  and Salary := 1000
  and Dept := derived)
```

The lower portion of the screen shows the inserted element, result of the evaluation. The derived attribute Dept is automatically inserted by the mkEmployee function.

Query

The following expression is an example of query: it returns name and birthdate of the employees earning more than 900.

```
for Employees
    with Salary > 900
    do Name := Name
       and BirthDate := BirthDate
```

_____

```
(Name := 'Sibille Ellis'
  and BirthDate := (Day := 15
                    and Month := 6
                    and Year := 1953))
```


Refinements

In the next example, PartTimeEmployees is a subclass of the Employees, and hence the type of its elements, PartTimeEmployee, is a specialization of the type Employee.

```
use
      PartTimeEmployees subset of Employees class
             PartTimeEmployee <->
                    is Employee
                    and PrivateData : string;


(PartTimeEmployees := [-]
 and mkPartTimeEmployee := function
 and repPartTimeEmployee := function)
```

Since PartTimeEmployees is a subclass of Employees, an element inserted in the
PartTimeEmployees class is also inserted in the Employees class and because of
the subtype relation all the functions defined on the type Employee are also
available on the type PartTimeEmployee.

Step by step evaluation

In this mode every intermediate result of evaluation is shown, together with the
(sub-)expression currently involved. The program cursor is moved upon the text
to show the execution path; at any step, the text (including the cursor) is
shown while in the low part of the screen the result of the evaluation of the
current expression appears. For example consider the case of quering the year of
birthdate of the employee denoted by SibilleEllis.

```
      Year of Birthdate of SibilleEllis ;

      _____

      _____
```

Giving the command of "step by step" evaluation, the various steps are
displayed. A message is printed in the middle part of the screen, to remember
that the evaluation is in progress.

```
Year of Birthdate of │SibilleEllis│ ;


─────────────────────────────────────────────────
                                  Step By Step Evaluation
─────────────────────────────────────────────────
(Name := 'Sibille Ellis'
 and BirthDate := (Day := 15
                   and Month := 6
                   and Year := 1953)
 and Salary := 1000
 and Dept := derived)
```

This step shows the data related to Sibille Ellis.

```
Year of │Birthdate of SibilleEllis│ ;


─────────────────────────────────────────────────
                                  Step By Step Evaluation
─────────────────────────────────────────────────
(Day := 15
 and Month := 6
 and Year := 1953)
```

This step shows the birthdate of Sibille Ellis.

```
│Year of Birthdate of SibilleEllis│ ;


─────────────────────────────────────────────────
                                  Finished Step By Step
─────────────────────────────────────────────────
1953
```

Together with the year of birthdate of Sibille Ellis, a message appears that
evaluation is terminated.

5. ARCHITECTURE

The architecture of the presented environment for conceptual design in Galileo
has been developed within a general software development environment, ISDE,

currently in progress at the Systems & Management Research and Development Division [11]. ISDE provides features of integration, incrementality, ease of use and extensibility, which are widely recognized as the basic features of any software development environment [12, 13, 19].

The key point in the architecture of ISDE is the unique representation of the program, based on the abstract syntax of the language. In our case, the internal representation of the program is the internal representation of a data base schema, query or any Galileo expression. The representation is a tree in which the nodes represent operators of the language. Attributes can be associated with the nodes, thus allowing a two-level description: the tree for the program structure (syntax), the attributes for the information generated by the application of the tools (semantics).

Integration among the environment tools is then achieved by means of the unique representation of the program. All the tools work on the same representation of the program.

Incrementality is achieved by means of the semantic information provided by the program representation. Using attributes, the environment tools can maintain all the relevant information on the tree, passing from one activation to a subsequent one. The program representation is then the "state" of the entire environment.

Ease of use results from a uniform user interface, the same for each environment tool, and from the generative style of editing programs, with the syntax directed editor which helps the user in writing programs.

Extensibility comes from the architecture which allows the implementation of new tools without involving the existing ones. On the other hand, the implementation of a new tool benefits from the environment providing the internal program representation on which the tool can operate and maintain its information.

Another important feature of ISDE's approach is the derivation of the environment tools for a specific language from a language-independent meta-environment. This fact arises from the consideration that some modules of the environment are language-independent, while tools concerned with syntactic aspects of the language can be obtained by means of a formal specification [8].

The environment presented in this paper is obtained by exploiting to a great extent ISDE facilities, as explained in the sequel. The resulting architecture of the workbench for conceptual design is:

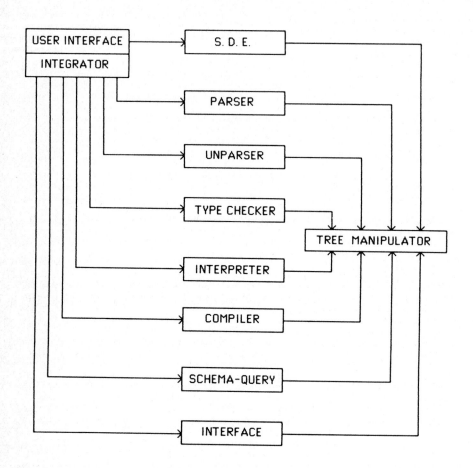

Let us briefly describe the environment modules currently available.

User interface

It acquires the user's command with a sophisticated terminal independent window system. It is a general tool provided by ISDE.

Integrator

It implements the command language, calling the various tools according . to the command issued by the user and acquired from the user interface. It is a general tool provided by ISDE.

Tree Manipulator

This is the kernel of the environment architecture and it is a general tool provided by ISDE. The Tree Manipulator makes available a set of functions to handle the internal representation of the program. All the other tools work on the internal representation by means of these functions, hence being independent from its implementation. In this sense the Tree Manipulator behaves like an abstract data type.

Syntax Directed Editor

It is automatically generated as an instantiation of an ISDE meta tool, by means of a formal description of the abstract syntax of Galileo.

Parser

It performs syntactic analysis of a Galileo expression represented as a string of characters. If no errors are detected an internal representation of the expression is constructed. The parser is an instantiation of the processors Lex and Yacc available in the Unix(*) operating system.

Unparser

The pretty printer Unparser maps the abstract syntax of a program into its concrete syntax. It gives the user the usual view of programs while leaving the internal representation to the various tools. It is automatically generated from an ISDE meta tool, specifying the mapping between the abstract and the concrete syntax.

Interpreter

It takes any Galileo expression and prints the result of its evaluation. In the debugging mode, it allows the user to follow the evaluation, showing the execution path on the program while printing the related results. The Interpreter is an ad-hoc realization for the Galileo language.

The implemented subset of the workbench is running on a Vax 750 under the Unix(*) operating system and is written in Berkeley Pascal.

6. CONCLUSIONS

An environment for prototyping data bases has been presented with the following features:

(1) the language upon which it is based, Galileo, allows a uniform description of data definition, query and manipulation.

(2) the environment fully integrates the tools related to the various aspects of programming. The basic tools are a syntactic analizer, a static semantic analizer (static consistency checker) and an interpreter to simulate data base operations. The environment has a high degree of interactivity to encourage incremental development of applications.

The implementation is still in an experimental phase and a lot has still to be done. At present, the results obtained encourage us to proceed in this

---

(*) Unix is a Trademark of Bell Laboratories.

direction and we believe that the stated features of the environment are a useful support for prototyping data bases applications. Work is in progress to:

- provide all the environment tools previously described, in particular the
  static semantic analizer.

- improve the user interaction, providing a graphical interface on a SUN
  workstation.

- cover all the phases of data base design. Of particular interest is the
  realization of an automatic tool to map a prototype into the implementation
  for the language of a specific DBMS.

REFERENCES:

[1] Albano A. and R. Orsini, An Interactive Integrated System to Design and Use
     Data Bases, Proc. Workshop on Data Abstraction, Data Bases and Conceptual
     Modelling, ACM SIGMOD Special Issue 11, 2 (1981) 91-93.

[2] Albano A., M. Capaccioli, M.E. Occhiuto and R. Orsini, A Modularization
     Mechanism for Conceptual Modeling, Proc. of 9th International Conference on
     Very Large Data Bases, Florence (1983) 232-240.

[3] Albano A., Types Hierarchies and Semantic Data Models, Proc. of the SIGPLAN
     '83 Symposium on Programming Language Issues in Software Systems, S. Fran-
     cisco, 1983, SIGPLAN Notices, 18, 6 (1983) 178-186.

[4] Albano A. and R. Orsini, Dialogo: An Interactive Environment for Conceptual
     Design in Galileo, in: Ceri S. (ed.), Methodology and Tools for Database
     Design (North-Holland, Amsterdam, 1983) 229-253.

[5] Albano A. and R. Orsini, A Prototyping Approach to Database Applications
     Development, IEEE DATA Engeneering (1984) (to appear).

[6] Albano A., L. Cardelli and Renzo Orsini, A Strongly Typed, Interactive Con-
     ceptual Lannguage, ACM Trans. on Database Systems (1985) (to appear).

[7] Balzer R., T.E. Cheatham and C. Green, Software Technology in the 1990's:
     Using a New Paradigm, Computer, November (1983) 39-45.

[8] Barbuti R., M. Bellia, E. Dameri, P. Degano, G.Levi, A. Martelli and C.
     Simonelli, Towards the Derivation of an Experimental Programming Environ-
     ment from Language Formal Specifications, Proc. of 15th Annual Hawaii
     International Conference on System Sciences (1982) 1-9.

[9] Borgida A., Features of Languages for the Development of Information Sys-
     tems at the Conceptual Level, IEEE Software (1984) (to appear).

[10] Ceri S. (ed.), Methodology and Tools for Database Design (North-Holland,
     Amsterdam, 1983).

[11] Chesi M., E. Dameri, M.P. Franceschi, M.G. Gatti and C. Simonelli, ISDE: An
     Interactive Software Development Environment, Proc. of ACM SIGSOFT/SIPLAN
     Symposium on Practical Development Environments, Pittsburg (1984).

[12] Donzeau-Gouge V., G. Huet, G. Kahn and B. Lang, Programming Environments
     Based on Structured Editors : the MENTOR Experience, Research Report, 26,
     INRIA (1980).

[13] Habermann N. and D.Notkin, The GANDALF Software Development Environment, Technical Report, Carnegie Mellon University (1982).

[14] Lum V., et al., 1978 New Orleans Data Base Design Workshop Report, Proc. 5th Int. Conf. on Very Large Data Bases, Rio de Janeiro (1979).

[15] Mylopoulos J., P.A. Bernstein and H.K.T. Wong, A Language Facility for Designing Database-Intensive Applications, ACM TODS 5, 2 (1980) 185-207.

[16] Navathe B.S., Information Modelling Tools for Data Base Design, Panel on Logical Database Design, Fort Lauderdale, Florida (1980).

[17] O'Brien P.D., An Integrated Interactive Design Environment for Taxis, Proc. SOFTFAIR: A Conference on Software Development Tecniques and Alternatives, Arlington, VA, 1983. Silver Spring , MD: IEEE Computer Society Press (1983) 298-306.

[18] Reiner D., M. Brodie, G. Brown, M. Chilenskas, M. Friedell, D. Kramlich, J. Lehman and A. Rosenthal, A Database Design and Evaluation Workbench: Preliminary Report, Proc. Int. Conf. on Systems Development and Requirements Specification, Gothenburg, Sweden (1984).

[19] Teitelbaum R. and T. Reps, The Cornell Program Synthesizer: A Syntax-Directed Programming Environment, CACM 24, 9 (1981) 563-573.

[20] Teory T.J. and Fry J.P., Design of Database Structures, Prentice-Hall, Englewood Cliffs, NewJersey (1982).

[21] Wasserman A.I., Automated Tools in the Information System Development Environment, Proc. IFIP WG 8.1 Working Conference on Authomatic Tools for Information Systems Design and Development, New Orleans, January (1982) 1-9.

[22] Yao S.B., B.S.Navathe and J.L. Weldon, An Integrated Approach to Logical Database Design, in NYU Symposium on Data Base Design, New York (1978) 1-14.

COMPUTER-AIDED DATABASE DESIGN: The DATAID Project
A. Albano, V. De Antonellis, and A. Di Leva (Editors)
© Elsevier Science Publishers B.V. (North-Holland), 1985

CHAPTER V

THE LOGICAL DESIGN IN THE DATAID
PROJECT: THE EASYMAP SYSTEM

M.N.Bert (*), G.Ciardo (*)(+), B.Demo (**), A.DiLeva (**),
P.Giolito (**), C.Iacobelli (*), V.Marrone (**)

(*) CSELT - Centro Studi e Laboratori Telecomunicazioni S.p.A.
     Via Guglielmo Reiss Romoli, 274 - 10148 TORINO (Italy)

(**) Dipartimento di Informatica - Universita´ di Torino
     Via Valperga Caluso, 37 - 10125 TORINO (Italy)

In this paper we focus on the system modules for logical
design. After a general description of the ISIDE
(Integrated System for Implementation DEsign) system,
developed within the DATAID project to support the logical and physical design phases, the structure of the
metadatabase, in which all the data relevant to the
design phases are stored, is described.
The system module, called Dynamic Analyzer, that evaluates the operation frequencies is then introduced, followed by the system modules, called EASYMAP, which
translates the conceptual database specification into
the corresponding logical specification, both for relational and CODASYL-like DBMS´s (Data Base Management
Systems).

1. INTRODUCTION

In recent years several tools have been produced to support the logical and physical phases of the database design (see [9] for an
exhaustive review), but it is difficult to find a general system
that supports all the steps of these phases according to a complete
and effective database design methodology. Usually, the tools
described in literature are confined to very restricted application
fields (e.g. see [22]). As far as general methodologies are concerned, the proposed tools are often oriented to document the
analysis of data and processes rather than to support the user in
this analysis, (see, for instance, DDSS [17], JSD [15], LBMS [14],
NIAM [24], SYSDOC [1], SASD [25]). In particular, at the implementation (logical and physical) level, some general metodologies, such
as ACM/PCM [5], ISAC [16], NIAM and SASD, do not support the user,
but give only guidelines for the conceptual-implementation conversion. JSD,for example, specifies the transformation from the conceptual specification to the operational system and some software su p-
port has been produced (e.g. the COBOL system implementation), but
it is mostly oriented towards process development.

(+) Presently at the Duke University - Durham N.C.

In this paper after introducing the ISIDE (Integrated System for Implementation DEsign) system, which supports both the logical and the physical design phases, we focus on the system modules for logical design. As regards ISIDE, we describe its general architecture and the structure of the metadatabase in which all the data relevant to the design phases are stored. For the logical design, we describe EASYMAP, i.e. the system module which translates the conceptual database specification into the corresponding logical specification, both for relational and CODASYL-like DBMS´s (Data Base Management Systems), and the Dynamics Analyzer i.e. the system module that evaluates the operation frequencies.

In developing ISIDE we have taken into account the following aspects:
- flexibility: in ISIDE the interface towards the conceptual design phase is neatly isolated so that different conceptual schema descriptions can be adopted. In particular, interfaces towards the EER model and the Galileo language have been developed.
- integration: ISIDE integrates the tools developed within the DATAID project to support the logical and physical design phases. To this purpose a Data Manipulation Interface (DMI) has been defined to be used as a low level DBMS to manipulate the metadatabase of the system. Through the DMI, interactions among the different tools become interactions between each tool and the metadatabase, facilitating the exchange of common information between tools.

2. GENERAL DESCRIPTION

The ISIDE system supports the logical and physical design phases and provides performance predictions. In this way, the database design can be tuned to meet the user requirements concerning the efficiency of the application, before its actual implementation.

The input to ISIDE is the conceptual description of the static and dynamic aspects of the application to be automated. It is composed by the global data schema, the operation schemata and the events schemata.

The **global data schema** is described by means of a conceptual data definition language (cddl). The data model used for the definition of the schema is the Enriched Entity Relationship Model (EERM), an extension of the Entity Relationship model and has been described in [7]. An example concerning the project management of a firm organization will be used in the rest of the paper; its conceptual schema is shown in Figure 1.

The **operation schemata**, defined by means of a conceptual data manipulation language (cdml), provides the database designer with the representation of processing requirements on data, that is: the access path performed on the data schema and the type of usage of the attributes.

In Figure 2 a simple operation is expressed by using the graphic representation of the operations introduced in [3].

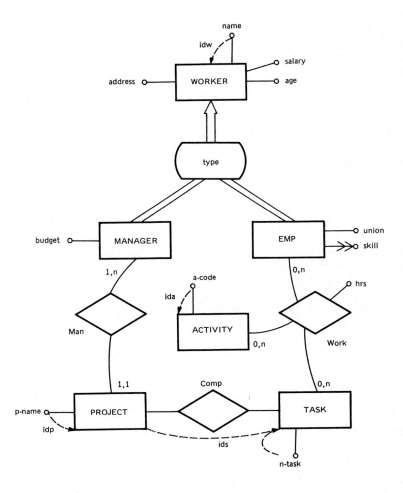

Fig. 1: The conceptual schema of the project management environment.

"Find name and address of the employees working on project X"

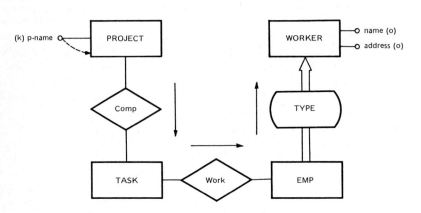

Fig.2 : Representation of the operation

The **events schemata** that represent the organization functions are described in a conceptual event description language (cedl).

The **quantitative parameters** related to the objects appearing in the conceptual description; i.e.:
- expected cardinality of entities and relationships;
- probability distribution of the values of the attributes. The Poisson, Gauss and Beta distribution may be used to model numerical values. Also the correlation between values of different attributes can be expressed by using a bidimensional distribution.

The output of ISIDE includes the logical and physical database schemata, according to the target DBMS, (in our case, both CODASYL-like and relational-like environments are considered) and performance predictions (i.e. the evaluated mean response time for each operation).

The ISIDE architecture, shown in Figure 3, has five main components: the Dynamics Analyzer, the Logical Designer (EASYMAP), the Relational Designer (IDEA), the CODASYL Designer (EROS, EOS) and the Metadatabase.

Both the **Relational Designer** and the CODASYL Designer generate a complete database specification from the logical description (output of the Logical Designer), i.e. they specify the physical parameters and access paths, and give an evaluation of the operations response time. These two components are both in operation and will be illustrated in other chapters of this book.

In the present paper, we focus on the other three components, in particular:
a) the **Metadatabase** (described in Section 3), that contains all the

information used and produced by the other components,
b) the **Dynamics Analyzer** (described in Section 4), that generates the operation frequencies (which are used in the logical and physical design) starting from the events graphs of the organization functions taken into account in the conceptual design phase. This component is not yet fully implemented.
c) The **Logical Designer** (described in Section 5), that converts the conceptual description of the database application into the logical description, input to the Relational or CODASYL Designer.

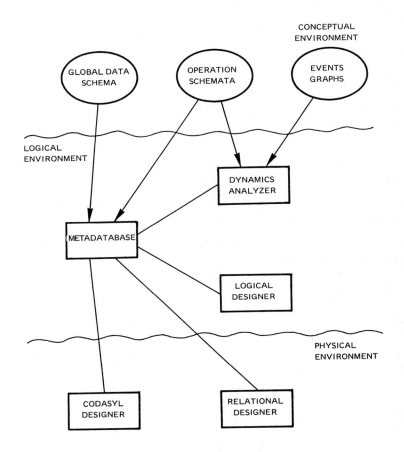

Fig. 3: ISIDE Architecture

3. THE METADATABASE OF ISIDE

The ISIDE system is based on a metadatabase which acts as a central repository of all the information being created and used during the different design phases. The Metadatabase component is made of a database (from now on referred to simply as "metadatabase") and a data manipulation interface (DMI).

All the inputs to ISIDE (global data schema, operation schemata, events graphs) are loaded into the metadatabase. The Logical Designer will then access the metadatabase in order to get the data it needs to produce the logical schema. The logical schema in turn will be stored into the metadatabase and used by the Relational or CODASYL Designer.

In Figure 4 a simplified description of the metadatabase schema is shown. The source (ER) model is described on the left-hand side, both final models (Relational and CODASYL) are described on the right-hand side, while the mappings between the ER model and the other two models are represented in the middle.

The ISIDE components interact with the metadatabase through a **data manipulation interface** (DMI), i.e. a set of commands for insertion, retrieval and modification of entities or relationships occurrences (or groups of them) in the metadatabase. We can say that DMI acts as a low level DML to manipulate a database via the ER model. Delete operations are not considered: data can only be updated but not erased, since it is important to maintain a complete trace of the whole design cycle, even of failures. The set of commands is callable from a program written in Pascal, which is the implementation language of all ISIDE components.

4.   THE DYNAMICS ANALYZER

The Dynamics Analyzer generates the operation frequencies (which are used in the implementation design) starting from the event graphs of the given set of organization functions.

The Petri nets used to represent events schemata in the DATAID approach are the basic C-E Petri nets [6]).

To characterize the organization dynamics, from a quantitative point of view we extend the events schemata, associating firing times with transitions.
In particular, two types of transition have been introduced in the model:
- operations, to be executed against the database that, upon enabling, take a finite amount of time to fire;
- controls, introduced in the net to express structures of concurrency and conflict, that immediately fire upon enabling.
In fact, as shown in [2], the Petri nets so extended and the related marking transition diagram can be considered as a network and flow analysis can be used to compute the mean number of times each opera-tion is activated within an execution of the net (relative frequen-cies).

The Dynamics Analyzer takes, from the metadatabase, an events schema described by means of the extended Petri net model and constructs the related marking transition diagram according to the initial assumptions given by the user. During the diagram construction, the system requests probability distributions in order to characterize conflict situations. As conflicts have been characterized, a flow

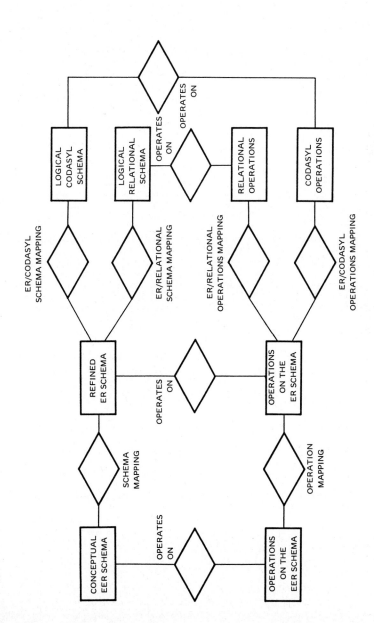

Fig. 4: Simplified description of the metadatabase schema.

analysis package is used to compute the relative frequency of each operation in the events schema. Once the frequency of the events schema is known, absolute frequencies are obtained. Quantitative parameters (such as the frequency) related to the events schemata are usually more reliable than those related to the operations, because events schemata correspond to the activities of the organization to be automated. The automatic derivation of the operation frequencies from the events schema frequency ensures the mutual consistency of these parameters that play a crucial role in the logical and physical design phases.

This module has not yet been fully implemented. A prototype module that constructs the marking diagrams and performs the flow analysis exists. It will be incorporated into an interactive system with a user friendly interface that supports the requirements collection and analysis at the organization level, presently under development.

5. THE LOGICAL DESIGNER: EASYMAP

The phase of logical design transforms the conceptual schema into a logical schema in which data structures are expressed either according to the CODASYL data model or to the relational model. In the following, a brief description of the Logical Designer module is given. For further details, the reader can refer to [4, 13].

The translation process is based on two fundamental tasks:
- simplification of the conceptual schema: data structures which cannot be directly transformated into the logical model (such as hierarchies and multiple relationships) are converted into simpler ones. This task produces a simplified schema which contains only non-hierarchical entities and binary relationships;
- refinement of the simplified schema: a set of transformations is applied on the simplified schema; performance measures are used to select from among different alternatives the solution which optimizes the execution of the most important operations.

Each translation step can produce several solutions that are inspected so as to reduce:
1 - the number of logical accesses of the operations to the entities (access number);
2 - the amount of data transferred in I/O activities between mass and core memory (transport volume).

In order to evaluate criteria 1 and 2, the conceptual schema is converted into an internal representation consisting of a flow graph. The nodes of the graph are the entities of the schema and the arcs represent the relationships connecting the entities. For each node, the number and the type of logical accesses of the operations to the related entity is evaluated. The number of accesses for each relationship is also evaluated and associated to the corresponding arc. Access numbers and transport volumes are calculated starting from the quantitative schema description that contains the statistical characteristics of the data schema [3] . A final task generates the database CODASYL and/or relational description, which comprises:
- the logical (relational or CODASYL) schema;
- a set of operation descriptions which translate the conceptual operations in the target (relational or CODASYL) model.

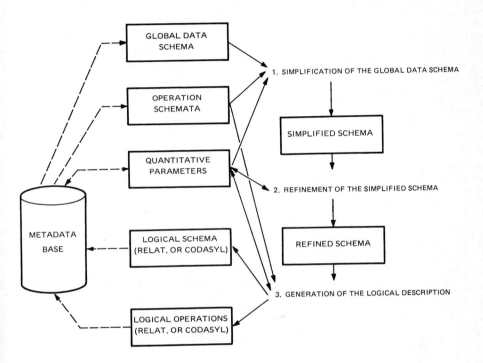

Fig. 5: Overall structure of the methodology.

5.1   Simplification of the global data schema

The aim of this task is to eliminate the following structures, which
cannot be directly translated into the logical model:
- hierarchies (both the generalization and the subset hierarchies);
- ring relationships (in which an entity has many roles), relationships having attributes and multiple relationships (relationships
  of an order greater than two); these relationships will be called
  complex relationships.

A complex relationship is transformed by introducing a   link   entity
which   inherits   the possible attributes of the complex relationship
and is externally identified by the entities that take part   in   the
complex relationship.

A hierarchy is translated by introducing   binary   1:1   relationships
between   the super-entity and the sub-entities; the sub-entities are
externally identified by the super-entity.   Each sub-entity can also
inherit   the attributes (and the relationships) of the super-entity,
giving rise to an alternative solution.

The last objective of this task is the selection of a principal
identifier for each entity in the simplified schema. The identifier
most frequently used by the operations for direct access to the
occurrences of the entity is selected; subsequent steps will
translate the principal identifier into the key of the record type
corresponding to the given entity.

5.2 Refinement of the simplified schema

The refinement process applies three kinds of transformation to the
simplified schema: merging and splitting of entities, and replication of attributes.

a) Merging of entities.

This kind of transformation is tried on all the sub-structures of
the schema composed of two entities connected by 1:1 relationship.
The entities are merged if the weight of the operations that use
both the entities is greather than the weight of the operations
when only one of the two entities is used.

The merging is achieved by transforming the two entities into a new
entity that inherits all the attributes and the relationships of the
older ones.

Merging of entities connected by a 1:n relationship (1:n merging) is
considered if one of the two entities is related to the rest of the
schema only through the relationship. In all the other cases, 1:n
or n:m merging is not considered because this kind of merging
involves complex restructuring of the schema and requires the introduction of new operations to preserve data integrity. Notice that
good performance results can be obtained in this case by clustering
physical records corresponding to the connected entities; this problem is then postponed to the physical design phase.

b) Splitting of entities

This kind of transformation is tried on all the entities of the
schema.

The transport volume related to an entity can be reduced if the
attributes of the entity are partitioned into different groups of
attributes used by disjointed classes of operations.

The problem of attribute partitioning has been considered by several
authors, e.g. [18, 20]. In our system, this problem is solved by
means of a cluster analysis algorithm that also investigates the
possibility of replicating some attributes in different attribute
clusters. The resulting clusters are good candidates for the construction of separate sub-entities that optimize operation execution. Each relationship in which the original entity takes part is
then transferred to the sub-entity which uses the same relationship
more frequently.

c) Replication of attributes.

Attributes of an entity can be replicated into another entity (connected to the first one), if this redundancy reduces the number of
logical accesses fo'r the most important operations.

It should be noted that the replication of an attribute introduces
data redundancy in the schema. Additional operations have to be
added to preserve the mutual consistency of the data and the replication will be accepted if the reduction in access cost is greater
than the maintenance cost introduced by the new operations.

Figure 6 shows the conceptual schema of Figure 1 after the simplification and the refinement steps.

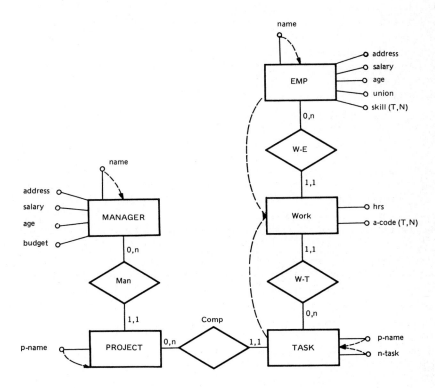

Fig. 6: The refined schema

5.3 Generation of the logical description

The aim of this task is to generate the logical description of the
database which includes:
- the logical (relational or CODASYL) schema, which describes the
  data structure of the database;
- a set of logical (relational or CODASYL) operation descriptions,
  which describes the workload on the database.

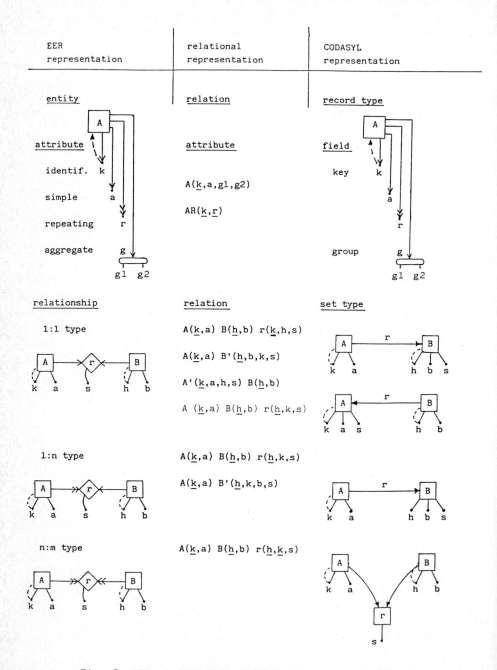

Fig. 7: EER, relational and CODASYL representations
         and translation rules

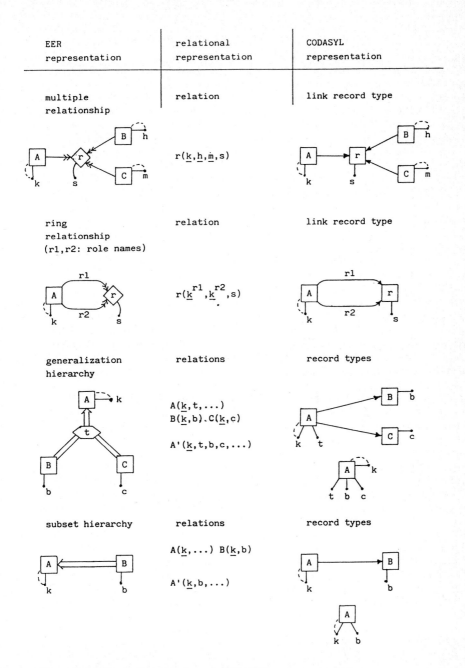

Fig. 7: EER, relational and CODASYL representations
and translation rules (cont.)

The CODASYL data model adopted at this stage to describe the logical
schema is a subset of the full CODASYL data description language
[10] which contains the structural and some of the integrity constraint characteristics of a schema. In the relational case, a set
of relations is derived. In Figure 7 the translation process is
summarized, both in the relational and in the CODASYL case. The
logical schemata corresponding to the global data schema of Figure 6
are given in Figure 8.

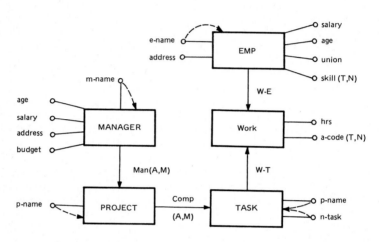

a) The CODASYL schema.

```
MANAGER      ( m-name, salary, age, address, budget)
EMP´         ( e-name, salary, age, address, union)
EMP"         ( e-name, skill)
PROJECT      ( p-name, m-name)
TASK         ( p-name, n-task)
WORK´        ( e-name, p-name, n-task, hrs)
WORK"        ( e-name, a-code, p-name, n-task)
```

b) The relational schema.

Fig. 8: The logical schemata

The operation schemata are automatically restructured according to
the logical schemata of Figure 8. The restructured operations are
described in terms of logical data manipulation languages (relational or CODASYL). In Figure 9 these languages are informally
illustrated with respect to the basic conceptual operations on the
refined schema (which contains 1:n or owner-member relationships
only). In the relational case, the QUEL [21] language is used.

```
conceptual access:    CODASYL description  relational description

to entities:
      k                 select x in X         range x is X
                          with id(....)         where K = "..."
      s                 foreach x in X        range x is X
      p                 foreach x in X        range x is X
                          where p               where p
      o/v               get x                 retrieve (x)
      d                 delete x              delete (x)
      w                 put x                 append (x)

to relationships:
   from x to y      foreach y in Y linked
                        to x in set R      range (x,y) is (X,Y)
   from y to x      find owner x of             where x.k = y.ky
                        in set R
```

Fig. 9 : The operations mapping

The restructured operations corresponding to the conceptual operation schema of Figure 2 are shown in Figure 10.

```
   select P in PROJECT with p-name = ´x´
      foreach T in TASK linked to P in set Comp
         foreach W in Work linked to T in set W-T
            find owner E of W in set W-E
            get E
            print ( E.name, E,address)
         end-for
      end-for
```

a) The restructured CODASYL operation.

```
   range (w,e) is (WORK´,EMP´)
      where w.p-name = ´x´
         and w.e-name = e.e-name
   retrieve (e.e-name, e.address)
```

b) The restructured relational operation.

Fig. 10 The restructured operations

6. CONCLUSIONS

In this paper, we have described the basic architecture of the ISIDE
system that supports the logical and physical database design phases
in the DATAID project. The nucleus of the system is a metadatabase
which contains all the static and dynamic database descriptions during the design process. The Dynamics Analyzer and the Logical
Designer have been also briefly illustrated.
Integration of these modules with the Relational and Codasyl
Designers is now under development and will produce an effective
tool for the implementation design and the performance predictions
of the object database.

Bibliography

[1]   Aschim F. and Mostue B.M. "IFIP WG 8.1 Case Solved using Sys-
      doc and Systemator", in [20] (1982).

[2]   Balbo G., Demo B., DiLeva A., Giolito P. "Dynamics Analysis in
      Database Design" Proc. IEEE Conf. COMPDEC, Los Angeles (1984).

[3]   Batini C., Lenzerini M., Moscarini M. "Views integration"
      chap.III of [8].

[4]   Bertaina P., DiLeva A., Giolito P., Iacobelli C., Marrone V.
      "An Automatic Tool for Logical Database Design" Proc. IEEE 1st
      Int. Conf. on Computers and Applications, Peking, p.385-391
      (1984).

[5]   Brodie M.L., Silva E. "Active and Passive Component Modelling"
      in [20] (1982).

[6]   Bussolati U., Ceri S., De Antonellis V., Zonta B. "Views Con-
      ceptual Design" chap.II of [7].

[7]   Ceri S. (ed.) "Methodology and Tools for Database Design",
      North-Holland (1983).

[8]   Chen P.S., "The Entity-Relationship Model: Toward a Unified
      View of Data" ACM-TODS, Vol.1, n.1, (1976).

[9]   Chen P.P., Chung I., "Survey of State of the Art Logical Data-
      base Design Tools" Preliminary Report, Grad. School of Mgt,
      UCLA (1983).

[10] CODASYL Data Description Language Committee, DDL Journal of
      Development, NBS Washington D.C. (1973).

[11] De Antonellis V., Zonta B. "Modelling Events in Data Base
      Applications Design", Proc. 7th Int. Conf. Very Large Data
      Bases, Cannes (1981).

[12] Demo B., Di Leva A. and Giolito P., "An Entity Relatioship
      Query Language" Proc. of Int. Conf. TFAIS, Barcelona, April
      (1985).

[13]   DiLeva A., Giolito P. "Automatic Logical Database Design in a
        CODASYL Environment" Proc. IEEE 4th Jerusalem Conf. on Infor-
        mation Technology, Jerusalem, p.350-357 (1984).

[14]   Hall J. "System Development Methodology", LBMS, (1981).

[15]   Jackson M. "System Development", Prentice-Hall, (1983).

[16]   Lundeburg M. "The ISAC Approach to Specification of Informa-
        tion Systems and its Application to the Organization of an
        IFIP Working Conference", in [20] (1982).

[17]   MacDonald I.G., and Palmer I.R. "System Development in a
        Shared Data Environment, theDDSS Methodology", in [20] (1982).

[18]   Navathe S., Ceri S., Wiederhold G., Dou J. "Vertical Parti-
        tioning for Physical and Distribution Design of Databases"
        Res. Report, Dep. of Computer Science, Stanford Univ. (1982).

[19]   Olle T.W., Sol H.G. and Verrijn-Stuart A.A. (Eds.) "Informa-
        tion Systems Design Methodologies: A comparative Review",
        Proc. of the IFIP TC 8 Working Conference, Noordwijkerhout,
        The Netherlands. North Holland, Amsterdam (1982)

[20]   Staniszkis W., Rullo P., Gaudioso M. "The Probabilistic
        Approach to the Evaluation of Data Manipulation Algorithms in
        a CODASYL Data Base Environment" Proc. ICOD-2 Conf., Cambridge
        (1983).

[21]   Stonebraker M.R., Wong E. and Kreps P. "The Design and Imple-
        mentation of INGRES", ACM TODS, vol.1, pp. 189-222 (1976).

[22]   Tsao J.H. "Enterprise Schema: An Approach to IMS Logical Data-
        base Design" Proc. Int. Conf. on Entity-Relationship Approach,
        Los Angeles, pp.446-462 (1979)

[23]   Van Griethuysen J.J., et al. "Concepts and Terminology for the
        Conceptual Schema", Preliminary Report, ISO, TC97/SC5/WG3
        (1981).

[24]   Verheijen G.M.A. and VanBekkum J. "NIAM: An Information
        Analysis Methodology", in [20] (1982).

[25]   Yourdon E.N. and Constantine L.L. "Structured Design", Yourdon
        Press and Prentice-Hall, (1978).

COMPUTER-AIDED DATABASE DESIGN: The DATAID Project
A. Albano, V. De Antonellis, and A. Di Leva (Editors)
© Elsevier Science Publishers B.V. (North-Holland), 1985

115

CHAPTER VI

ARCHITECTURE OF A PHYSICAL DESIGN TOOL FOR RELATIONAL DBMSs

Dario MAIO, Claudio SARTORI, Maria Rita SCALAS

Università di Bologna - Facoltà di Ingegneria
Centro Di Studio per l'Interazione Operatore-Calcolatore - C.N.R.
Viale Risorgimento 2 - 40136 BOLOGNA - ITALY

ABSTRACT

Relational DBMSs enable application programmers and users to operate on data at logical view level, via high level non-procedural query languages. The operations are performed with low programming effort and disregarding the physical aspects of data organization and retrieval. Nevertheless the physical aspects, together with a good logical organization choice, heavily affect the system performances. One of the current research areas is now directed towards the developement of completely integrated and automated logical and physical design tools. In this chapter the physical design tool IDEA for relational DBMS is described. The adoption of performance evaluation techniques as a last step of the physical design process is also presented.

1. INTRODUCTION

In the last few years a considerable effort has been made in developing automated tools for data base design both at logical and physical level. This new research area has assumed remarkable interest owing to the increasing popularity of general purpose DBMSs, and consequently to the greater complexity of the applications involved. High level non procedural query languages enable the application programmer and the end-user to operate at logical view level, with low programming effort, disregarding the physical aspects of data organization and retrieval. Anyway these aspects, together with a good logical organization choice, heavily affect the performances.

At present the DBMSs cannot completely relieve the data base designer of the task of making logical and physical decisions and tradeoffs. Yet some software tools covering particular aspects of the DB design are becoming available. For example, DBDSGN [1] is a physical data base design tool, developed for System-R [2, 3, 4], that suggests which indexes should be built on the DB relations for a given collection of SQL statements [5].

The research is now evolving and is directed to the development of completely integrated and automated design tools. Following this trend we implemented a package for the physical design of relational data bases, which can be used both alone and closely connected with the logical design tool presented in the previous chapters of this book. Specifically our tool IDEA (Index DEsign Algorithm) produces an efficient set of indexes to the stored data, on the basis of a description of the logical data structure and the collection of the queries that are expected to be representative of the workload on the data base, under storage and response time constraints. It must be noticed that the choice of an optimal set is made by means of the same criteria used by the DBMS to choose a particular access path among those available, when executing a query. Moreover the package has a modular structure that allows to be fitted to the characteristics of the particular relational DBMS adopted. The adaptability is limited to a farily wide class of systems, as will be described in detail later. The input required can be expressed in an internal form, when deriving from the output of the logical design tool, or in high level Data Description and Manipulation Languages, similar to those used by the DBMS, when the tool is used alone. At present the implementation is oriented to System-R like relational DBMSs.

As illustrated in Figure 1, a last step of the design process should be to test how the choices effected influence the system performances. In this way we would obtain a layered model intended to provide a framework on which to examine the interrelations between various design decisions, using, at the lowest level, models which are able to capture architectural aspects of the DBMS and of the host system. In this respect our research is also devoted to produce an interface between the output of the physical design and the input to a general purpose performance prediction package previously developed [6], based on the analytical solution of queueing network models.

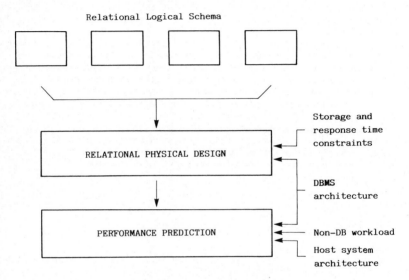

Fig. 1 - Logical and physical design process

Section 2 deals with a general overview of the peculiarities of the relational DBMSs which sensibly affect the physical design process. In Section 3 IDEA is presented in detail. Section 4 briefly illustrates the basic concepts of performance prediction and the few attempts made to include this aspect in physical design tools.

In the following we suppose the reader to be familiar with the relational model concepts and with the related terminology. A complete review on this subject can be found in [7, 8].

2. BACKGROUND

This section is devoted to clarifying some aspects of the relational data base systems (RDBMS) which must be taken into account in order to perform the physical design. From a general point of view, the physical design involves, among others, the following main aspects:

a) the choice of the file structures,

b) the allocation of the files on mass storage devices,

c) the setting of some system parameters, such as the size of the DBMS buffer pool.

Yet, it must be noticed that b) and c) are usually disregarded by the so-called physical design tools, while they are separately considered during a further performance optimization step. The main reason for this division of tasks is the difficulty of approaching the whole problem in a single integrated design phase, due to the high number of parameters involved. Moreover, another reason may be found in the different knowledge and experience necessary to deal with the various aspects of the problem. We defer to Section 4 for a brief discussion of the few attempts towards the construction of an integrated layered model. Therefore, from now on, with physical design we shall intend only aspect a).

As far as the file structures are concerned, we point out that some choices are strictly dependent on the particular DBMS concerned. As an example, relational DBMSs differ for the kind of alternate access paths available to access a relation. The most commonly used access paths, built in order to improve the performance for some transactions, are indexes, links and hashing [2, 9]. In particular indexed files are supported by all the RDBMSs, but they are implemented by using different techniques, such as inverted lists and tree structures [10]. Anyway, all the RDBMSs provide the optimization facility. In other words, given a set of access structures, the selection of an efficient access plan to the stored data related to a query, is the task of a RDBMS software module which is commonly named optimizer [2, 11, 12, 13]. Once the DB designer has built the suitable set of access paths, the presence and the use of these structures remains completely transparent both to the end-user and to the application programmer. The relational model combined with the optimizer facility allows the operations on the DB to be expressed by non-navigational query languages, the effectiveness of the physical design being responsible for the system performance. For the sake of exposition, before introducing the reader to the design problem, we make some considerations on the relational DBMS's architecture, referring, for simplicity, to the functional structure of System-R. Figure 2 gives a functional view of System-R major interfaces and components interacting with the host operating system [2, 3].

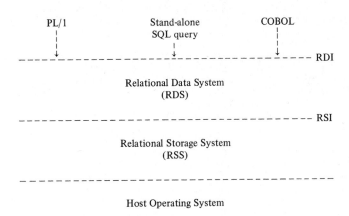

Fig. 2 - Functional view of System-R

The relational Data System (RDS) implements the Relational Data Interface (RDI), which provides high-level data independent facilities for data retrieval, manipulation, definition and control. The major components of RDS are listed below:
— parsing
— authorization checking
— integrity constraints
— catalog
— access path selection (optimizer)
— code generation.

One of the basic goals of System-R is to support two different categories of processing: (1) SQL stand-alone statements, which are usually executed once in a while, and (2) canned programs, which are executed hundreds of times [14]. For this reason, the RDS module is splitted into two distinct functions:

- a precompiler to precompile host-language programs and install them as «canned programs» under System-R;
- an execution time system which controls the execution of canned programs and also provides the execution of SQL statements for the ad hoc terminal user.

After the precompilation and the consequent compilation of a modified host-language program, an access module, that is a machine code ready to run on RSS, is generated. On the contrary an ad hoc statement is run-time optimized, and its corresponding access module is dynamically generated. The Relational Storage System (RSS) implements the Research Storage Interface (RSI) which provides simple record-at-a-time primitives on the relations. Operators are also supported for data recovery, transaction management and data definition. Inside the RSS component a paged buffer pool acts as a «cache memory», preserving the most recently used pages. The major functions performed by RSS are listed below:

- space/device management
- index management
- link management
- concurrency control (locking)
- logging and recovery.

RSS is responsible for the execution of the access modules produced by RDS.

Now, in order to illustrate the physical design aspects included in the previously mentioned point a), let us briefly summarize the main aspects concerning the optimizer module, which represents the major distinctive point between file systems and relational DBMSs.

For a given query the optimizer effects the choice of the access plan to adopt during the execution of the access modules. Abandoning the details related to System-R, we outline the major features of an optimizer. An access plan is chosen on the basis of cost estimates taking into account both the CPU time and the I/O requests. In particular, the estimation of the number of I/O operations is effected by considering the selection predicates involved in the query and assuming a statistical model of the values distribution in the definition domain and in the data pages. Anyway, the optimizer is a program that is able to deal with any DB. Consequently, even by making suitable choices as a rule, some of its criteria may not exactly match with the workload characteristics. In fact, present optimizers estimate costs by making general assumptions on correlations and distributions of attribute values which may be quite different from real statistics for a specific DB.

The most common approach relies on the simplifying assumptions of uniform distributions and mutual independence of the attribute values [11, 15, 16]. Different assumptions for the distribution of column values require refined knowledge of the data; the system catalogs should store adequate distribution parameters and the optimizer should be able to use appropriate evaluation formulas. An interesting research area is devoted to the refinement of cost models and, more generally, to the development of «intelligent optimizers» [17, 18].

Apart from the statistical model, the optimizer's criteria are influenced by the access path structures available and by the access algorithms implemented. As an example, we can classify algorithms based on intersection lists construction and on the use of a single index per relation. Moreover many different algorithms can be found to solve operations involving more than one relation. The most common join methods are the nested loop, the sort-merging scan and the TID-algorithms [19, 20].

Coming bach to the physical design we can now individuate a general framework of the major steps to be followed in solving the access path design problem, as in Figure 3. In particular, step 1 includes precise consideration of: a) the physical implementations of access structures (i.e. indexes based on tuple identifiers or on page identifiers, B + trees, inverted lists, etc.); b) the access methods; c) the strategies used in solving transactions, e.g. join methods and index maintenance techniques; d) optimizer algorithms and criteria, i.e., it should never happen that the designer suggest an access path which would never be chosen by the optimizer.

step 0: specification of the DB statistics, the workload characteristics and the storage constraints;

step 1: estimate of the expected cost for each class of transactions and for each possible access path;

step 2: comparison of the access path effectiveness, in order to eliminate the obviously useless ones or those providing minor benefits when the others are present;

step 3: generation of an optimal set of access paths.

Fig. 3 - Physical design process

3. AN ARCHITECTURAL OVERVIEW OF IDEA

IDEA takes as inputs the logical relational schema together with the workload characteristics, both derived from the logical design phase, and it determines an optimal set of indexes. Moreover, because of the close dependence of the physical design on the RDBMS architecture and, in particular, on the optimizer criteria, we have primarily addressed our tool to RDBMSs whose characteristics are similar to those of System-R, though more limited. On the other hand a good modularity makes it possible to adjust the tool in order to meet the characteristics of other systems.

3.1. Assumptions and definitions

We assume that the RDBMS being considered provides the following features:

1) Each relation may be accessed by using a sequential scan or by using only one of the indexes built on the relation itself.

2) The indexes are structured as B + trees and the leaves contain all the key values, each followed by the set of tuple identifiers (TIDs) where the value appears [21]. Furthermore, an index cannot be built by using compound keys. At most one index per relation may be recognized by the system as clustered, that is, built on a sorted column [22].

3) An index cannot be used to access tuples for an update statement that modifies the indexed column, since this way might lead to hitting the same tuple more than once [22].

4) Joins are performed according to separable or approximately separable methods [12, 23, 24, 25], and particularly:

   a) by using the nested loop;
   b) the relations are assigned to each nesting level by following the same order as they are referenced in the specification of the operations;

5) the RDBMS optimizer estimates execution costs hypothesizing uniform distributions, i.e.:

   a) distribution of column values: the values of each column are uniformly distributed over the relation tuples; furthermore, column values are uniformly distributed over the domain;
   b) distribution of the tuples with a given value over the relation pages: two cases are considered for

a given relation;

b1) the stored column, where it exists, forces a correspondence between data pages and column values;

b2) the unsorted column, where column values are assumed uniformly distributed over the relation tuples and, consequently, over the data pages.

These last assumptions are justified since monitoring and maintaining statistics are complex operations, excepted for those cases that are easily represented by well-known distributions.

The assumptions 1, 2, 3 and 5 meet the requirements of many of the actual systems. The assumption 4) does not fit to those systems which use other join methods, as for example systems which adopt the TID intersection algorithm. Furthermore the hypothesis 4b, suitable for most of the RDBMSs, is justified because it constrains the system to access relations in the same order specified by the user, an order that is presumably significant for the application. In any case the major reason for this assumption is that the separability concept allows the design tool to univocally split a join into a group of statements which act on a single relation. This results in a considerable reduction in the complexity of the solution generation procedure, as will be described below. Similar considerations lead us to neglect, at this design level, any effect produced by the concurrency of the operations in a real time environment.

In the following we will name «operation» a single statement of an interactive language for database manipulation, involving one or more relations. Instead, the term «transaction» is reserved to indicate a more general collection of statements to be executed not independently. IDEA does not perform an automatic splitting of transactions into single separate operations: this is still a task of the DB designer.

3.2. Operation decomposition

In order to clarify the join decomposition rule adopted by IDEA, let us introduce the following notations:

Q   a generic statement which refers to one or more relations;

w   a weight, associated with Q, function of:

— the frequency of execution over the period of time t during which the workload is not expected to change substantially;
— the distribution of the execution of Q during t;
— particular needs for response time;

REL   a generic relation subject to the physical design;

NKEY[REL,COL]   the number of different values of the column named COL for the relation REL;

NTPL[REL]   the cardinality of the relation REL;

f[COL,PRED]   the selectivity factor of a predicate PRED related to the column COL.

Given the following two relations, about the customers of a bank and the kind of banking relationships, respectively:

CUSTOMER (CUST-COD, NAME, ACTIVITY)

RELATIONSHIP (REL-COD, CUST-COD, REL-TYPE)

let us consider the following operation Q, expressed in SQL, with the weight w:

Q: select (NAME, REL-COD)
   from CUSTOMER, RELATIONSHIP
   where ACTIVITY = «CLERK»
   and REL-TYPE = «CREDIT»
   and CUSTOMER. CUST-COD = RELATIONSHIP. CUST-COD

Q is decomposed by applying the separability concept and assuming the nested loop algorithm as the join method. First of all we consider the selection of tuples of the first relation (external relation), according to its local predicates. The following sub-operation Qe, with the same weight of the original operation, comes out:

Qe: select (NAME, CUST-COD)
    from CUSTOMER
    where ACTIVITY = «CLERK»

Qe selects the clerks of the relation CUSTOMER one at a time. The expected number of selected tuples is given by:

$$ETPL[Qe] = NTPL[CUSTOMER] * f[ACTIVITY, PRED].$$

Where the selectivity factor of the equality predicate (PRED : ACTIVITY = «CLERK») is estimated, as a consequence of the uniform distribution assumptions, as:

$$f[ACTIVITY, PRED] = 1/NKEY[CUSTOMER, ACTIVITY].$$

It is worth noting that, at this level, the join predicate has no selection effect on the external relation. For each tuple so far selected, the following internal sub-operation Qi is generated on RELATIONSHIP:

Qi: select (REL-COD)
    from RELATIONSHIP
    where REL-TYPE = «CREDIT»
    and RELATIONSHIP. CUST-COD = «value»

From the design point of view, because of the assumpitons 4 and 6 of Section 3.1, the original join Q is equivalent to the pair Qe and Qi, provided that the Qi frequency is assumed as w * ETPL[Qe]. Note that the join predicate CUSTOMER. CUST-COD = RELATIONSHIP. CUST-COD has been transformed into the predicate, local to the internal sub-operation Qi, RELATIONSHIP. CUST-COD = «value». This last predicate is parametric, in the sense that «value» assumes an actual value for each execution of Qi, as a consequence of the actual CUSTOMER. REL-COD occurrence contained in the tuple selected by Qe.

The extension to joins invonving more than two relations is straightforward; furthermore an analogous decomposition process can be applied also to nested operations [26].

3.3. Cost estimation

After the decomposition of the workload into a set of operations involving a single relation, the design goes on with the estimation of the execution costs, according to the following algorithm.

```
FOR each operation Q (on a relation R) of the workload DO
        compute the cost of a sequential access to R;
        FOR each field of R DO
            IF there is a selection predicate on the field
                THEN compute data and index access costs
                        for clustered and unclustered cases
                ELSE set the cost to the sequential one;
            IF Q modifies R
                THEN compute the relation and index maintenance cost;
```

The algorithm generates cost matrices that become the input to the procedure of generation of the optimal index set.

For example, referring to the operation Qe of the previous section, the possible reasonable access paths to be evaluated are:

a) the sequential scan
b) the index on CUSTOMER.ACTIVITY, either if clustered or not.

To evaluate the efficiency of an access structure, in the algorith two major cost functions are considered: I/O cost for retrieving tuples and cost for tuple and index updating, if the requested operation is a data base modification. Insert and delete statements are handled as particular instances of update statements. In [27] all the drawbacks and CPU time consumption due to the I/O operations have been pointed out. Considerations of a similar nature probably led other authors to take into account only the number of I/O operations, in comparing access methods, disregarding the CPU time. In IDEA we also adopt the same approach.

As an example of cost evaluation we assume a statistical model of the data as described in Section 3.1, and we consider the relations CUSTOMER and RELATIONSHIP, and the operation Q, decomposed into Qe and Qi, introduced in Section 3.2.

Let us assume that:

NPAG[CUSTOMER]   is the number of data pages in CUSTOMER;

NTPL[CUSTOMER]   is the number of tuples in CUSTOMER;

NKEY[ACTIVITY]   is the number of different activities;

NLEAF[ACTIVITY]   is the number of leaves of the index on ACTIVITY (the intermediate levels are, for simplicity, disregarded).

NPAG[RELATIONSHIP]   is the number of data pages in RELATIONSHIP

NTPL[RELATIONSHIP]   is the number of tuples in RELATIONSHIP;

NKEY[REL–TYPE]   is the number of different relation types;

NLEAF[REL-TYPE]   is the number of leaves of the index on REL-TYPE;

NKEY[CUST-COD]   is the number of different customer codes;

NLEAF[CUST-COD]   is the number of leaves of the index on CUST-COD;

For Qe, the expected number of tuples satisfying the predicate ACTIVITY = «CLERK» is

$$ETe = (1/NKEY[ACTIVITY]) * NTPL[CUSTOMER]$$

and the expected number of leaves to be accessed, if the index is used, is

$$ELe = (1/NKEY[ACTIVITY]) * NLEAF[ACTIVITY]$$

Finally, the expected number of data pages to be accessed is computed by the CARDENAS' formula [15]:

$$EPe = NPAG[CUSTOMER] * (1 - (1 - 1/NPAG[CUSTOMER]) ** ETe)$$

and the expected number of I/O operations necessary to execute the operation is ETOTe = EPe + ELe. For Qi we apply the same formulas in the two cases, depending on which index (on REL-TYPE or on CUST-COD) is used.

Accessing via REL-TYPE we obtain:

$$ETi\_r = (1/NKEY[REL\text{-}TYPE]) * NTPL[RELATIONSHIP]$$

$$ELi\_r = (1/NKEY[REL\text{-}TYPE]) * NLEAF[REL\text{-}TYPE]$$

$$EPi\_r = NPAG[RELATIONSHIP] * (1 - (1 - 1/NPAG[RELATIONSHIP]) ** ETi\_r)$$

$$ETOTi\_r = EPi\_r + ELi\_r$$

and accessing via CUST-COD, the formulas are:

$$ETi\_c = (1/NKEY[CUST\text{-}COD] * NTPL[RELATIONSHIP]$$

$$ELi\_c = (1/NKEY[CUST\text{-}COD] * NLEAF[CUST\text{-}COD]$$

$$EPi\_c = NPAG[RELATIONSHIP] * (1 - (1 - 1/NPAG[RELATIONSHIP]) ** ETi\_c)$$

$$ETOTi\_c = EPi\_c + ELi\_c$$

Qi is the internal operation deriving from the decomposition of a join and is re-executed for each tuple of CUSTOMER selected by Qe; for this reason the total I/O cost is to be computed, in the two cases, as:

$$ETOT'i\_r = ETe * ETOTi\_r$$

$$ETOT'i\_c = ETe * ETOTi\_c$$

For predicates other than «equality», different formulas, either empirical or analytical, depending on the knowledge available on the data model, are shown in [11, 22, 28]. A more detailed description of the commonly used formulas can be found in Appendix.

3.4. Index selection

Our physical design procedure selects the secondary indexes that ensure the minimal global cost under the constraints imposed by the DBA on the memory. This problem has been shown in [29] to be NP-hard, even for simple cost criteria. In [22] the design tool utilizes an algorithm which requires an exponential exploration of all the possible index subsets, if applied without restrictions. More recently, in [30], it was shown that the index selection problem can be solved by solving a properly chosen instance of the «knapsack problem» (KP). In the context of a query processing model which assumes the use of intersection lists, the paper presents, for a single relation, an approximation algorithm which solves the KP in polynomial time. The Secondary Index Selection method (SIS) adopted in IDEA, based on the optimal assignement principles, has been presented in [31]. It explores a number of combinations linearly proportional to the cardinality of the candidate indexes set. The method is applied in a multiple relation environment, provided that join methods are separable. To show the operation principles of SIS, let us define:

ISET: the set of the secondary indexes which are candidates to be built on the relations subject to the design;

BSET: a subset of ISET which represents the optimal solution.

Each index in ISET involves:

a) a potential reduction of the data access cost;
b) a maintenance cost;
c) a storage cost.

The selection problem is approached as a minimization of an «objective function», which takes into account the cost a) and b), the minimization is subject to a user defined index storage constraint, involving the consideration of c).

SIS operates an initial choice of BSET guaranteeing, for each operation, the index (clustered or unclustered) providing the minimum access cost. The approximation algorithm is essentially composed of two parts: the first one (p1) finds an optimal solution without memory constraint, the second part (p2) operates when the unconstrained solution does not fit in the memory available for the indexes. Since the initial solution was found without considering the update costs , part p1 tries to remove from BSET the indexes with higher update cost. In this phase indexes can be simply removed from BSET or substituted with others that were not considered initially. All the indexes are considered in order to minimize the objective function. Part p2 removes from BSET the indexes whose memory requirement (weighted by a function defined by the user) multiplied by its global cost is maximum. Then, it is substituted by another index whose ratio between the global execution cost increase and the memory gain is minimum. The substitutions are repeated until the indexes in BSET satisfy the memory limit.

Presently in SIS the choice of the columns on which the relations must be clustered is assumed to be already made. IDEA first adopts a heuristic approach to reduce the set of candidate clustered indexes, then, for each surviving combination of clustered choices, it applies SIS. As a last step, the various solutions obtained are compared to produce an optimal set of clustered and unclustered indexes.

3.5. Implementation, inputs and outputs

IDEA has been written in Pascal and runs on VAX/VMS, while SIS has been written in Fortran, to obtain better response times. At present the following modules of IDEA are not yet operational:

1) the interface to describe the workload in a high level language;
2) the automatic decomposition of the transactions;
3) the automatic choice of the clustered indexes.

To use IDEA the following data must be provided from the designer, in order to perform the unclustered index selection:

a) The secondary storage available for the indexes.

b) For each relation

   — the cardinality, the tuple length, the mean number of tuples per data page;
   — the column on which a clustered index is already designed;
   — for each column of the relation, the length of the field, the number of different values, the range (if available and only for numeric fields).

c) For each operation

   — a weight, taking into account the frequence of the operation in the workload;
   — the selection predicates and their logical connection;
   — for each predicate, the column involved and the relational operator;
   — ordering required for the output.

The outputs provided by IDEA are:

   — for each operation, the list of the indexes that could be used to access the data and, for each of these, the expected number of page fetches to retrieve data and index leaves and, if necessary, the number of page rewritings to update data and indexes;

— the set of indexes producing the lowest overall cost and fitting in the index space available.

4. TOWARDS PERFORMANCE PREDICTION

This section is devoted to surveying some of the few known attempts to make an overall model able to capture the effects on resource consumption, throughput and response time of the various physical and logical data base design decisions.

In [32] a layered model intended to provide a framework in which to examine the interdependencies among various design decisions is proposed. The study is conducted with reference to many commercial systems: in particular the design of prediction packages for the Micro-Relational System (MRS) and for the hierarchical System 2000 is described. The major peculiarity of the proposed approach is the choice, at the lowest level, of a queueing network model which accepts as input the logical data base description and a characterization of the workload in terms of transaction classes.

Two data base system performance prediction tools, whose architecture reflects the generality of the framework proposed in [32], have been developed inside the DATAID Project: EOS and IDEA [6, 33]. Let us explain in more detail the performance prediction step as an extention of IDEA, while for EOS see [33]. Referring to the System-R architecture, we hypothesize an interactive environment in which a set of user terminals submits stand-alone SQL statements and pre-optimized canned programs to the system. Then we apply analytical techniques based on queueing network models [34]. Modelling a computer system with queueing networks means to model:

a) the configuration, which specifies the individual characteristics of the devices (speed, allowed parallelism, scheduling algorithms, etc.) and their interconnections;

b) the workload, which specifies the characteristics of the resource demands placed on the devices by jobs (mean number of CPU instructions, mean number of I/O operations, etc.) and the routing behaviour through the network. Usually the jobs are grouped into classes, according to their similar resource demands, and into chains, according to their routing behaviour.

To solve a queueing model means to analyze the relationships between the models a) and b) and to compute performance parameters, such as response times for each job class, throughputs, queueing lenght distributions. Reference [35] is a tutorial for the best known applications and solutions techniques of queueing network models. When the overall model is too complex, the decomposition allows to simplify problems through modularization. Applying the decomposition/aggregation approach consists in solving portions of the overall model in isolation («offline») and gathering the results together («online»), as illustrated in Figure 4, for a system with a single job class. In the offline experiment the subsystem is operated under all the possible different load conditions (N jobs inside the subsystem) and the related throughput X(N) is derived. Now the subsystem can be replaced in the original system by an «equivalent server» with a load-dependent service time $S(N) = 1/X(N)$. In some cases this strategy will cause some errors, because the aggregation does not totally capture the interactions between the various isolated portions. On the other hand this approach is the only feasible when the queueing network does not belong to a particular category («product form») for which a complete analytical solution is already known.

Referring to the system under analysis, we have built a model whose overall structure is that of a closed queueing network with several job classes and two distinct routing chains, one grouping classes of stand-alone statements and one grouping classes of canned programs. We solve the overall model by applying the decomposition/aggregation approach and we use an iteration algorithm to correct the inaccuracy in subnetwork representation. The overall model is analyzed in three stages.

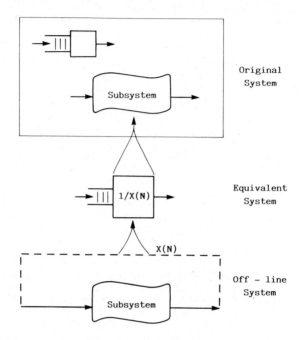

Fig. 4 - Decomposition / Aggregation

Stage a

We analyze the CPU-I/O subsystem obtaining an equivalent server with four service classes, representing the following four system operations, respectively:

QP: analysis and optimization of a stand-alone operation and generation of an access module;
QA: execution of an access module for a stand-alone operation;
CP: execution of non-data base operations in canned programs;
CA: execution fo access modules for a canned program.

Note that, at this stage, a key role is played by the physical design choices: in other words the information available about the files structure, the kind of access paths, the operations of the workload, the number of expected read and write requests for each operation, the operation concurrency and the locking constraints should be traslated into queueing network parameters, such as service time and routing probabilities at the various devices of the computer system for the various transaction (job) classes.

Stage b

We perform an analysis of the model of Figure 5 by using appropriate iterative algorithms. This submodel takes into account the buffer pool contemption and evidentiates the different behaviour of the two transaction chains inside the CPU-I/O subsystem analyzed in Stage a. Stand alone operations, after the compilation and optimization, require an access module execution phase. Canned programs after execution of non-data base operations require with 1-P probability the execution of an access module.

Stage c

We solve, by using iterative methods, an external level model, somewhat similar to the previous one, which is able to capture the memory queue effects.

Concluding this section we remark that such performance prediction tool, even if based on gross simplifying assumptions, can be a good guidance to the designer in making physical choices such as the buffer pool size and so on. On the other hand the inaccuracy of the assumptions made in the previous levels of the design justify at this level the use of a not very detailed macro-model.

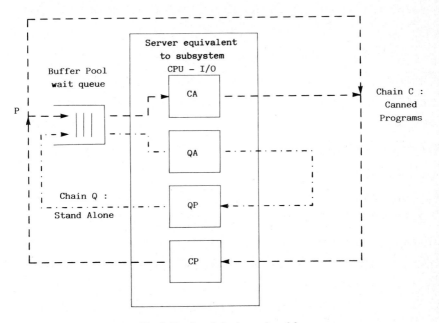

Fig. 5 - Database behaviour submodel

5. CONCLUSIONS

The goal of the physical data base design is to provide an optimal set of access path structures in order to minimize the time spent in I/O operations, taking into account the maintenance cost, the memory constraints and the workload characteristics. Within the DATAID project we developed a tool for the selection of an optimal set of indexes to be built on the DB relations. A major distinctive aspect of IDEA is that the choice is effected by heuristic algorithms, based on the separability concept. IDEA finds a near optimal solution which tends to minimize the global I/O traffic.

More accurate performance analyses can be effected only by including considerations on the resource contemption, whose effects are usually not well considered at logical and physical design levels. To overcome these drawbacks we have investigated the possibility of using queueing network models to evaluate the quality of the physical design. A performance evaluation tool has been implemented which has proved effective in modelling the most important aspects of the DBMS functional architecture. Future work in this area will involve the implementation of workload characterization techniques which bridge the gap between the logical-physical description level and the more detailed workload description needed as an input for a queueing network model.

D. Maio et al.

APPENDIX

SELECTIVITY FACTORS USED FOR THE COMPUTATION OF THE NUMBER OF TUPLES SELEC-
TED BY THE VARIOUS RELATIONAL OPERATORS

E : empirical selectivity factors for columns whose range and number of different values are unknown;

A : analytical selectivity factors for columns with a uniform distribution of the values between MINKEY
and MAXKEY and with NKEY different column values

PREDICATE	E	A
COL < value	1/3	$\dfrac{\text{value-MINKEY}}{\text{MAXKEY - MINKEY}}$
COL = value	1/10	1/NKEY
COL > value	1/3	$\dfrac{\text{MAXKEY - value}}{\text{MAXKEY - MINKEY}}$
COL between (value 1, value 2)	1/4	$\dfrac{\text{value 2 - value 1}}{\text{MAXKEY - MINKEY}}$
COL in (list of values)	$\dfrac{\text{(numbers of values in list)}}{10}$	$\dfrac{\text{number of values in list}}{\text{NKEY}}$

SELECTIVITY FACTORS PRODUCED BY A LOGICAL COMBINATION OF PREDICATES

AND   f(COL 1, PRED 1) * f(COL 2, PRED 2)

OR   f(COL 1, PRED 1) + f(COL 2, PRED 2) − f(COL 1, PRED 1) * f(COL 2, PRED 2)

NOT   1 − f(COL, PRED)

ACKNOWLEDGEMENTS

The Authors are very grateful to Professor Paolo Tiberio for the profiquous discussions and suggestions during the development of the project.

BIBLIOGRAPHY

[1] Finkelstein, S.J., Schkolnick, M. and Tiberio P., DBDSGN - a Physical Data Base Design Tool for System R., IEEE Database Engineering, 5, 1 (1982) 9 - 11.

[2] Astrahan, M.M. et al., System-R, a Relational Approach to Data Base Management, ACM TODS, 1, 2 (1976) 68 - 90.

[3] Blasgen, M.W. et al., System R: an Architectural Overview, IBM Syst. J., 20, 1 (1981) 41 - 62.

[4] Chamberlin, D.D. et al., A History and Evaluation of System R, Comm. ACM, 24, 10 (1981) 632 - 646.

[5] Chamberlin, D.D. et al., SEQUEL2: a Unified Approach to Data Definition, Manipulation and Control, IBM J. Res. Dev., 11 (1976) 560 - 575.

[6] Maio, D. and Sartori, C., A Queueing Network Model Approach for Evaluating Relational Data Base Performances, Proc. 4-th IASTED Int. Symposium and Course on Modelling and Simulation, Lugano, Switzerland (1983).

[7] Date, C.J., An Introduction to Database Systems (Addison-Wesley, London, 1981).

[8] Schmidt, J.W. and Brodie, M.L., Relational Database Systems (Springer-Verlag, Berlin, 1983).

[9] Held, G. and Stonebraker, M., B-trees re-examined, Comm. ACM, 21, 2 (1978) 139 - 143.

[10] Knuth, D., The Art of Computer Programming, 3: Sorting and Searching (Addison-Wesley, London, 1973).

[11] Selinger, P.G. et al., Access Path Selection in Relational Database Management Systems, Proc. ACM. SIGMOD Conf., Boston (1979) 23 - 34.

[12] Wong, E. and Youssefi, K., Decomposition - a Strategy for Query Processing, ACM TODS, 1, 3 (1976) 223 - 241.

[13] Bonfatti, F. et al., An Indexing Technique for Relational Data Bases, Proc. IEEE COMPSAC, Chicago (1980) 784 - 791.

[14] Chamberlin, D.D. et al., Support for Repetitive Transaction and Ad Hoc Queries in System R, ACM TODS, 6, 1 (1981) 70 - 94.

[15] Cardenas, A.F., Analysis and Performance of Inverted Data Base Structures, Comm. ACM, 18, 5 (1975) 253 - 263.

[16] Yao, S.B., Approximating Block Accesses in Data Base Operations, Comm. ACM, 20, 4 (1977) 260 - 261.

[17] Christodoulakis, S., Estimating Record Selectivities, Information Systems, 8, 2 (1983) 105 - 115.

[18] Maio, D., Scalas, M.R. and Tiberio P., A Note on Estimating Access Costs in Relational Data Bases, Information Processing letters, 19 (1984) 157 - 161.

[19] Yao, S.B., Optimization of Query Evaluation Algorithms, ACM TODS, 4, 2 (1979) 133 - 155.

[20] Blasgen, M.W. and Eswaran, K.P.F., Storage and Access in Relational Databases, IBM System Journal, 16, 4 (1977) 363 - 377.

[21] Comer, D., The Ubiquitous B-tree, Computing Surveys, 11, 2 (1979) 397 - 434.

[22] Schkolnick, M. and Tiberio, P., A Note on Estimating the Maintenance Cost in a Relational Database, ACM TODS, to appear.

[23] Whang, K.Y., Wiederhold, G. and Sagalowicz, D., Separability - an Approach to Physical Database Design, IEEE Transactions on Computers, C-33, 3 (1984) 209 - 222.

[24] Whang, K.Y., Wiederhold, G. and Sagalowicz, D., The Property of Separability and its Application to Physical Database Design, Query Processing in Database System, (Springer-Verlag, Berlin, to appear).

[25] Bonfatti, F., Maio, D. and Tiberio, P., A Separability - Based Method for Secondary Index Selection, in Ceri, S. (ed.), Methodology and Tools for Data Base Design (North-Holland, Amsterdam, 1983) 149 - 160.

[26] Kim, W., On Optimizing an SQL-like Nested Query, ACM TODS, 7, 3 (1982) 443 - 469.

[27] Severance, D. and Dunhe, R., A Practitioner's Guide to Addressing Algorithms, Comm. ACM, 19, 6 (1976) 409 - 418.

[28] Schkolnick, M. and Tiberio, P., Considerations in Developing a Design Tool for a Relational DBMS, Proc. IEEE COMPSAC Conf., Chicago, (1979) 228 - 235.

[29] Comer, D., The Difficulty of Optimum Index Selection, ACM TODS, 3, 4 (1978) 440 - 445.

[30] Ip, M.Y.L. et al., An Approximation Algorithm for the Index Selection Problem, IEEE COMPSAC Conf., Chicago (1981) 43 - 49.

[31] Bonanno, R., Maio D. and Tiberio P., An Approximation Algorithm for Secondary Index Selection in Relational Database Physical Design, The Computer Journal, to appear (1985).

[32] Sevcik, K.C., Data Base System Performance Prediction Usign an Analytical Model, Proc. 7-th VLDB Conf. (1981) 182 - 198.

[33] Orlando, S., Rullo, P., Saccà, D. and Staniszkis W., Integrated Tools for Physical Data Base Design in CODASYL Environment, in this volume.

[34] Baskett, F., Chandy, K.M., Muntz, R.R. and Palacios, F., Open, Closed and Mixed Networks of Queues with Different Classes of Customers, JACM, 22, 2 (1975) 248 - 260.

[35] ACM Computing Surveys, 10, 3, Sep. 1978.

COMPUTER-AIDED DATABASE DESIGN: The DATAID Project
A. Albano, V. De Antonellis, and A. Di Leva (Editors)
© Elsevier Science Publishers B.V. (North-Holland), 1985

CHAPTER VII

INTEGRATED TOOLS
FOR PHYSICAL DATABASE DESIGN IN CODASYL ENVIRONMENT

S. Orlando, P. Rullo, D. Saccà, W. Staniszkis

CRAI
via Bernini 5
87030 Rende, Italy

Physical database design plays a central role in the implementation of database applications. Many current research efforts are directed towards development of automated tools to support physical database design methodologies. The use of automated tools is motivated by the complexity of the physical database design process, in particular by the high number of decision variables and the complex characterization of database performance. In this paper two automated tools supporting physical database design in CODASYL environment are presented. The first tool, System EOS, is a database performance predictor based on analytical evaluation models, which allows to precisely characterize the application workload and the database performance behaviour. The second tool, System EROS, is an physical database designer based on optimization models, which uses the evaluation models of EOS to estimate the cost of alternative implementation solutions. The two tools are the integrated components of a workbench for the selection and evaluation of database implementations.

1. INTRODUCTION

The recent years have witnessed the rapid growth of size and complexity of databases. As a consequence, several methodologies for database design have been proposed (see, for instance, [2,14]). Manual database design methodologies are not powerful enough to cope with present design requirements, characterized by semantic complexity and stringent user requirements with respect to data availability and application performance. Hence, many recent research efforts have concentrated on automated database design tools.

In this paper, we are concerned with automated tools for physical database design. Two broad classes of physical database design tools are currently subject to intensive research and development efforts, namely, those based on *performance evaluation models* (which estimate the performance of a given specific design) and those based on *optimization models* (which select the best design with respect to some performance criteria, among a number of alternative solutions).

A number of database performance evaluation models have been proposed in the literature. A comprehensive survey of them may be found in [20]. Most of such models are based on mathematical models of database systems and are applied to specific database design problems. Besides, they do not significantly study workload characterization.

As far as optimization models are concerned, there are several tools dealing with single aspects of physical database design (like storage structure, access path, storage hierarchies, etc.). A survey of the whole field can be found in [3, 16, 18].

In this paper, we present two integrated automated tools, namely, EOS and EROS, which support the physical database design phase in CODASYL environment.

EOS is a database performance predictor tool, based on performance evaluation models, which allows to precisely characterize the application workload and the application performance behaviour. Starting from the logical and physical description of a given database schema, the description of transactions, the quantitative database description, DBMS and hardware characteristics, EOS estimates performance measures such as page references, throughputs, utilizations, mean queue length and mean response time under different scenarios of concurrent transactions. The general architecture of EOS is similar to that proposed in [20]. However, in EOS much more emphasys has been put on workload evaluation. Research results pertaining to workload evaluation are reported in [12,13] and, more recently, in [6,7,11,25]. The above techniques concentrated on evaluation of single Data Manipulation Language (DML) statements, whose frequencies are specified by the user. Instead EOS uses an operational description and a probabilistic evaluation of transactions to derive individual DML statement frequencies. To this end, EOS provides for precise definition of database statistical characteristics, including various data item value distribution types, as well as possible correlations between values of distinct data items. Advantages of such an approach have been demonstrated in [4]. EOS considers the complete set of CODASYL DML statements together with their options as defined in [5,8,9]. The workload evaluation of EOS consists of 1) expanding each DML statement in a number of atomic physical operations (using an expansion model similar to the one proposed in [27]), 2) computing DML statement workloads in terms of number of page transfers (using physical operation cost equations), and 3) deriving the overall workload of each transaction (using DML statement workloads and frequencies). At the lowest level, the performance parameters of the estimated transaction workload are evaluated by a closed queueing network model similar to those presented in [1,10].

EROS is an automated tool for physical database design based on optimization models, which uses the evaluation models of EOS to estimate the cost of alternative design solutions. EROS allows for a high level transaction specification which is completely independent from the physical implementation of the database; it provides an "optimal" physical schema and, on the base of it, the actual implementation of transactions. The idea of integrating an optimization tool with an evaluation model has been often used in the literature. For instance, the database designer in [19] selects the optimal design for a relational database on the basis of costs computed by the query optimizer, which acts as an evaluation model. In a similar way, EROS selects the CODASYL physical database implementation, which has the best performance according to the evaluation of EOS; besides the designer can enforce constraints on the final design, in order to limit the search space of the optimal solution. While the designer in [19] is only devoted to determine the optimal set of indices for a given relational schema, EROS design models cover the whole spectrum of physical database design decisions, namely, physical access paths (including indices), placement strategy, storage allocation and area allocation. We note that also the CODASYL database designer presented in [16] covers most of the above-mentioned design decisions. However, the automated designer of [16] evaluates workloads of single DML statements, while EROS uses transaction analysis of EOS to compute frequencies and workloads of DML statements. The repertoire of physical data structures supported by EROS is a superset of that allowed by commercial CODASYL DBMSs.

The two tools, EOS and EROS, are fully integrated not only because EROS is based on the evaluation model of EOS, as we pointed out before, but also because they can be used together during the database design process. For instance, the designer may start from using EROS to obtain a first optimal solution (we stress that this solution is determined by heuristic techniques and is not the optimum). Then he can try to improve this solution by proposing some additional implementation strategies based on his experience and knowledge of applications. By means of EOS, the designer has the possibility to compare the final alternative designs and to select the best solution on the basis of EOS detailed performance measures. More in general, the designer can switch from one tool to the other during the physical design process, according to some particular design strategy. Design strategies may vary from the use of only system EROS (and in this case the physical design is fully automated) to the use of only system EOS (and in this case the designer selects the best solution among few alternative designs or according to a performance-oriented database design methodology as the one presented in [22]). Our belief is that a good strategy should make a combined use of both tools.

In Section 2 we discuss the physical design problems and the role of EOS and EROS in their solution. In Sections 3 and 4 we present a description of EOS and EROS, respectively. In Section 5 we give the conclusion and discuss further work.

2.   INTEGRATED TOOLS FOR PHYSICAL DATABASE DESIGN

2.1 *The Physical Database Design Process*

The logical database design phase produces a DBMS-processible schema, which satisfies user requirements but which is not necesseraly the best implementation as far as performance is concerned. The goal of physical database design is to refine the logical schema by means of the specification of physical data structures and to define the actual implementation of the database applications.

The taxonomy and the general characteristics of the physical database design process in the CODASYL DBMS environment have been discussed in [17,23].

The main input to the physical database phase (see Figure 1) is 1) the logical schema and transaction descriptions, provided by the logical design, and 2) quantitative data and characteristics of both DBMS and hardware. The output of the phase is the definition and allocation of physical structures, which determine the actual implementation of the database, and the performance evaluation of this implementation. The physical database design process consists of selecting an implementation with good performance behaviour; therefore, this process is based on performance evaluation models (which describe a database implementation in terms of measures such as transaction workload, page transfers and response time) and on optimization models (which take design decisions).

Performance evaluation models consider a database system to be a collection of interacting agents, such as application software (transactions), a database, control software (DBMS, operating system) and hardware devices. Performance of database systems is determined by behaviour of each of the above agents as well as by their interaction. Transactions generate requests (DML statements) for DBMS services. Transaction workload depends on the frequencies of such requests and on the complexity of data management functions that service the requests. Such complexity depends on the calling DML statement parameters and on the database design. Transaction workload is expressed in terms of the number of physical operations that have to be executed to implement data management functions. Physical operations issue I/O transfer requests with respect to the various I/O devices containing database areas. The number of such requests depends on the physical operation type and on the quantitative data characteristics. Additionally, a number of CPU instructions is executed within each logical and physical operation execution. The DBMS control functions, such as concurrency control and page buffer management functions, influence the number of actually effected I/O transfers. The former group of control functions usually increases such number, whereas the latter group may, in some cases, have the reverse effect. The operating system represents an overhead with respect to the CPU requests as well as the I/O transfer requests (i.e., paging). Duration of the above operations (response time) is determined by the CPU and I/O device service rates as well as by contention on these devices resulting from multiprogramming. In some cases, delays resulting from database locks (concurrency control) may influence transaction performance.

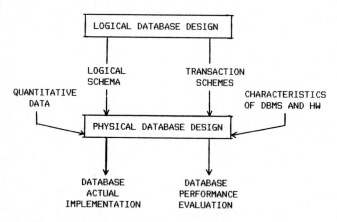

Fig. 1. Physical Database Design Phase

As far as optimization models are concerned, design decisions may be subdivided into two levels: *data implementation optimization level*, and *area allocation optimization level*.

The data implementation optimization level defines the physical data structures (records, files, and allocation of records on files) which minimize the workload generated by transactions, and consists of the following three broad decision areas ([17,23]):

i) *Placement strategy decisions*, which deal with creation of an optimal scheme for record implementation. The possible placement strategies are either clustering record occurrences within a particular CODASYL set (LOCATION MODE VIA set-name) or dispersing record occurrences in database areas via hashing algorithms (LOCATION MODE CALC). Implementations of records define their primary access paths.

ii) *Access path support decisions*, which are concerned with selection of physical data structures such as indices (implemented as B-trees), CODASYL set implementation types (chain, pointer-array and B-tree data structures), singular sets. Secondary access paths are specified through SET IMPLEMENTATION and SEARCH KEY clauses.

iii) *Storage allocation decisions*, which deal with selection of database areas (files) for storing record occurrences, indices and pointer-arrays. Page size and number of pages for each area have to be specified. These values are strongly connected with the record clustering decisions. Record allocation on database areas is specified, in a CODASYL system, through the WITHIN AREA clause.

The area allocation optimization level defines the allocation of areas on hardware devices. The objective of this design level is to minimize single I/O operation costs (and response times) by reducing the level of contention on I/O devices of the hardware configuration.

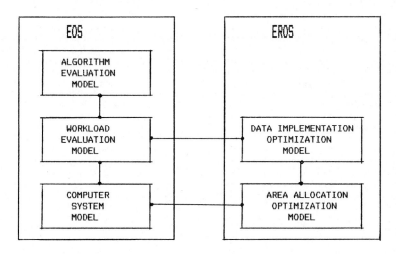

Fig. 2. Models of EOS and EROS

2.2 *Automated Physical Database Design*

In order to support the physical database design phase, we present two automated tools which cover all aspects of physical design process in CODASYL environment: the Database Performance Predictor EOS and the Physical Database Designer EROS, based on evaluation models and on optimization models, respectively. The models of EOS and EROS and their interactions are shown in Figure 2.

EOS is a database performance predictor which gives a complete description of the behaviour of a database implementation by means of the following evaluation models: the *Algorithm Evaluation Model*, the *Workload Evaluation Model* and the *Computer System Model*.

The **Algorithm Evaluation Model** analyses transaction descriptions and determines the execution frequencies of DML statements of each transaction.

The **Workload Model** predicts behaviour of the DBMS control software servicing data manipulation requests issued by each transaction. The performance measure returned by this model is the number of database page requests issued by DBMS control software, as well as the CPU requirements of a given data manipulation request. The CPU requirements are expressed in terms of the expected number of CPU instructions per one page request. The above performance measure is computed by expanding DML statements into a collection of logical operations which, in turn, are expanded into a number of physical operations, and by computing the cost of each physical operation (expressed in terms of number of page requests). Expansion of a data manipulation statement into a collection of logical operations is determined by the logical database schema definition, particulary by the data manipulation support features defined in the logical database schema (set order, set occurrence selection, virtual data items etc.) and by integrity constraints (insertion/deletion criteria, value checking etc.). The expansion of a logical operation and the cost of physical operations are determined by the physical database design decisions, namely, the access path support, placement strategy and storage allocation decisions.

The workload evaluation results, performed individually for each transaction regardless of the number of its concurrent occurrences, provide a useful relative measure to evaluate the possible design refinements regarding the object transaction, as well as the corresponding logical data structure and its physical implementation strategy. Yet, the workload measure does not necessarily coincide with the actual response time of a transaction. The transaction response time is determined by the service times of the utilized hardware devices (CPU and I/O devices), as well as by the interference of the concurrently processed transactions resulting in congestion on the various elements of the hardware configuration. Hence, realistic prediction of transaction respose times may only be performed in the context of a particular processing scenario with the use of the Computer System model.

The **Computer System Model** considers as input a) the workload generated by a processing scenario (i.e., the mix of jobs to be concurrently executed in the computer system), b) the mean service time of each I/O device (evaluated by means of technical data such as disk scheduling discipline, the seek and latency times, the number and capacity of disk cylinders), and c) the volume configuration (i.e., placement of database areas on I/O devices). The model evaluates the mean waiting time (time in queue plus the service time), the average queue length and utilization of each device specified in the object computer system configuration. The performance measures established by the Computer System Model coupled with the transaction type workload information are the basis for calculation of the response times (transaction response time, DML statement response times) for each transaction participating in a given processing scenario.

EROS is a physical database designer which selects a good database implementation by means of heuristic optimization techniques for the search of alternative solutions. The evaluation of alternatives is made by using the performance evaluation models of

EOS. EROS contains two optimization models: the *Data Implementation Optimization Level* and the *Area Allocation Optimization Model*.

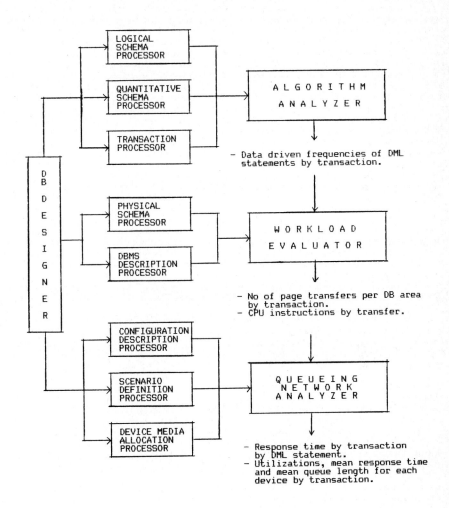

Fig. 3. Architecture of EOS

The **Data Implementation Optimization Model** decides the placement strategy for each schema record (LOCATION MODE of each record), the access path supports (indices, CODASYL set implementation, singular sets) and the storage allocation (number of database areas, page size and number of pages for each area, allocation of records on areas). The objective of this model is to minimize the workload generated by transactions, thus number of page transfers. We point out that this objective does not depend on the allocation of files on hardware devices. The model is based on heuristic optimization algorithms which use the Workload Model of EOS as cost evaluation function.

The **Area Allocation Optimization Model** decides the allocation of areas on hardware devices for the database implementation provided by the previous optimization model. The allocation of areas on the available disks is aimed at minimizing the response time of various scenarios of transactions. This model uses the Computer System Model of EOS as cost evaluation function.

We point out that, in general, the database implementation with the best performance does not necessarily coincide with the implementation with the minimal workload. This means that the exact solution of the physical database design problem should be found by means of an optimization model which makes all decisions in only one step. Unfortunately, this model is very hard to be implemented. For this reason, the approach of EROS uses two separated optimization models, where decisions are made by heuristic algorithms. This is also the very reason for which we have provided something like a workbench (as described in [24]), where the database designer may use the two integrated tools EOS and EROS according to some ad-hoc strategy, based on his experience and knowledge of applications.

3.   CODASYL DATABASE PERFORMANCE PREDICTOR EOS

The architecture of EOS, shown in Figure 3, reflects the major steps of the physical database design process. The modules *Algorithm Analyzer*, *Workload Evaluator* and *Queueing Network Analyzer* implement the Algorithm Evaluation Model, the Workload Evaluation Model and the Computer System Model, respectively. In addition, there are some modules for the database description (which comprises the logical schema definition, the physical schema definition, quantitative data and the device/media allocation definition) and the transaction description (which comprises definition of transactions and various transaction scenarios).

The logical and the physical database schemata are defined with the use of interactive, menu-driven processors (respectively, **Logical Schema Processor** and **Physical Schema Processor**). The logical schema description reflects the facilities provided by the Data Description Language proposed by the CODASYL DDLC ([5,9]). The physical schema description refers to the physical data structure implementation techniques used in the major CODASYL DBMSs.

By using the **Quantitative Schema Processor**, the database designer provides the basic information for the physical database structure design as well as for the performance evaluation of a database applications. Since a facility to define the quantitative properties of data is not available in the current CODASYL systems, we propose the *Quantitative Data Description Language* (the logical schema and a fragment of the quantitative schema pertaining to a University database are shown in Figure 4 and 5, respectively).

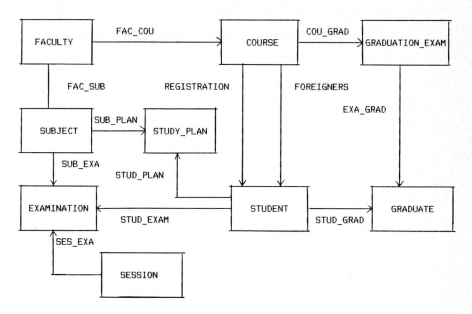

Fig. 4. University Database Schema

Quantitative data refer to:

i) *Definitions of records and sets.* The expected cardinality values with respect to all record types described in the logical data description are defined. The set participation probability and the empty set probability are defined for set types. The set conditions may be specified either directly as the probability of the condition being true or as a boolean expression defining the condition. Default values are assumed equal to 1 and 0, respectively. Set types with the AUTOMATIC/MANDATORY membership have the participation probability equal to 1.

ii) *Definitions of the data item value distributions.* The data item value is considered to be either a numeric value or a character string. The Poisson, Gaussian and Beta-distribution probability density functions may be used to model the numerical data item value distributions. Discrete numerical data item values may be approximated to continuous random variables. In the case of correlated data items, the multivariate Gaussian distribution may be used. The correlation definition specifies the correlation coefficients between correlated data items. The character string data item values are treated in an different way by considering selectivity, defined as the probability that a particular string will be found in an object record type occurrence. The string selectivity definition may be specified as an exhaustive list together with the associated probability, or as an incomplete list with the UNIFORM

option.   In   the   former   case,   all   the   probabilities
associated with the listed character strings must have a
total of 1.   The uniform selectivity is assumed for the
remaining N character strings (N is defined as an integer in
the UNIFORM option).

```
                    {RECORD SECTION}
    Record FACULTY has Cardinality Constant = 5;
        Data_Item NAME has Selectivity Uniform for 5.
    Record COURSE has Cardinality Constant = 15;
        Data_Item Name has Selectivity Uniform for 15;
        Data_Item COURSE_DURATION has Selectivity
                "4" 0.4, "5" 0.6.
    Record STUDENT has Cardinality Mean = 10000;
        Data_Item Name has Selectivity Uniform for 10000;
        Data_Item SEX has Selectivity
                "male" 0.6, "female" 0.4;
        Data_Item YEAR_COURSE has Selectivity
                "1" 0.33, "2" 0.23, "3" 0.17, "4" 0.14, "5" 0.13;
        Data_Item AGE has Min=18, Max=35, Mode=23, Unit=1;
        Data_Item NATIONALITY has Selectivity
                "Italian" 0.9, Uniform for 10.
    Record SUBJECT has Cardinality Constant = 100;
        Data_Item Name has Selectivity Uniform for 100.
    Record EXAMINATION has Cardinality Mean = 150000;
        Data_Item GRADE has Min=18, Max=30, Mode=25, Unit=1.
                        . . .

                    {SET SECTION}
    Set FOREIGNERS has Membership Not NATIONALITY in ["italian"].
    Set STUD_GRAD has Empty Probability = 0.9.
    Set STUD_EXAM has Empty Probability = 0.05.
```

*Fig. 5. A Fragment of the Quantitative Schema for the
          University Database*

By means of the **Transaction Processor** the database designer
provides   definitions   of   all   transactions that will be used in the
processing scenarios. Transactions are defined using a structured
Transaction Definition Language (TDL), which allows for DML statement
specification based on DBTG April 1971 proposal ([8]).   Transaction
descriptions,   coupled   with   the   definition   of   database and
quantitative schemata, provide ample information for   estimation of
DML statement execution frequencies.   The basic characteristics of
the TDL control structures are listed below:

-   The termination condition in the *iteration* control statement
    is determined by the cardinality of a database structure
    element (a set or a record type).

-   The selection condition specified in *if-then-else* and *case*
    control statements may be specified as boolean expressions,
    set predicates or as explicit branching probability values.
    The selection condition may be also used with a single DML
    statement.

- The boolean expressions are specified in the disjunctive
  normal form, that is, as a disjunction of conjunctive
  conditions (boolean terms) and predicates. A predicate may
  be defined as a simple data item condition of the form:
  <data-item-identifier > <relational-operator > <value >.
  The term *<value >* may be a constant (of the numeric or
  character string type), a value-range (for numerical values
  only), a data-item-identifier or a parameter-identifier.

- The set predicates define set conditions that are to be
  evaluated. They correspond to the set conditions specified
  in the quantitative data description, and the branching
  probability evaluation of these conditions is based on the
  respective probabilities given or evaluated in the
  quantitative schema.

A sample transaction definition, pertaining to the University
database schema shown in Figure 4, is presented in Figure 6.

```
TRANSACTION LIST_STUD.
 { Print for each foreign student of a given faculty
   the list of examinations with grade greater than 24. }

 begin LIST_STUD
  Find Calc Record FACULTY;
  begin FACULTY_COURSE do Cardinality of Set FAC_COU;
   Find Next Record COURSE Set FAC_COU;
   begin COURSE_STUDENTS do Cardinality of Set REGISTRATION;
      Find Next Record STUDENT Set REGISTRATION;
      if  not NATIONALITY in ["italian"]  then FOREIGNER_EXAM;
      begin FOREIGNER_EXAM do Cardinality of Set STUD_EXAM;
         Find Next Record EXAMINATION Set STUD_EXAM;
         if  GRADE in [24,30]  then PRINT_GRADE;
            begin PRINT_GRADE;
              Get EXAMINATION;
              end { PRINT_GRADE };
      end { FOREIGNER_EXAM };
   end { FOREIGNER_STUDENTS };
  end { FACULTY_COURSE };
 end  { LIST_STUD}.
```

Fig. 6. Sample Transaction Definition.

Implementation characteristics of the CODASYL DBMS are provided
by the database designer by using the **DBMS Description Processor**.
The DBMS implementation parameters must be given in order to account
for the implementation differences that exist among the various
CODASYL systems. The physical data structure parameters, such as the
database key length, the pointer length and the pointer-array
utilization factor (expressed as the proportion of the pointer-array
segment space expected to be utilized) are to be provided.

Technical parameters of the respective hardware devices are
given using the **Configuration Description Processor.** The CPU is
defined in terms of the mean number of instructions per microsecond,
possibly modified for taking into account the operating system
overhead. The characteristics of the I/O devices comprise the
minimum and the maximum seek times, the latency time, the track
length, the number of cylinders as well as the disk scheduling

policy. The FCFS (First Come First Served), SSTF (Short Seek Time First) or SCAN scheduling policies may be specified. The first scheduling policy will result in treating the I/O device as a load independent device and the two latter ones express the load dependency. Additionally, the CPU requirements of each logical operation type (expressed in terms of the mean number of CPU instructions executed for one page reference) must be specified. These measures must be established as a result of a performance study of the target DBMS. A catalogue of hardware devices and the major CODASYL DBMSs is maintained by EOS.

All of the above parameters, coupled with the Device/Media Allocation information (provided by the database designer by using the **Device Media Allocation Processor**), allow for calculation of the service times to be used in the queueing network model of the computer configuration.

Finally, using the **Scenario Definition Processors**, the database designer defines the processing scenarios to be evaluated. Transactions participating in a given processing scenario must be indicated and the number of concurrently executed tasks must be given for each transaction type. In general, the designer specifies several processing scenarios in order to have a complete characterization of database performance.

The **Algorithm Analyzer** evaluates transaction definitions in order to establish the data-driven frequencies of each of the DML statements. The detailed description of the probabilistic evaluation of data manipulation algorithms may be found in [21].

The **Workload Evaluator** analyses each DML statement comprised in a transaction, expands each statement into a collection of logical operations, that, in turn, are expanded into collections of physical operations. The physical operations are considered to be atomic operations and they are evaluated by the respective cost equations. The cost of each physical operation is expressed in terms of the expected number of page references to be performed with respect to a database area. The sum of all physical operation costs (grouped by database areas) is considered to be the workload of the DML statement. Transaction workload is computed using workloads and frequencies of all DML statements in the transaction. Detailed description of the workload evaluation may be found in [15].

The **Queueing Network Analyzer** (QNA) provides a model of the computer system and generates performance quantities characterizing its behaviour under the workload resulting from a particular processing scenario. The queueing network model is the central server model [1,10] and the normalization constant approach is used to calculate the required performance quantities. The queueing networks considered in the model are the multiple job class, closed queueing network models with a finite number of stations. The CPU (only one) is considered as a station with the PS (Processing Sharing) service discipline and the I/O devices are considered as stations with the FCFS service discipline. In some cases (depending on the disk unit scheduling policy), the I/O device service time are considered to be load dependent and the respective load dependency factors are input to the model. A job class corresponds to a transaction type and its workload characteristics are represented by the respective transaction workload vector. All jobs have the same exponential service time distribution at a FCFS service center, whereas each class of jobs may have a distinct service time distribution at the PS station.

The performance quantities, evaluated by the QNA, are the marginal queue length distribution, the throughput, the utilization , the mean queue length and the mean waiting time for each station per

job class as well as the mean response time for each job class.   The
mean waiting time is used to compute the response times of   each   DML
statement   specified   in   the   respective   transaction   device access
matrix.   The proportion of the transaction execution time used   by   a
particular DML statement may also be computed.

D M L C O M M A N D			PAGE REFERENCES	
No	T Y P E	FREQ.	INDIVIDUAL	GLOBAL
1	Find Calc Record FACULTY	1.	1.00	1.
2	Find Next Record COURSE Set FAC_COU	3.	1.00	3.
3	Find Next Record STUDENT Set REGISTRATION	200.	1.00	200.
4	Find Next Record EXAMINATION Set STUD_EXAM	3158.	0.02	63.
5	Get EXAMINATION	1989.	0.00	0.
		5351.		267.

Fig. 7. The Transaction Workload Report

The principal reports generated by EOS are:

- *Transaction workload report*, which is   generated   for   each
  transaction.   Workload is expressed in terms of frequencies
  and workloads (i.e., page references) of   DML   statements.
  The   workload report of the transaction in Figure 6 is shown
  in Figure 7.

DML	COMMAND		RESPONSE TIME msec	TIME IN EXECUTION msec	% TIME EXECUT
No	TYPE	FREQ.			
1	Find	1.	67.64	68.	0.3
2	Find	3.	67.64	203.	1.0
3	Find	200.	67.64	13528.	69.9
4	Find	3158.	1.76	5559.	28.7
5	Get	1989.	0.00	0.	0.0

TRANSACTION RESPONSE TIME - MIN: 0 SEC: 19 MSEC: 357

Fig. 8. The Transaction Performance Report

- *Storage Performance Parameter Report*, which comprises the
  set clustering factor, the resord splitting factor, the
  record location cost, the calc-chain length and the
  pointer-array splitting factor.   These parameters are
  calculated for each of the database areas defined in the
  database schema and for each record type and set type
  (whenever applicable).   Additionally, such information as
  the database area size (in bytes), the allocation on I/O
  devices, the area utilization and the number of Kbytes used
  for data and pointers are provided.

-   *Transaction Performance Report*, which is generated for each
    transaction type participating in the current scenario. It
    is considered to be one of the principal reports of a
    performance prediction study. The transaction performance
    report of the transaction shown in Figure 6, for a sample
    processing scenario (reported in [22]), is presented in
    Figure 8.

-   *Configuration Performance Report*, which provides global
    performance measures of the computer system under the
    workload generated for the current scenario. The CPU and
    the I/O devices are identified by the internal names defined
    in the configuration specification. For each device the
    queueing discipline and the load dependency are indicated.
    The configuration performance report corresponding to a
    sample case study reported in [22] is shown in Figure 9.

DEVICE	QUEUEING DISCIPLINE	LOAD DEP.	MEAN SERVICE TIME msec	VISITS (I/O TRANS)	UTILIZATION FACTOR	AVERAGE WAITING TIME msec	AVERAGE QUEUE LENGTH
CPU_1	PS	LI	2.00	9248.69	0.20	2.48	0.25
IO_1	FCFS	LI	20.82	3040.69	0.68	51.77	1.69
IO_2	FCFS	LI	24.61	3167.31	0.90	92.48	3.37
IO_3	FCFS	LI	20.82	3040.69	0.68	51.77	1.69
IO_4	FCFS	LI	0.00	0.00	0.00	0.00	0.00

Fig. 9. The configuration performance report

A number of optional reports are also available to allow for
more detailed analysis of the data manipulation statements. Reports
summarizing various parts of the database description may also be
generated by the system.

4.   THE PHYSICAL DATABASE DESIGNER EROS

4.1 *Architecture of EROS*

The architecture of EROS, shown in Figure 10, consists of three
levels: the *Parameter Description Level*, the *Data Implementation
Level* and the *Area Allocation Level*. The Parameter Description level
allows for the specification of the parameter description, namely,
the logical schema, the transaction specification, the quantitative
schema, the DBMS parameter description and the hardware configuration
description. The Data Implementation and the Area Allocation levels
implement the two corresponding optimization models described in
Section 2.2. These two levels also provide interface modules which
allow the designer to enforce constraints on design decision
variables.
At the *Parameter Description* level the database designer
provides all inputs to the database design process but possible
design constraints that will be eventually specified using ad-hoc
interfaces. The Parameter Description Level consists of six modules

which are also present in the architecure of EOS: the *Quantitative Schema Processor*, the *DBMS Description Processor*, the *Configuration Description Processor*, the *Transaction Processor*, the *Logical Schema Processor* and the *Algorithm Analyzer*. Since the former three modules are the same as in EOS, we only describe the latter three modules.

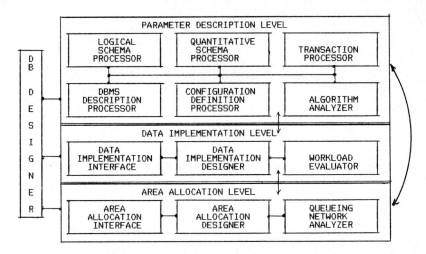

Fig. 10. *Architecture of Eros*

The **Logical Schema Processor** is an interactive processor which accepts the logical database schema description and produces an internal schema representation. This module differs from the corresponding module , of EOS because it does not consider physical descriptions of the schema (for instance, there is no specification of LOCATION MODE and SET IMPLEMENTATION clauses). The logical schema description reflects the facilities provided by the CODASYL 78 proposal.

```
TRANSACTION PRINT_EXAM.
{ List all examinations with grade=30 }
begin
   Find All Records EXAMINATION where GRADE=30;
end.
```

Fig. 11. *A Transaction Defined in the TDL of EROS*

The **Transaction Processor** and the **Algorithm Analyzer** accept transaction descriptions specified using Transaction Definition Language (TDL). This language is similar to the TDL of EOS.

However, the TDL of EROS can be independent on actual physical database implementation. An example of a TDL transaction pertaining to the University schema in Figure 4 is shown in Figure 11. The transaction will be refined after the physical database design process. For instance, by adding to the schema a singular set (called SYS_EXAM) on the record EXAMINATION which links all the occurrences having grade=30, the refinement of the above transaction is shown in Figure 12.

```
Transaction PRINT_EXAM.
  { List all examinations with grade=30 }
    begin PRINT_EXAM do Cardinality of Set SYS_EXAM
      Find Next Record EXAMINATION Set SYS_EXAM;
      Get EXAMINATION;
    end {PRINT_EXAM}.
```

Fig. 12. Refinement of the Transaction in Figure 10

The *Data Implementation* level decides the placement strategy for each schema record, access path supports and the storage allocation. The objective of the above decisions is to minimize the workload generated by transactions. This level consists of the following modules: the *Data Implementation Interface*, the *Workload Evaluator* and the *Data Implementation Designer*.

The **Data Implementation Interface** allows the designer to enforce constraints on the following design variables: LOCATION MODE, SET IMPLEMENTATION, SEARCH KEY (indices). In this way the space of search for the optimal solution can be reduced; besides, by enforcing some decisions, the designer can use EROS according to some strategy based on his esperience and knowledge of applications and he can make a combined usage of EROS and EOS. In addition, the module returns the data implementation decisions obtained as result of the design optimization.

The **Workload Evaluator** implements the cost evaluation function of the Data Implementation Optimization Model. This module extends the Workload Evaluator of system **EOS** in the following way. At the beginning of a data implementation design section, all DML statements are expanded into a sequence of logical operations according to the parameters specified in TDL transactions, which do not include physical design decisions. Later on, for each record to be designed, the Workload Evaluator is invoked in order to expand all logical operations, dealing with the record, into a sequence of physical operations, according to the physical implementation design decisions currently being examined for the record. Transaction execution frequencies are also taken into account (while in EOS they are only considered in scenario descriptions for the Queueing Network Analyzer).

The **Data Implementation Designer** implements the heuristic algorithms for the minimization of the cost function. At each step of the optimization process, the module invokes the Workload Evaluator for the evaluation of the cost of the current decision-tree node. Physical data structures are selected according to DBMS characteristic definition.

Example. We now present an example of usage of the Data Implementation level of EROS. Let us consider the subschema of the University Database shown in Figure 13, the quantitative schema in Figure 5 and the following transactions (transaction frequencies are shown in parenthesis):

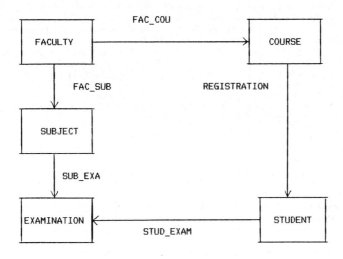

Fig. 13. A Subschema of the University Database

T1. *List all subjects of a given faculty* (3000);

T2. *List all students who passed the examinations of a given subject* (1000);

T3. *List all subjects passed by a given student* (1000);

T4. *List all students of a given faculty* (2500);

T5. *List all examinations (including subject and student) with grade=30* (2500);

T6. *Insert examination of a given student for a given subject* (2000).

As far as decisions about LOCATION MODE of records are concerned, we decide to enforce that record FACULTY is CALC on FACULTY_NAME data-item and record COURSE is VIA SET FAC_COU. The automated designer decides the following placement strategies for the other records:

-   SUBJECT is VIA FAC_SUB

-   EXAMINATION is VIA SUB_EXAM

-   STUDENT is VIA REGISTRATION

Concerning the SET IMPLEMENTATION and SEARCH KEY clauses, we decide to enforce the implementation of sets FAC_COU and SUB_EXA as unidirectional chain and chain linked to owner, respectively. The automated designer decides to implement all other schema sets as unidirectional chains, except the STUD_EXAM set which is also linked to owner; moreover, it introduces an index on the STUDENT record (implemented by means of a singular set) and a singular set (of type MANUAL/OPTIONAL) on the EXAMINATION record which links all the occurrences with data-item GRADE equal to 30.

Record occurrences are allocated within areas by the automated designer with care taken not to loose the effect of the clustering. In particular, records FACULTY, COURSE and SUBJECT are allocated within the same area, whereas STUDENT and EXAMINATION record occurrences are allocated within two different areas.

The workload for the implementation decided by the automated designer, expressed in terms of page references, is shown in Figure 14.

TRANSACTION NAME	WORKLOAD	FREQUENCY	GLOBAL WORKLOAD
T1	1	3000	3000
T2	1510	1000	1510000
T3	19	1000	19000
T4	13	2500	32500
T5	202	2500	505000
T6	8	2000	16000
TOTAL			2085500

Fig. 13. The Transaction Workload for the Database Implementation Provided by EROS

Let us consider another reasonable physical implementation of the same schema, where the records have the following LOCATION MODE values:

- FACULTY and STUDENT are CALC;

- SUBJECT is VIA FAC_SUB;

- EXAMINATION is VIA STUD_EXAM;

- COURSE is VIA FAC_COU.

All CODASYL sets are implemented as unidirectional chains and no indices are introduced. Records are allocated within areas as in the above implementation. The transaction workload of this implementation is shown in Figure 15. We note that the workload for the solution provided by the automated designer is 88% less than the manual solution. ∎

The *Area Allocation* level decides the allocation of areas on hardware devices for the database implementation provided by the Data Implementation level. The objective of the above decisions is to minimize the response time of various scenarios of transactions.

This level consists of the following modules: the *Area Allocation Interface*, the *Queueing Network Analyzer* and the *Area Allocation Designer*.

TRANSACTION NAME	WORKLOAD	FREQUENCY	GLOBAL WORKLOAD
T1	1	3000	3000
T2	3003	1000	3003000
T3	2	1000	2000
T4	2002	2500	5005000
T5	3570	2500	9375000
T6	5	2000	10000
TOTAL			17421000

Fig. 14. The Transaction Workload for a Straigthforward Database Implementation

The **Area Allocation Interface** is the interface module with the designer.   It accepts constraints on the allocation of areas on I/O devices and the maximum number of areas allowed.   On the other side, it returns the area allocation schema obtained as result of the automated design.

The **Queueing Network Analyzer** is an implementation of the cost evaluation function of the Area Allocation Optimization model.   It evaluates, on the basis of the "optimal" transaction workload selected   at Data Implementation Level, the queue length distribution at the I/O devices, used in the formulation of the objective function, and other performance parameters of the computer system used for the evaluation of the transaction response times.   This module is the same as in EOS.

The **Area Allocation Designer** implements the heuristic algorithms for minimization of the level of contention on I/O devices.   At each step, the module invokes the Queueing Network Analyzer for evaluation of the current value of the objective function.

Since the implementation of the Area Allocation level is not yet completed, we do not present any example of usage of this level.

4.2 *The Optimization Models of EROS*

The response time of a transaction is determined by the workload, expressed in terms of I/O operations required during its execution, and the cost of I/O operations.   While the former is determined by the physical data structures designed to implement the logical database schema, the latter depends on the service times of the hardware devices as well as on the area allocation on I/O devices, which determines the level of contention on the components of the hardware configuration.

According to the above considerations, we have introduced two different   levels   of   physical   design   decisions :   the *data*

implementation level and the *area allocation* level.
    Each of the proposed design levels is characterized by a cost
evaluation function **f** such that

$$c = f\ (\bar{v}, \bar{p})$$

where **c** is the estimated cost associated to each instance of the
design decision variable vector $\bar{v}$, for a given parameter vector $\bar{p}$.
Parameters represent logical design decisions, such as the logical
database   schema   and   the   data   manipulation   algorithms, and
characteristics of the modeled system, such as the quantitative data
and the descriptions of the DBMS and the hardware configuration.
    The design activity, at each of the above mentionned two levels,
can be formulated, in a very general way, as follows:

$$\operatorname*{Min}_{\bar{v}}\ f\ (\bar{v}, \bar{p})$$

    The idea behind **EROS** is to utilize the evaluation model of
system **EOS** as the performance cost functions, and to provide
heuristic optimization algorithms for the automated selection of the
"best" design, on both physical database design levels, which
"minimizes" the cost functions.
    At the *Data Implementation* level, the objective of the heuristic
optimization model is to select the physical data structures which
"minimize" the global transaction workload using the Workload
Evaluator as cost evaluation function.
    The heuristic approach is based on the separability assumption,
proposed in [26] for relational systems, later extended in [25] to
network systems. A separability-based design methodology has been
also reported in [23]. The theory of separability proves that, if
certain conditions are satisfied, the problem of designing the
optimal physical database can be reduced to the subproblem of
optimizing individual record types independently of one another.
    Let R_i, $Op_i = \{DML_1, \ldots, DML_k\}$ and $Ef_i = \{ef_1, \ldots, ef_k\}$ be,
respectively, the i-th record type, the set of DML operations
performed on it and the execution frequency of each operation.   The
separability assumption allows for reducing the global optimization
design problem to the following local optimization problem:

$$\operatorname*{Min}_{R_i}\ f(R_i, Op_i, Ef_i) \qquad V = 1..n$$

where **f** is the transaction workload cost function and **n** is the number
of database record types.   Once the problem has been partitioned,
designing a single record R_i means selecting primary and secondary
access paths as well as record allocation within a database area.
More precisely, let us consider a record type as a relation

$$R_i = \langle Key, A_1, \ldots, A_s, \ldots, A_m, fk_1, \ldots, fk_r, \ldots, fk_n \rangle$$

where **Key** is the record database key, A_s is the s-th data item of the
record and fk_r is the r-th foreign key (corresponding to the database
key of the record which is owner in the r-th set having R_i as
member).   **Key**, $fk_1, \ldots,$ fk_n are fictitious data-items of R_i. The
objectives of the physical record design are:

    - *Defining the placement strategy* of R_i, either by dispersing
      record occurrences via hashing algorithms or by clustering
      them according to one of data-items **Key**, fk_1, $\ldots$, fk_n.

- *Implementing access paths* to the record using each of the above-mentioned fictitious data-items as key. For each fictitious data-item **fk$_r$**, an access path (chain, pointer-array or B-tree) must be introduced, which implements the r-th set having R$_i$ as member. Defining an access path through **Key** corresponds to the introduction of a singular set.

- *Selecting indices* on data-items **A$_i$** *(record indices)* and/or on compound data-items <fk$_r$,A$_i$> *(set indices)*.

In this way the physical implementation of CODASYL records represents the extension of the index selection on relations for relational databases ([19]).

The heuristic optimization is based on both a generator of all possible implementations of the record R$_i$ and a variety of rules which improve the performance of the search within the set of all possibilities. These rules, on the basis of the logical access paths to each record type, promote candidate implementations eliminating paths of investigation that have little chance of success. Some simple examples of physical database design rules are listed below:

- direct accesses to a record type are best supported by hashing algorithm access method;

- scanning CODASYL set occurrences is fast if they are clustered;

- a record type which is accessed both directly and sequentially, may require some index.

The evaluation of candidate implementations are made using the Workload Evaluator, which plays the same role of the optimizer in relational physical database design.

At the **Area Allocation** level, the aim of the heuristic optimization model is to provide the area allocation schema which "minimizes" the level of contention on I/O devices.

The minimization problem may be formulated as follows:

Min var (Q)

where the objective is to "minimize" the variance of the distribution queue lengths $Q_1, \ldots, Q_r$ on the r I/O devices. These values, togheter with other performance quantities, such as the mean waiting times of requests to to the components of the computer system and the respective utilization factors, are provided by the Queueing Network Analyzer. The heuristic approach is based on a greedy algorithm.

5. CONCLUSIONS

In this paper we have presented the automated tools EOS (a database performance predictor) and EROS (a physical database designer) which can be used during the physical database design process. The tools are fully integrated since both EROS is based on evaluation models of EOS and it is possible to make a combined usage of them in the design process. The architecture of the two tools and an example of their capabilities were also reported.

Presently, EOS is fully implemented in a prototype version on VAX 11/780 under VMS operating system. The prototype is written in

Pascal. In addition, a prototype version of EROS is also available in the same environment, the only part to be still completed being the Area Allocation level.

Further research work will be devoted to extend the design capabilities of EROS and, in particular, to complete the implementation of the Area Allocation level.

ACKNOWLEDGMENTS

We are gratefull to G. Balbo, R. Bonanno, M. Gaudioso and S. Scrivano for their cooperation in design and implementation of EOS. We are also indebted to C. Zhong for his cooperation in implementation of EROS. Finally we wish to thank A. Albano for a careful reading and many useful comments on preliminary drafts of this paper.

REFERENCES

[1]   Bruell,S.C., Balbo,G., *Computational Algorithms for Closed Queueing Networks* (North-Holland, Amsterdam, 1980).

[2]   Ceri,S. (ed.) *Methodology and Tools for Database Design* (North-Holland, Amsterdam, 1983).

[3]   Chen,P.P., Yao,S.B., Design and Performance Tools for Data Base Systems, *Proc. 3rd VLDB Conf.*, Tokio, Japan (1977) 3-15.

[4]   Christodoulakis,S., Estimating Record Selectivities, *Information Systems* 8 (1983) 105-115.

[5]   CODASYL DDLC Journal of Development 1978, Dept.of Supply and Services, Canadian Government, Quebeck, Canada (1978).

[6]   Dahl,R., Bubenko,J.A., IDBD: An Interactive Design Tool for CODASYL-DBTG-Type Data Bases, *Proc. 8th VLDB Conf.*, Mexico City, Mexico (1982) 108-121.

[7]   Dayal,U., Goodman,N., Query Optimization for CODASYL Data Base Systems, *Proc. ACM SIGMOD Conf.*, Orlando, Florida (1982) 138-150.

[8]   DBGT 71 Report ,ACM, New York, NY (1971).

[9]   DDLC 73 Report, National Bureau of Standards, Washington D.C. (1973).

[10] Denning,P.J., Buzen,J.P., The Operational Analysis of Queueing Network Models, *Computing Surveys 10* (1978) 225-261.

[11] Effelsberg,W., Haerder,T., Reuter,A., Measurement and Evaluation of Techniques for Implementing Cosets - a Case Study, *Proc. 1st Int. Conf. on Data Bases*, Aberdeen, UK (1980) 135-159.

[12] Gambino,T.J., Gerritsen,R., A Data Base Design Support System, *Proc. 3rd VLDB Conf.*, Tokyo, Japan (1977) 534-544.

[13] Gerritsen,R., Understanding Data Structures, Ph.D. Diss., Carnegie-Mellon Univ., Pittsburg, Pa. (1975).

[14] Lum,V., et al., 1978 New Orleans Data Base Design Workshop Report, *Proc. 5th VLDB Conf.*, Rio de Janeiro, Brasil (1979) 328-339.

[15] Orlando,S., Rullo,P., Staniszkis,W., Transaction Workload Evaluation in the CODASYL Database Environment, *Proc. IEEE Int. Conf. on Data Engineering*, Los Angeles, California (1984) 562-569.

[16] Reuter,A., Kinzinger,H., Automatic Design of the Internal Schema for a CODASYL Database System, *IEEE Trans. Software Eng.*, 4 (1984) 358-375.

[17] Sacca',D., Staniszkis,W., Physical Data Base Design in CODASYL Environment, *Proc. AICA Annual Conf.*, Pavia, Italy (1981) 835-845.

[18] Schkolnick,M., A Survey of Physical Database Design Methodology and Techniques, *Proc. 4th VLDB Conf.*, Berlin, Germany (1978), 479-487.

[19] Schkolnick,M., Tiberio,P., Considerations in Developing a Design Tool for a Relational DBMS, *Proc. IEEE COMPSAC Conf.*, Chicago, Ill. (1979) 228-235.

[20] Sevcik,K.C., Data Base Performance Prediction Using an Analytical Model, *Proc. 7th VLDB Conf.*, Cannes, France (1981) 182-198.

[21] Staniszkis,W., Rullo,P., Gaudioso,M., Orlando,S., Probabilistic Approach to Evaluation of Data Manipulation Algorithms in a CODASYL Data Base Environment, *Proc. 2nd Int. Conf. on Databases*, Cambridge, UK (1983) 332-357.

[22] Staniszkis,W., Rullo,P., Orlando,S., Performance-Oriented Database Design Laboratory, in: Bell,D.A. (Ed.), *Infotec State-of-the-art Report: Database Performance* (Pergamon Press, London, 1984) 132-160.

[23] Staniszkis,W., Sacca',D., Manfredi,F., Mecchia,A., Physical Data Base Design for CODASYL DBMS, in: Ceri,S. (ed.), *Methodology and Tools for Data Base Design* (North-Holland, Amsterdam 1983) 119-148.

[24] Teorey,E., et al., Systems and Techniques for Research in Physical Database Design, *IEEE Database Engineering 5* (1982) 22-30.

[25] Whang Kyu-Young, Wiederhold,G., Sagalowicz,D., Physical Design of Network Model Databases Using the Property of Separability, *Proc. 8th VLDB Conf.*, Mexico City, Mexico (1982) 98-107.

[26] Whang Kyu-Young, Wiederhold, G., Sagalowicz, D., Separability: An Approach to Physical Database Design, *Proc. 8th VLDB Conf.*, Cannes, France (1981) 320-332.

[27] Yeh,R.T., Baker,J.W., Toward a Design Methodology for DBMS: A Software Engineering Approach, *Proc. 3rd VLDB Conf.*, Tokyo, Japan (1977) 16-27.

PART II
DATAID METHODOLOGY

CHAPTER VIII

DATAID-D:
METHODOLOGY FOR DISTRIBUTED DATABASE DESIGN

S. CERI[*], B. PERNICI[**]

* Dipartimento di Elettronica   ** CSISEI-CNR
Politecnico di Milano
Piazza L. Da Vinci, 32
20133 Milano, Italy

This paper presents DATAID-D, the extension of DATAID-1 to the
design of distributed databases. Two new phases are presented:
"analysis of distribution requirements" and "distribution
design". The problems considered during distribution design are
horizontal and vertical partitioning of relations, allocation of
fragments, and reconstruction of local schemata at sites. An
example of application of DATAID-D is presented in detail.

1. INTRODUCTION

The design of distributed databases is becoming more and more important:
distributed information systems constitute one of the most important technological
developments of the present days, and the problem of designing and implementing a
distributed database system will therefore become a major challenge for many
organizations [1]. Presently, there are very few distributed database systems
available, mostly developed in the academic environment or in research centers of
computer companies [2-3]; however, most software producers are developing
extensions to their commercial database systems in order to support distribution
[4-7], and it is easy to predict that, in a few years, distributed databases with
full capabilities will enter the commercial market. With this scenario, the
database designer will have to face a new design problem, i.e. to determine the
distribution of data which reflects more accurately the needs of their
organization. This paper is concerned with a methodology for making the
appropriate distribution design decisions.

The design of distributed databases has been deeply investigated in the past, and
several contributions to the literature on this topic have been given also in the
framework of the DATAID project [12-19]. The emphasis in the previous works was on
the understanding, formulation, and solution of specific design problems, often
approached from an operations research viewpoint. In this paper, instead, the
emphasis is placed on providing a methodological framework to the designer,
indicating the relevant design problems, which parameters are required in order to
solve each of them, and how each problem can be "easily" approached manually,
without using a computer-based solution method. In this way, the "optimality" of
the approach is sacrificed to the practicability and ease of application.

Distributed databases can have very different features:

a. Distributed database systems typically use local systems which are based upon
   commercial, nondistributed systems; they can be based on any of the three more
   commonly used data models (hierarchical, network, and relational).

b. The database can be **homogeneous**, i.e., with the same database system at each
   site, or **heterogeneous**, i.e., with at least two different data base systems.

c. The database can be built on a **local** network, which connects several computers within a small area with a very fast and reliable communication link, or on a **geographical** network, with geographically dispersed computers connected by slower and less reliable links.

In this paper, we will present methodological problems which are common to all the above distributed database environments, thus assuming a general approach; DATAID-D can be tailored to a specific environment in which all these features (and many other) are fixed.

This paper is organized as follows. Section 2 describes the architecture of DATAID-D and indicates its role within DATAID-1. Section 3 describes the phase of "Distribution Requirement Collection". Section 4 describes the phase of "Distribution Design". The methodology is exemplified on a case study, describing a distributed manufactoring control system.

2. ARCHITECTURE OF DATAID-D

The proposed methodology constitutes an extension of DATAID-1 towards distribution. This extension requires the addition of two phases to the original DATAID-1 architecture, as shown in Figure 1:

a. **Analysis of distribution requirements.** This phase is required in order to collect information about distribution. With respect to Requirements Analysis of DATAID-1, this phase collects additional information, such as the frequency of activation of each operation from each site. However, it is required to know the structure of data and operations in order to collect information about their geographical properties. Thus, distribution requirements are collected starting from some of the results of the conceptual design: the global data schema and the global operation schemata.

b. **Distribution Design.** This phase starts from the specification of the integrated database schema and from the collected distribution requirements, and produces several database schemata, one for each site of the distributed database, each one describing the portion of data that will be allocated to that site. The input of Distribution Design is an integrated database schema described using a simplified version of the EER model, including only entities and binary relationships. This choice allows us to limit the complexity of the distribution design phase, and to take profit of the results of the first two steps of Logical Design in DATAID-1, having precisely the purpose of producing a simplified schema (eliminating generalization hierarchies and complex relationships).

Figure 1 shows that distribution design separates two major activities in the design of a Distributed Database. The first one consists in the traditional design of an integrated database schema starting from the collection of all the requirements. The second one consists in the logical and physical design for each partial database schema at each site.

2.1 Example: a distributed manufacturing control system.

The phases of DATAID-D will be shown on a distributed manufacturing system. Manufacturing control is an application which typically shows strong distribution properties, when the manufacturing system is itself distributed [26]. In our example, we assume that an Italian semiconductor company has 4 production departments, two specialized in assembling keyboards and displays respectively, and the other two which assemble other systems. The company has also two sale distribution departments, which control the north and the south areas, and 3 warehouses. Figure 2 shows that the distributed information system of the company has 5 sites connected through a geographic communication network; each site is

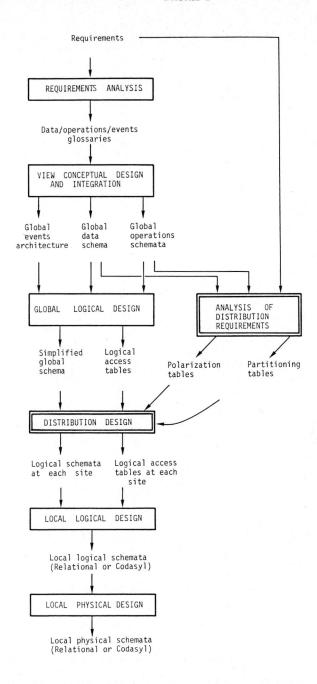

Fig. 1. Phases of DATAID-D within the architecture of DATAID-1

located close to one or more departments of the company.

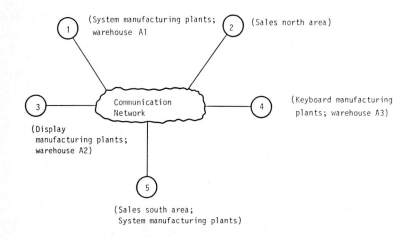

Fig. 2. Distributed information system in proposed example

In Figure 2, basic information about the geographical placement of each site with respect to the company departments is also shown; thus, for instance, in the location of site 1 we have system manufacturing plants and warehouse A1.

Figure 3 shows the ER conceptual schema of the data constituting the distributed database. The entity PRODUCT describes product features, the entity PRODUCTION describes the (many) production processes for each product.

Each PRODUCTION instance is related through the PROD_SCHEDULE relationship to just one PRODUCT instance; one attribute of PRODUCTION indicates the number of units of products to be produced (P_QUANTITY). The bill of material for each product is simply represented by using the entity MATERIAL, describing each material required for the production process, and a many-to-many relationship between the entities MATERIAL and PRODUCT, showing the composition of each product. The sale data are represented by an entity SALE_DEPARTMENT describing the points of sale of the company and a relationship NEEDS between PRODUCT and SALE_DEPARTMENT, which indicates the quantity and date at which products must be available to each sale department. Clearly, this database schema is a very simple one in terms of number of entities, attributes, and relationships; however, it is sufficient for showing several interesting and nontrivial distribution design problems.

Figure 4 shows the operation schemata for the operations that will be considered in the distributed database application.

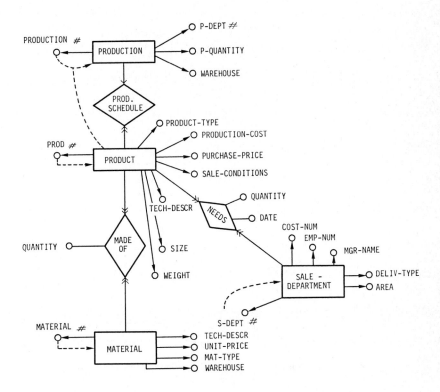

Fig. 3. Entity-Relationship example schema

a. Report R1 requires the scheduled productions and required materials for some selected products. We recall from [9] that the numbers in the box representing entities correspond to the total number of instances of the entity and to the number of instances which are selected by an operation, respectively. We also recall that the arrows on the relationships indicate the paths to access entities. Thus, report R1 selects initially 100 out of 10,000 instances of products, and for those instances selects 150 material instances and 300 production instances, by following the PROD_SCHEDULE and MADE_OF relationship.

b. Update transaction U1 changes the production schedule for 10 selected products.

c. Update transaction U2 changes the bill of material. It is possible that the changes only affect the quantity required of a given material (operation (a)) or require the insertion of a new product or material instance (operation (b)).

d. Report R2 retrieves the sale conditions of products requested at given sale departments.

e. Report R3 retrieves information about all productions and materials which are stored at given warehouses.

Operation R1 : For some products, retrieve scheduled productions and
required materials.

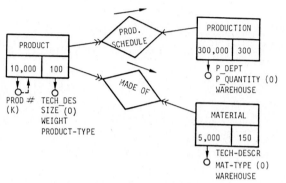

Operation U1: Change production schedule

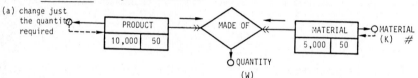

Operation U2: Change bill of material

(a) change just
    the quantity
    required

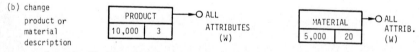

(b) change
    product or
    material
    description

Operation R2: For some sale departments, retrieve sale conditions of products

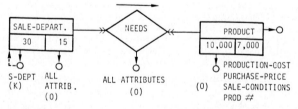

Operation R3: Retrieve production and material information stored at given
warehouse

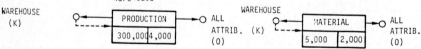

Fig. 4. Global operation schemata in the example

Figure 5 shows the Entity Access tables for the 4 entities of the schema, built according to the method described in [9] (we omit, for brevity, the Relationship Access tables).

These tables summarize how operations use attributes (K indicates keyed access, O indicates output, W indicates write), and how many instances of each entity are accessed by each operation.

3. ANALYSIS OF DISTRIBUTION REQUIREMENTS

The collection of distribution requirements is divided into two tasks: the determination of distribution predicates, and the determination of polarization. The first task requires to determine the logical properties of data which have an impact on distribution; the second task corresponds to the collection of quantitative data, based on the properties determined above. Figure 6 indicates the diagram of the tasks of this phase.

3.1 Determination of distribution predicates

Initially, it is important to understand the **locality properties** of operations. Therefore, assuming that each operation can be issued from different sites, it is required to collect the frequency of activation of each operation from each site. Figure 7 shows a table which reports the frequency of activation of each operation from each site.

Note that some sites have a null frequency of activation for some operations; this means that the operation is never executed from that site. In general, operation frequency reflects the particular need for information of the activities performed at that site; so, for instance, sites 1, 3, 4, and 5, where production departments are located, activate operation R1, which performs an enquiry on production plans.

The major effort of this task consists in building the Partitioning Tables, shown in Figure 8.

These tables describe candidate partitionings which might apply to each entity; as it will be shown in Section 4, the horizontal fragmentation of entities is largely based on this information.

Each partition consists of a set of selection predicates which properly define a partition of the set of all the instances of a given entity. Therefore, each partition must satisfy the following constraints:

1. Predicates must be disjoint;

2. Predicates must be mutually exclusive;

3. All instances of an entity must satisfy at least one partitioning predicate.

For instance, the entity PRODUCT can be partitioned according to PRODUCT_TYPE by the following 3 predicates:

- TYPE="SYSTEM";

- TYPE="KEYBOARD";

- TYPE="DISPLAY".

Table 8 indicates this partitioning in the first row; to each predicate, it is also associated a predicate selectivity.

The criteria that lead to the determination of partitioning predicates are to

Entity:PRODUCT

Attributes	OPERATIONS				
	R1	U1	U2a	U2b	R2
PROD. #	K	K	K	W	O
TECH-DES, SIZE, WEIGHT, TYPE	O			W	
PRODUCTION-COST PURCHASE-PRICE SALE-CONDITIONS				W	O
RA					NEEDS
HA					
AN	100	10	50	3	7,000

Entity:PRODUCTION

Attributes	OPERATIONS		
	R1	U1	R3
PRODUCTION #		W	O
P-DEPT # P-QUANTITY	O	W	O
WAREHOUSE	O	W	K
RA	PROD. SCHEDULE	PROD. SCHED.	
HA			
AN	300	100	4,000

Entity:SALE-DEPARTMENT

Attributes	OPERATIONS
	R2
S-DEPT #	K
CUST-NUM EMP-NUM MGR-NAME AREA DELIV-TYPE	O
RA	
HA	
AN	15

Entity: MATERIAL

Attributes	OPERATIONS			
	R1	U2a	U2b	R3
MATERIAL #		K	W	K,O
TECH-DESCR MAT-TYPE WAREHOUSE	O		W	O
RA	MADE-OF			
HA				
AN	150	50	20	2,000

Fig. 5. Entity access tables

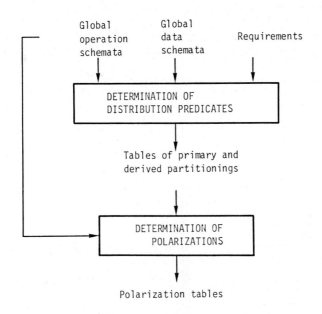

Fig. 6. Analysis of distribution requirements

Frequency Table		Sites				
		1	2	3	4	5
Operations	R1	50	0	40	40	50
	U1	50	20	50	50	60
	U2	5	0	3	3	0
	R2	0	15	0	0	15
	R3	20	0	20	10	0

Fig. 7. Frequency table

produce subsets of data which are accessed with a greater probability than by assuming an average distribution of accesses. Thus, for instance, the predicate TYPE="SYSTEM" describes a subset of the PRODUCT entities which is accessed with high probability by the operation R1 activated from sites 1 and 5; recall that these sites are located at the production departments specialized in system

Primary Partitioning Table

Entity	Partition Name	Predicates	Predicate Selectivity
PRODUCT	PRODUCT-TYPE	TYPE = SYSTEM TYPE = DISPLAY TYPE = KEYBOARD	50 30 20
MATERIAL	STORAGE	WAREHOUSE = A1* WAREHOUSE = A2* WAREHOUSE = A3*	35 40 25
PRODUCTION	STORAGE	WAREHOUSE = A1* WAREHOUSE = A2* WAREHOUSE = A3*	30 35 35
PRODUCT	PRICE-CLASS	PURCHASE-PRICE<100$ PURCHASE-PRICE>100$	80 20
SALE-DEPARTMENT	SALE-AREA	AREA = N AREA = S	45 55

Derived Partitioning Table

Entity	Association for the derivation	Base Entity	Partition Name	Predicate Selectivity
PRODUCTION	PROD-SCHEDULE	PRODUCT	PRODUCT-TYPE	SAME

Fig. 8. Partitioning tables

assembling. Similarly, the predicate TYPE="DISPLAY" describes a subset of entities which are largely used at site 3, where displays are built. In general, partitionings are defined to reflect a structural decomposition of data into subsets according to the distribution of operations over sites and to the pattern of access of operations to data.

It is possible to determine more than one partitioning criteria for each entity. In general, this happens because different operations, with different distribution features, affect the same entity. Thus, for instance, the entity PRODUCT is also partitioned on the basis of its PRICE_CLASS. Similarly, the entity PRODUCTION can be partitioned according to two criteria. It is important to collect the potential partitionings which lead to large differences with respect to an homogeneous distribution of accesses, disregarding those that only marginally affect it.

Partitionings can be primary or derived; the derived partitioning of an entity A is built by considering the partitioning of an entity B and the association between B and A. The following conditions must apply:

Let $P=\{p1,p2,..pn\}$ be a set of partitioning predicates for the entity B, $I_A(p1)$ be the subset of the instances of A for which p1 holds, $I_B(p1)$ the subset of instances of B which are related (through the association) to at least one element of $I_A(p1)$. Then, the subsets $I_A(p1)$, $I_A(p2)...$, $I_A(pn)$ must be a partition of the entity A in order for the derived partitioning to be correct. Figure 9 shows this condition.

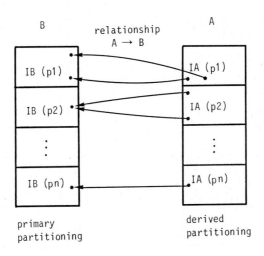

Fig. **9.** Derived partitioning

A sufficient condition for ensuring the correctness of a partition requires that:

a. The relationship B-A is functional (i.e., each instance of A is related just to one instance of B);

b. The relationship B-A is mandatory for A (i.e., each entity of A belongs to the relationship).

In our example, it is possible to introduce a derived partitioning on the entity PRODUCTION, by deriving the partitioning from the entity PRODUCT partitioned by PRODUCT_TYPE and from the relationship PROD_SCHEDULE. The derived partitioning corresponds to the intuitive concept of partitioning PRODUCTION data in the same way as PRODUCT data, i.e., of determining the subsets of all productions related to products of the types "SYSTEM", "DISPLAY", and "KEYBOARD", respectively. Note that this example satisfies the above condition. In Section 4, we will see that derived partitionings are particularly useful for avoiding costly joins between horizontally partitioned relations.

3.2 Determination of polarizations

After having collected the specifications of partitioning predicates, it is important to associate to them a quantitative measure that allows to evaluate the "polarizations", i.e., the difference with respect to homogeneous distribution due to the introduction of the partitioning.

The Polarization Table in Figure 10 collects the data about polarizations, reported as **deviations from the uniformity assumption.**

		R1 1	R1 3	R1 4	R1 5	U1 1	U1 2	U1 3	U1 4	U1 5	U2 1	U2 3	U2 4	R2 2	R2 5	R3 1	R3 3	R3 4
PRODUCT BY PRODUCT-TYPE	p1	80			80	60				60	90					✕	✕	✕
	p2	(12)	95					50				95				✕	✕	✕
	p3	(8)		95					50				95			✕	✕	✕
PRODUCT BY PRICE CLASS	p1															✕	✕	✕
	p2													80	80			
PRODUCTION BY PRODUCT-TYPE	p1	80			80	60				60	✕	✕	✕	✕	✕	✕	✕	✕
	p2		95					50			✕	✕	✕	✕	✕	✕	✕	✕
	p3			95					50		✕	✕	✕	✕	✕	✕	✕	✕
PRODUCTION BY STORAGE	p1										✕	✕	✕	✕	✕	100		
	p2										✕	✕	✕	✕	✕		100	
	p3										✕	✕	✕	✕	✕			100
MATERIAL BY STORAGE	p1					✕	✕	✕	✕	✕	✕	✕	✕	✕	✕	100		
	p2					✕	✕	✕	✕	✕	✕	✕	✕	✕	✕		100	
	p3					✕	✕	✕	✕	✕	✕	✕	✕	✕	✕			100
SALE-DEPARTMENT BY SALE-AREA	p1					✕	✕	✕	✕	✕	✕	✕	✕	90		✕	✕	✕
	p2					✕	✕	✕	✕	✕	✕	✕	✕		90	✕	✕	✕

Fig. **10.** Polarization tables

Each operation is compared with each partitioning; if the operation is affected by the partitioning criterion, then the intersection area is further organized in a matrix which shows the sites at which the operation is activated and the predicates used for the partitioning. The polarization coefficient 80 shown at the intersection between activation of R1 at site 1 and predicate P1 of the PRODUCT by PRODUCT_TYPE partitioning indicates that 80% of accesses of the operations R1 activated from site 1 are addressed to data which satisfies predicate p1. This is a deviation from the uniformity assumption, because predicate p1 corresponds just to 50% of the entities. In practice, products of the type "SYSTEM" are more likely to be accessed from operations R1 activated at site 1. The residual 20% of accesses are distributed in the residual 50% of entities homogeneously; thus, 12%

(i.e., 30/50*0.2) of accesses are related to products of the type "DISPLAY", and 8% (i.e., 20/50*0.2) of accesses to products of the type "KEYBOARD". Since this information can be deduced from the selectivity information associated to predicates, it needs not to be specified.

Some operations do not use entities for which a partitioning was defined, and therefore clearly it is not possible to observe any polarization property; in this case, the corresponding positions of the polarization matrix are crossed. For instance, the area between U1 and the partitioning on MATERIAL is crossed, since U1 does not use that entity.

Some other operations might use an entity and yet have no polarization property with respect to other partitioning criteria; in this case, the corresponding positions of the polarization matrix are left empty. For instance, the operation U2 which changes the bill of material of PRODUCTs is not affected by the PRICE_CLASS of products; thus, the area at the intersection between PRODUCT partitioned by PRICE_CLASS and the operation U2 is left empty.

Frequency, partitioning, and polarization tables (shown in Figures 7, 8, and 10) contain the information required for taking distribution design decisions.

4. SCHEMA DISTRIBUTION

Trying to optimally decompose the global schema on N sites is a very hard problem. The number of variables that could be considered to specify the problem completely is very large, since every possible fragmentation and allocation (possibly redundant) of the fragments obtained from the schema entities should be considered.

The purpose of the distribution design phase for a manual design methodology, such as DATAID-D, is to offer a methodological help for data distribution to the designer and not an algorithm which, given the requirements, allocates data in an optimal way.

The problem is decomposed in sequential tasks (Figure 11):

1. iterative horizontal and vertical partitioning, for a non-redundant allocation of the schema

2. redundant data allocation

3. reconstruction of local logical schemata

This approach to schema decomposition introduces a simplifying assumption. The schema is initially partitioned (by applying horizontal and vertical partitioning) with the goal of allocating data in a non-redundant way. Redundancy is considered only in the following task, so the resulting schemata are obtained as a post-optimization of those obtained in the first task.

The separation of problems sacrifices "optimality" to practicability of the approach, and is particularly acceptable with a non-automated methodology (though it is also suggested with automatic tools [18], [27]).

The global schema is constituted of entities and relationships which can be allocated to sites following different optimization criteria. As a general consideration, the more complex is the evaluation performed, the more can the model be tailored to a specific type of system.

The following distribution criteria can be considered:

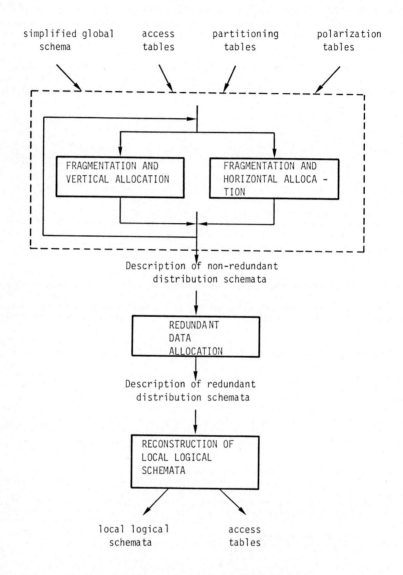

Fig. 11. Tasks in distribution design

1. Locality
   According to this criterion, the data objects obtained from the first task of
   the distribution phase are allocated to the site where they are more often
   required. Allocation models based on maximal locality are described in [13,
   16].

2. Complete locality
    Data are allocated to sites so that most operations are executed at a single
    site. This model is included in the class of models which maximize locality of
    operation, but encourages operations where all the required data are local at
    the starting site, while operations where only some of the data are local are
    discouraged. A model based on this criterion is described in [14].

3. Transmission cost minimization
    The transmission costs required for executing operations are evaluated for
    each possible distribution, and the distribution associated to the minimum
    cost is selected. Transmission costs depend on the quantity of data
    transmitted and the characteristics of the network. When this criterion is
    used, operation schemata are used as a basis to evaluate operation execution
    costs. In fact, even if costs are dependent on operation execution strategies,
    it is very difficult to perform at the same time both data allocation and
    operation optimization.

4. General models
    These models consider also costs not due to transmission; recent experimental
    evaluations revealed that, in particular on local networks, transmission costs
    are comparable to I/O and CPU costs. These models, for instance, consider the
    costs of execution of expensive operations due to the distribution, such as
    joins on entities allocated to different sites. An allocation model based on
    this criterion is described in [17].

4.1 Types of fragmentation of data objects

In this subsection we briefly describe the two types of fragmentation which can be
applied to entities to obtain fragments: vertical partitioning and horizontal
partitioning.

4.1.1 Vertical partitioning

Vertical partitioning is performed on entities, splitting non-identifying
attributes in non-overlapping sets. Each resulting fragment is defined by the
identifying attributes (key) and by the non-identifying attributes belonging to
one of the sets. An example of vertical partitioning for the entity PRODUCT is
shown in Figure 12: the entity PRODUCT is partitioned by decomposing it into
PRODUCT/1 (which has attributes related to the production environment) and
PRODUCT/2 (which stores the attributes related to the sales environment).

The entity PRODUCT as a whole can be reconstructed using its key, which is present
in both fragments, with a join operation. This possibility is represented through
the relationship JOINS between the two fragments. Incorporating the key attributes
in each fragment is a practical method used in all distributed database prototypes
and in commercial distributed systems [2-7].

4.1.2 Horizontal partitioning

An entity is partitioned horizontally when its instances are split in subsets
(fragments) which satisfy a partitioning predicate.

In Figure 13 the entity MATERIAL is partitioned horizontally according to the
attribute 'WAREHOUSE', which can assume the values A1, A2, and A3.

The set of selection predicates define a partition of the entity, as shown in
Section 3. The fragmentation of an entity can depend either on primary predicates
(in this case the partition is called primary) or on derived predicates (in this
case the partition is called secondary). A fragment has a derived horizontal

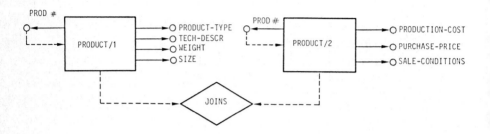

Fig. 12. Vertical partitioning applied to the entity product

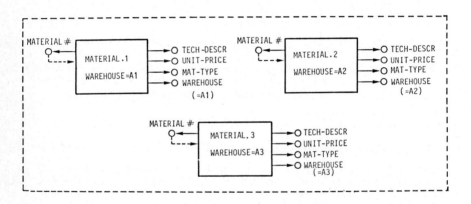

Fig. 13. Horizontal partitioning applied to the entity MATERIAL

partition when the partition is not based on the original fragment's properties, but is induced by attributes of another entity, connected with a relationship; for instance, in Figure 14 the entity PRODUCTION is fragmented horizontally according to the 'PRODUCT_TYPE' which is an attribute of PRODUCT.

4.1.3 Mixed partitioning

It is possible to partition an entity iteratively, using the partitioning operations described above.

In general, it is possible to describe the entire fragmentation of an entity through a fragmentation tree. Figure 15 shows how the entity PRODUCT, which is vertically partitioned as in Figure 12, is further partitioned horizontally, with appropriate predicates on the attributes of each fragment.

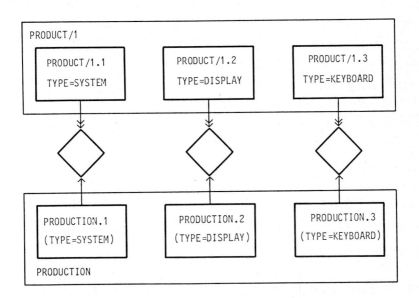

Fig. 14. Derived partitioning for entity PRODUCTION

4.2 Fragmentation design

Goal of this task is to determine the fragmentation of each entity in the schema.

Vertical and horizontal partitioning are applied on entities or groups of entities which are related; they are performed iteratively, choosing at each iteration the more adequate partitioning operation. The designer stops the iterative process when no further partitioning of the existing fragments would be beneficial.

Vertical partitioning

The effect of the vertical partitioning of an entity is shown for instance in Figure 12, where entity PRODUCT is split in subentities PRODUCT/1 and PRODUCT/2. When vertical partitioning is applied, new one-to-one relationships are created between fragments of the original entities. Original relationships linking the considered entity to other entities need to be associated to just one of the vertical fragments. The result of vertical partitioning is an extended global schema which can be used in the following iterations.

The rationale of vertical partitioning is to produce fragments which are used by different operations on the database, so that attributes required by specific operations are grouped in distinct data objects. To identify attributes used separately by different operations, the global operation schemata of Figure 4 are examined. An ideal vertical fragmentation exists when operations use sets of attributes which have no intersection; otherwise, some conflicts arise: by deciding of including the intersection attributes into one fragment, one operation is disadvantaged, as it will need to access two fragments.

The operation schemata of Figure 4 have to be reinterpreted in order to be used in

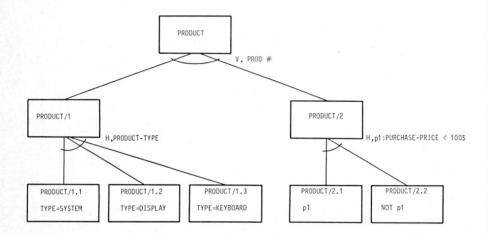

Fig. 15. Fragmentation tree for entity PRODUCT

the following evaluations, as well as the polarization tables of Figure 10. In case of a previous vertical fragmentation, fragments which are really used in the operations replace the original entities (see Figure 16).

Vertical partitioning should be used in order to increase processing locality of operations; this happens when the partition is such that operations activated at each site mostly use one specific fragment. The increase of processing locality is obtained by allocating each vertical fragment at the site where it is mostly used.

A quantitative evaluation can be done about the overall convenience of a vertical partitioning. Two numbers should be evaluated: the number of accesses of operations which require just one of the two partitions, and the number of accesses of operations which require both partitions. If the latter number is null (i.e, there are no conflicts), then the partitioning is certainly beneficial, because it will be possible to allocate each partition at the site where most operations using it are activated, thus having an increase of processing locality. In order for the vertical partition to be potentially advantageous, the difference between the former and the latter number must be positive. In fact, a more complex evaluation should take into account the overhead of performing the merging of fragments (one-to-one join).

Considering again the partitioning of PRODUCT of Figure 12, R1 and R2 use disjoints sets of attributes, and thus indicate the potential vertical fragmentation. Figure 16 shows that, by decomposing PRODUCT into the two fragments, all operations except U2 (b) require only one fragment, and the above difference is: 100*180+7000*30-11*3, clearly positive.

Operation R1

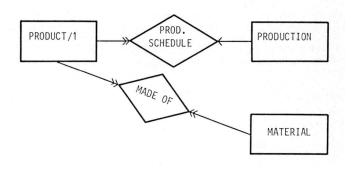

Operation U2.b.1

Operation R2

Fig. **16.** Operations with entity PRODUCT vertically partitioned

At this point of the design, no final allocation is attempted yet. Locality considerations for operations are the basis of this transformation of the global schema, but the allocation of fragments is decided only when the fragmentation task is terminated. The allocation is performed on the final fragments because they represent data which have the same features with respect to every operation performed on the database, so that every fragment is a good "unit of allocation".

Horizontal partitioning

Partitioning predicates are the basis for deciding on horizontal partitioning; these predicates are usually not limited to a single entity, but involve groups of entities.

The major problems in evaluating the convenience of horizontal partitioning are:

a. Evaluating the alternative of partitioning an entity or maintaining it non partitioned. Notice that a weak polarization observed on an entity might not be a sufficient condition for partitioning the entity, because the management of partitioned data is in general more complex than the management of non-partitioned data (for instance, it becomes more difficult to access catalog information, or to distribute access operations).

b. In presence of two alternative candidate partitionings, selecting one of them. Notice that, in general, it is not required to select one alternative; it is also possible to combine several partitioning criteria into a single one, which uses as partitioning predicates all the possible conjunctions between predicates which define the original partitionings.

It is possible to use an algorithm for horizontal partitioning in order to solve problem (b) above; in general, this algorithm will produce as a result an horizontal fragmentation even with very small polarization, and therefore the designer must evaluate problem (a) above independently. The algorithm proceeds as follows:

1. Consider all possible partitionings of a given entity. Build all the conjunction of predicates obtained by taking ordinately one predicate from each partitioning set. Regard the set of instances for which the conjunction predicate holds as a **minterm fragment.**

2. Evaluate the accesses which are performed from each site to the minterm fragment. These accesses would become local accesses if the minterm fragment were allocated to that particular site. Associate each minterm fragment to the site which has the maximum number.

3. Group all minterm fragments associated to the same site into a same, final fragment. Each final fragment is also associated to a storage site, to be interpreted as the "candidate" allocation site for that fragment. The candidate site of a fragment F will be designed as final storage site if no additional fragmentation of F will occurr during the design.

The rationale of this algorithm is based on the consideration that the final allocation of the fragment will be the one produced by the algorithm, unless the fragment is further partitioned, and therefore the proposed fragmentation will maximize the locality of processing.

We use the entity PRODUCTION to exemplify the algorithm. This entity can be fragmented directly through its attribute 'WAREHOUSE' and in a derived way through attribute 'PRODUCT_TYPE' of PRODUCT, as shown in Figure 8. For each of the 9 minterm fragments obtained from the two partitions, Figure 17a shows the total number of accesses from each site for each operation. For instance, the first measure at the top left, corresponding to the minterm fragment associated to the predicate: TYPE="SYSTEM AND WAREHOUSE="A1", is computed as follows:

.80 * .30 * 50 * 300 = 3600

(i.e. locality from Polarization Table * fraction from Partioning Table * frequency of operation from Frequency Table * number of access from Figure 4).

Figure 17b shows the global results of this computation, and the consequent allocation of PRODUCTION, partitioned only according to 'PRODUCTION_TYPE'; this result shows that one of the two partitioning criteria dominates the other.

Let us consider Figure 15, which shows two applications of horizontal partitioning to the entities PRODUCT/1 and PRODUCT/2. Notice from Figure 8 that two alternative partitioning criteria were possible for PRODUCT, based on PRODUCT_TYPE and on

Production Frequency x # accesses

		R1				U1					R3		
		1	3	4	5	1	2	3	4	5	1	3	4
S	A1	3600	120	120	3600	900	300	540	470	1080	40000		
	A2	4200	150	120	4200	1050	350	630	550	1260	24000		
	A3	4200	150	120	4200	1050	350	630	550	1260	16000		
D	A1	540	3420	70	540	360	180	750	280	430		40000	
	A2	630	4000	80	630	420	210	880	330	500		24000	
	A3	630	4000	80	630	420	210	880	330	500		16000	
K	A1	360	50	3420	360	240	120	220	750	290			20000
	A2	420	60	4000	420	280	140	250	880	340			12000
	A3	420	60	4000	420	280	140	250	880	340			8000

Fig. 17.a) Total number of accesses

Sites

		1	2	3	4	5	Chosen Site
S	A1	44500	300	660	590	4680	1
	A2	23250	350	780	670	5460	1
	A3	21250	350	780	670	5460	1
D	A1	900	180	44170	350	970	3
	A2	1050	210	28880	410	1130	3
	A3	1050	210	20880	40	1130	3
K	A1	600	120	270	23420	650	4
	A2	700	140	310	16940	760	4
	A3	700	140	310	12880	760	4

Final partition of PRODUCTION by 'production-type'

Production-type = systems   site 1
                = displays   site 3
                = keyboards   site 4

Fig. 17.b) Allocation of PRODUCTION

PRICE CLASS. Without vertical partitioning, we should have to evaluate also in this case the trade-off (b); however, the vertical partitioning determines two fragments which deal with production and sale data, and thus the PRODUCT_TYPE partitioning is applied to PRODUCT/1, while the PRICE_CLASS partitioning is applied to PRODUCT/2. Notice that in this case the decision of performing vertical partitioning first is very critical; this decision is left to the experience of the database designer.

In general, horizontal and vertical partitioning are applied iteratively, until the fragments show uniform behavior with respect to all the global operations, and can therefore be considered proper "units of allocation".

Subschemata are then allocated, non redundantly, to one of the sites, following one of the optimization criteria described in the Section 4.1. Frequency tables for global operations are used to compute the optimal allocation of entities and relationships to sites. In general, the last partitioning step predetermines the final allocation.

In our example, fragments PRODUCTION.1, PRODUCT/1.1 and MATERIAL.1 are allocated at site 1, fragment SALES_DEPT.1 is allocated at site 2, fragments PRODUCTION.2, PRODUCT/1.2, and MATERIAL.2 are allocated at site 3, fragments PRODUCTION.3, PRODUCT/1.3, and MATERIAL.3 are allocated at site 4, and fragments PRODUCT/2 and SALES_DEPT.2 are allocated at site 5.

4.3 Redundant allocation design

Redundancy is introduced in distributed systems to improve reliability and availability.

Efficiency is improved if fragments which are only read by operations are replicated at operation sites, because in this way remote accesses are avoided. Reliability is improved by the possibility of performing operations also when some of the system elements are failed; for instance, when a network site is failed, it is possible to access the same data replicated at other sites. On the other hand, redundancy of data causes the problem of maintaining data consistency between redundant copies.

In general, the benefit of redundancy depends directly on the ratio between read-only and update operations on the data: the greater this ratio, the greater the convenience of replicating data. The frequency tables for global operations are the basis to compute the convenience of replicated data. However, the way in which replication is managed by the system is also very important. In distributed database systems there are very many possible ways of managing redundant data; there is a clear trade-off between:

a. allowing inconsistencies and therefore gaining in efficiency and availability;

b. preserving consistency of copies and therefore loosing in efficiency and availability.

Let us consider the two extreme alternative cases:

a. maintaining a primary copy with deferred updates to all other copies;

b. maintaining consistent updates on all the copies.

In the first case, update operations and consistency checks are performed at the site where the primary copy is located, and updates are propagated only later to the other copies. Thus, this case does not penalize updates very much, and the redundant solution might be acceptable even with low values of the ratio between read-only and update applications. Notice that the usage of non-primary copies leads to inconsistent reads; for many applications, where the timeliness and accuracy of data is not a requirement, this solution may be acceptable.

When all the copies must be consistent, updates must be propagated to all the copies by operations, thus the number of read operations must largely outbalance the number of update operations. The problem of allocating a fragment in a redundant way with consistent updates has been studied in [21], using both transmission costs and storage costs; the problem has been demonstrated to be NP-hard.

In DATAID-D, redundancy is introduced as a post-optimization, starting from non-redundant allocation of fragments. An iterative process is suggested also in this case. Schema elements are replicated at sites where they are often required and then the evaluation criterion used in the previous task is applied again. If the new allocation is positively evaluated by the designer, then the new allocation is assumed; the same process is repeated until the designer decides that no further improvement may be achieved. Obviously, not all candidate allocations are considered, but only those which are more important, using the operation frequency table.

In our example, fragment PRODUCT/2 can be allocated redundantly to sites 2 and 5, which access it frequently with read-only operations. Moreover, since the timeliness and accuracy of information about PRODUCTs is not very important, the decision is taken of establishing one primary copy at site 5, which will be used by update operations, and performing deferred updates to the other copy at fixed times (for instance, at the end of the day).

4.4 Reconstruction of local schemata design

This step produces the final output of the distribution phase, i.e. the local subschemata. Notice that, after Task 2, at each site there is a list of groups of entities, not a local subschema yet. In this task, the local schemata are reconstructed, i.e. a local subschema is built containing all the entities and relationships allocated at each site, based on the extended global schema.

Relationships among sites have also to be allocated in order to be able to reconstruct the global schema, allowing any type of operation which would have been possible on the original global schema.

The allocation of relationships can be based on a simple idea: consider two entities A and B allocated at different sites and relationship R between them. Given that the identifiers of entities will need to be transmitted, allocate R to the site of the entity which has the largest cardinality; in this case the identifiers of the other entity will be transmitted.

Figure 18 shows the final local subschemata at sites.

At site 1, fragments of entities PRODUCTION and PRODUCT with TYPE="SYSTEM", and MATERIAL with WAREHOUSE="A1" are stored and are connected by the original relationships. This allocation is very reasonable, since at site 1 the company has a production department specialized in system assembling and warehouse A1. PRODUCT is linked to MATERIAL fragments allocated to other sites (3 and 4) and this relationship is allocated to site 1, since the entity PRODUCT has the largest number of instances. MATERIAL is linked to PRODUCT at sites 3 and 4, and in this case the relationship is allocated at those sites for the same reason. Sites 3 and 4 have a local subschema similar to that on site 1.

Site 5 contains the data of the southern sales department with fragments of the entities SALES_DEPARTMENT and PRODUCT. These entities are linked by the original relationship between them, and PRODUCT/2 is further linked to PRODUCT/1 fragments

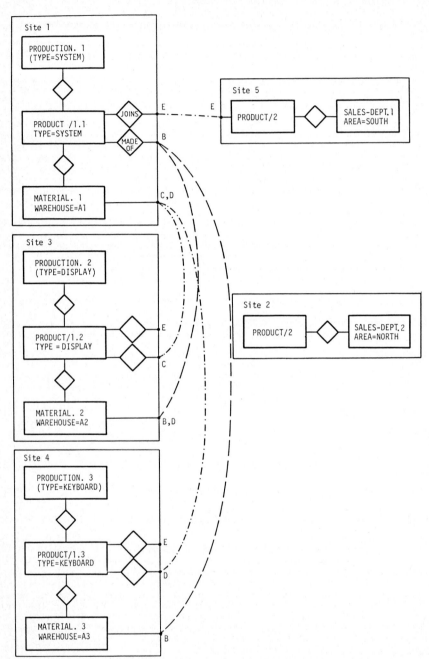

Fig. 18. Result of distribution design: local schemata for sites 1-5

at sites 1, 3, and 4. Site 2 has a subschemata similar to site 2. The replicated entity PRODUCT/2 is considered in this case to be a secondary copy, so that all updates to it are deferred and come from site 2; due to this redundancy, at site 5 it is possible to reconstruct the whole entity PRODUCT.

To each local schema produced in this way it is possible to apply the original DATAID-1 methodology, in particular by performing the last 2 tasks of logical design and the physical design.

5. CONCLUSIONS

In this paper, we have shown DATAID-D, a methodology for the distribution of a database schema which is fully integrated with DATAID-1.

The major objective of this paper is to give a precise definition of the design problems to be faced and to outline a practical and feasible way for solving each of them. Several solution methods based on analytical models attain an "optimal" design for each specific problem; however, these methods require sophisticated solution algorithms and their practicability is often compromised by the difficulty of collecting accurate input parameters. Conversely, the proposed methodology can be applied without using a computer and requires simple input parameters, whose collection has been carefully described. Algorithms for deciding about horizontal and vertical fragmentation are simple.

Recent investigations in the direction of integrating the algorithms for solving individual distribution design problems are described in [27]; this integration will produce a major advance in the direction of producing usable tools for the design of distributed databases, which might in future be coupled to DATAID-D.

REFERENCES

[1]   Ceri, S. and Pelagatti, G., Distributed Databases: Principles and Systems,
      (McGraw-Hill, New York, 1984).

[2]   Williams, R. et al., R*: an Overview of the Architecture, IBM Res. Rep.
      R3325 (40082), San Jose, CA (1982).

[3]   Devor, C. and Weeldreyer, J., DDTS: A Testbed for Distributed Database
      Research, Honeywell Report HR-80-274, Honeywell Corporate Computer Science
      Center, Bloomington, MN (1980).

[4]   Borr, A.J., Transaction Monitoring in Encompass: Reliable Distributed
      Transaction Processing, Proc. 7th Int. Conf. on Very Large Data Bases,
      Cannes (1981).

[5]   Acker, R.D. and Seaman, P.H., Modelling Distributed Processing across
      Multiple CICS/VS Sites, IBM Systems Journal, Vol. 21, N. 4 (1982).

[6]   Special Issue on Highly Available Systems, Database Engineering, Vol. 6, N.
      2 (1983).

[7]   Gray, J.P., Homan, P., Hansen, P.J., Lerner, M.A., and Pozefsky, M., SNA's
      Advanced Program-to-Program Communication, IBM Systems Journal (1984).

[8]   Ceri, S. (ed.), Methodology and Tools for Database Design, (North Holland,
      Amsterdam, 1983).

[9]   Bertaina, P., Di Leva, A., and Giolito, P., Logical Design in Codasyl and
      Relational Environment, in: Ceri, S. (ed.), Methodology and Tools for
      Database Design, (North Holland, Amsterdam, 1983).

[10] De Antonellis, V. and Di Leva, A., DATAID-1: A Database Design Methodology
      to appear on Information Systems, Vol. 10, N. 1 (1985).

[11] Bertino, E. et al., DATANET/Hermes: A Distributed Database System, Proc.
      AICA Conf., Pavia 1981 (in Italian).

[12] Bussolati, U., Ceri, S., and Pernici, B., A Methodology for Schema
      Distribution in the Design of Distributed Databases, Proc. AICA Conf.,
      Padova 1982 (in Italian).

[13] Ceri, S., Martella, G., and Pelagatti, G., Optimal File Allocation on a
      Network of Minicomputers: A Solution Method Based on the Knapsack Problem,
      Computer Networks, Vol. 6, N. 5 (1982).

[14] Ceri, S. and Pelagatti, G., A Solution Method for the Non-additive Resource
      Allocation Problem in Distributed System Design, Information Processing
      Letters, Vol. 15, N. 4 (1982).

[15] Ceri, S. and Pelagatti, G., Allocation of Operations in Distributed Database
      Access, IEEE-TC, Vol. C-31, N. 1 (1982).

[16] Ceri, S., Negri, M., and Pelagatti, G., Horizontal Data Partitioning in Database Design, Proc. ACM-SIGMOD Conference, Orlando, FL (1982).

[17] Ceri, S., Navathe, S.B., and Wiederhold, G., Distribution Design of Logical Database Schemas, IEEE-Transactions on Software Engineering, Vol. SE-9, N. 4 (July 1983).

[18] Ceri, S. and Navathe, S.B., A Methodology for the Distribution Design of Databases, Proc. Spring Compcon 1983, Chicago (1983), and Mohan, M. (ed.) IEEE-Recent Advances in Distributed Data Base Management, (May 1984).

[19] Navathe, S.B., Ceri, S., Wiederhold, G., and Dou, J., Vertical Partitioning for Physical and Distribution Design of Databases, Stanford University, Report No. STAN-CS-82-957, January 83, to appear on ACM-Transactions on Database Systems.

[20] Apers, P.M.G., Redundant Allocation of Relations in Communication Networks, Proc. 5th Berkeley Workshop on Distr. Data Manag. and Comp. Netw., Berkeley (1981).

[21] Eswaran, K.P., Placement of Records in a File and File Allocation in a Computer Network, Information Processing, (1974).

[22] Hammer, M. and Niamir, B., A Heuristic Approach to Attribute Partitioning, Proc. ACM-SIGMOD Conference, Boston (1979).

[23] Mahmoud, S. and Riordon, J.S., Optimal Allocation of Resources in Distributed Information Networks, ACM-TODS, Vol. 1, N. 1 (1976).

[24] Morgan, H.L. and Levin, J.D., Optimal Program and Data Location in Computer Networks, CACM, Vol. 20, N. 5 (1977).

[25] Ramamoorthy, C.V. and Wah, B.W., The Placement of Relations in a Distributed Relational Database, Proc. 1st Int. Conf. on Distributed Computing Systems, Hountsville (1979).

[26] Norman, A. and Anderton, M., EMPACT: A Distributed Database Application, Proc. National Computer Conference (1983).

[27] Ceri, S., Pernici, B., and Wiederhold, G., An Overview of Research in the Design of Distributed Databases, to appear on IEEE Database Engineering, special issue on Database Design (1985).

COMPUTER-AIDED DATABASE DESIGN: The DATAID Project
A. Albano, V. De Antonellis, and A. Di Leva (Editors)
© Elsevier Science Publishers B.V. (North-Holland), 1985

CHAPTER IX

DYNAMICS IN LOGICAL DATABASE DESIGN

B. G. Demo, A. DiLeva, P. Giolito

Dipartimento di Informatica - Universita` di Torino
via V. Caluso 37 - 10125 TORINO (Italy)

A consistent specification of quantitative processing characteristics is of crucial importance
to obtain an efficient logical and physical database design. In this paper a formal model for
dynamics description is introduced. The model is
based on an extension of the Petri Net model and
is used to derive the frequencies of both the
functions and the operations that describe the
organization dynamics.

1. INTRODUCTION

Growing attention is presently being paid to dynamics modeling in
modern database design methodologies [8,12,13].

There are many reasons for the introduction of dynamics modeling in
database design.   In conceptual design, it can be used to describe
the behavior of database applications.   In logical and physical
(implementation) design, it can be used to construct an operational
model of the database application in order to validate the design
choices [10].

In the DATAID project [8,9], dynamics modeling is used, at the conceptual level, to represent the organization functions and to test
the completeness and consistency of the overall design. The organization functions are then analyzed to identify the operations and the
causal dependencies/independencies between them. At the implementation level, dynamics modeling is used for the analysis of quantitative data that drive the logical and physical design phases [5,6,15].

Among quantitative data, the frequencies of the operations defined in
the database application assume a crucial role. Unfortunately, practical experience has shown that to give frequency operation information is a very difficult task because operations within organization
structures are usually mutually correlated in fairly complex ways.
Taking into account these correlations is not easy and the risk of
specifying inconsistent frequency values is high.

In this paper, we suggest a systematic approach for automatically
deriving the operation frequencies. The first step of this approach
is a structured analysis of the organization to obtain a high level
description of the organization behaviour. A stepwise refinement
process is then introduced, starting from the gross abstract description of the organization environments, and proceeding to derive the
frequencies of the component functions. Finally, a flow analysis of
the function representation allows the derivation of the operation

frequencies.

The paper is organized as follows. Section 2 presents the dynamics representation formalism. Section 3 describes the mathematical treatment of the operation frequency derivation problem. Section 4 describes the extension of the DATAID methodology to take into account the organization environment dynamics and Section 5 states our conclusions.

2. DYNAMICS REPRESENTATION IN THE DATAID PROJECT

As described in [8], the DATAID methodology requires that the organization in which the database application will be developed has already been subdivided into several environments: they constitute the sectors of the organization that are homogeneous as regards the functions performed. A function is a set of operations, with the associated execution conditions, which must be executed to achieve a given organization goal. A functions/environments cross reference form summarizes the organization structure.

In the requirements analysis and the conceptual design phases, the database application dynamics is expressed by means of a set of operation schemata (workload description) and an events schema for each environment [4]. An event schema is the description of the causal dependencies among the operations of the organization environment. It is expressed by means of the condition-event Petri Net (PN) formalism and is derived by combining a set of events graphs that correspond to the environment functions [7,14].

In the logical and physical design phases the dynamics description is used to drive the conversion process from the conceptual data schema to the logical and physical data schemata. A set of performance oriented transformations is applied to the conceptual schema to restructure the conceptual structures so that the logical and physical schemata are optimized with respect to the workload specification.

Execution costs are evaluated starting from the quantitative specification of the database workload which provides statistical information regarding the data structures and the processing characteristics. In particular, for each operation the frequency (number of executions over a unit period of time) must be given and this information assumes a crucial role in execution cost calculations.

Practical experience has shown that is very difficult to give frequency operation information because operations are usually mutually correlated in fairly complex ways and to take into account these correlations is not easy.

In the rest of this section we will analyze the PN formalism used in the DATAID methodology to describe the organization dynamics and its extension introduced to derive operation frequencies.

According to the PN formalism, an event is determined by the conditions (places) which cease to hold (preconditions) and by those which begin to hold (postconditions) when the related operation (transition) fires. The holding of a condition is represented by a token (indicated as a dot) in the corresponding place.

An events graph describes the causal dependencies between the

operations of the object function. It can contain two types of transitions: operations (represented as continuous lines) and controls
(represented as dashed lines) which are introduced to express structures of concurrency and conflict within the PN notation.

The basic PN model has been extended, to derive the operation frequencies, by associating a firing time to the transitions [3]. The
firing of operation transitions is assumed to take a finite amount of
time from the moment of their enabling. Control transitions differ
from operation transitions because they fire immediately upon enabling.

The state of an events graph is defined by its marking, that is by
the distribution of tokens in the places of the corresponding PN net.
A marking M is denoted by the subset {pl,p2,...,pk} of places containing the tokens.   The firing of a transition (operation or control) changes the state of the net. Consequently, the execution of
the net can be expressed by means of a marking transition diagram.
This diagram is a directed graph; markings are the nodes of the graph
and an arc exists between nodes Mh and Mk if there is a transition
that takes the net from Mh to Mk.

By associating firing times with transitions, time characteristics
are induced in the PN net markings too. There will in fact be markings in which the net (usually) spends a non zero amount of time and
markings from which the net exits in zero time. Markings of the
former type will be called tangible while those of the latter type
are called vanishing.

To precisely specify the relations existing between transition and
marking classifications we introduce the following PN firing rules:

a) when a marking enables different transitions, only one of these
   transitions is allowed to fire;

b) when a marking enables only timed transitions, a probability density function must be defined over the set of the enabled transitions to specify which of these transitions fires. This probability density function is part of the description of the net and
   must then be specified by the user;

c) when a marking enables timed and immediate transitions, only the
   immediate transitions are allowed to fire (timed transitions do
   not get the chance to fire). A probability density function must
   be defined over the set of enabled immediate transitions to
   specify which of these transitions fires. Again, this probability
   density function must be specified by the user.

Figure 1 shows an events graph (represented by the net R): the token
in place 1 represents the initial condition for an execution of the
events graph. The related marking transition diagram is also shown
in Figure 1.   The arcs are labelled with the corresponding transitions and the related probability density function values.

The transition probability matrix is the stochastic matrix associated
with the marking transition diagram. In our case this stochastic
matrix is shown in Figure 2 .

From the marking diagram and the transition probability matrix, the
firing matrix W can be easily derived. An element Wij of the firing
matrix gives the probability that the transition j will fire when the
net is in the marking Mi.   In our example, we obtain the firing

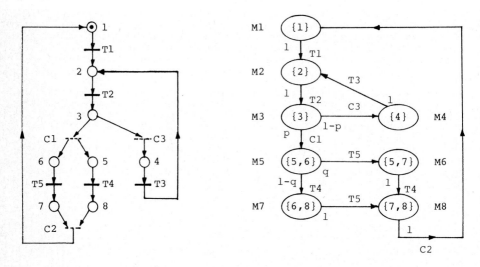

Fig. 1 : A net R and the marking transition diagram M(R).

matrix shown in Figure 3 .

3. A GENERAL METHOD FOR OPERATION FREQUENCY DERIVATION

A general way of computing the mean number of times that each operation is activated during an execution of the events schema is to
analyze the marking transition diagram as a flow network to compute
the number of visits to each node (see, for example, [11]). In our
context, markings represent events, and the flow through a node can
be interpreted as the number of times the corresponding event occurs.
The flow analysis is feasible under the following conditions:

1) the system is in equilibrium conditions (we analyze the general
   statistical properties of the system);

2) the marking diagram is free from absorbing loops, that is no markings (or group of markings) exist in which the activity can be
   trapped. In terms of the original PN net this means that, besides
   being significant, the net must be such that if loops among tangible or vanishing states exist, it must be possible for the net to
   exit from such loops with a non-zero probability.

The flow X_i (i=2,3,...,m) through each of the m nodes of the marking
diagram, under the above assumptions, is given by the balance flow
equation:

$$X = X * T \qquad \text{(T is the transition probability matrix)}$$

	M1	M2	M3	M4	M5	M6	M7	M8
M1		1						
M2			1					
M3				1-p	p			
M4		1						
M5						q	1-q	
M6								1
M7								1
M8	1							

Fig. 2 : The transition probability T matrix for the net R .

	Operations					Controls		
	T1	T2	T3	T4	T5	C1	C2	C3
M1	1							
M2		1						
M3						p		1-p
M4			1					
M5				1-q	q			
M6				1				
M7					1			
M8							1	

Fig. 3 : The firing matrix W for the net R .

The ratio between any two flows X_i/X_j provides the mean number of visits a "visitor" entering the network in M1 (initial marking) makes to node M_i between two subsequent visits to node M_j. If we use the entry node as a reference point, then the visit vector:

$V_i = X_i / X_1 = \langle 1, V_2, V_3, \ldots, V_m \rangle$, $(i=1,2,\ldots,m)$

can be obtained by solving the system of linear equations:

$V = V * T$

In our case, we have:

```
      T1    T2    T3      T4      T5   C1   C2   C3
V = < 1 , 1/p , 1 , (1-p)/p , 1/p , q , 1-q , 1 >
```

To evaluate the mean number of firing times of each transition Fj (j=1,2,...,n), given the visit numbers Vi (i=1,2,...,m), we have to know the probability (given by the firing matrix W) that the operation j will fire when the net is in the marking Mi. We have then:

F = V * W

In our case we obtain:

```
      T1    T2      T3    T4  T5  C1  C2      C3
F = < 1 , 1/p , (1-p)/p , 1 , 1 , 1 , 1 , (1-p)/p >
```

The operation frequencies, to be used in the logical and physical design phases, are obtained by multiplying each component Fj by the frequency of the overall events schema.

The solution method proposed is computationally acceptable whenever the size Kv of the set of vanishing markings is small compared with the size Kt of the set of tangible markings. However this method requires the computation of the control frequencies that are not used in the subsequent design phases. Moreover, controls not only require useless calculations but, by enlarging the size of the transition probability matrix, make the computation of the frequencies expensive and, in some cases, even impossible to obtain.

To reduce the computational effort to the operation frequencies only, let us consider the following process [2].

First of all, the transition probability matrix (for instance, the matrix T of Figure 2) is rearranged (see Figure 4) into submatrix blocks C,F,D and E that contain respectively:

C   the transition probabilities between vanishing markings only;

F   the transition probabilities between tangible markings only;

D,E the transition probabilities from a vanishing to a tangible marking and viceversa.

Let Crs, Drj, Eis and Fij be the general elements of the submatrices C, D, E and F; we can construct the following matrix S:

$$Sij = Fij + \sum_{r \in U} Eir * P(r-->j)$$

where U is the set of vanishing markings and P(r-->j) represents the probability that a vanishing marking r moves to a tangible marking j in an arbitrary number of steps, following a path through vanishing markings only.

In [2], it is shown that the matrix S can be interpreted as the transition probability matrix between tangible markings only, and can be obtained (in a computational efficient way) by means of the following expression:

S = F + E * G

	M1	M2	M4	M5	M6	M7	M3	M8
M1		1						
M2							1	
M4		1						
M5					q	1-q		
M6								1
M7								1
M3			1-p	p				
M8	1							

Fig. 4 : The rearranged transition probability matrix.

where each component of G is the explicit expression of the above mentioned probability P(r-->j).

In our exmple, G is equal to the matrix D because we have no possible vanishing path (all the elements of C are equal to zero). The final result is shown in Figure 5, where the new elements in matrix S with respect to matrix F represent the paths on the marking diagram M(R) of Figure 2 connecting two tangible markings through vanishing marking only.

	M1	M2	M4	M5	M6	M7
M1		1				
M2			1-p	p		
M4		1				
M5					q	1-q
M6	1					
M7	1					

Fig. 5 : The tangible transition probability matrix S.

The solution of the operation frequency problem is then:

  V' = V' * S

in which V' is the visit vector restricted to the tangible markings.

The advantage of this method of solution is twofold.

First, the time and space complexity of the solution is reduced, since instead of solving a system of Kv + Kt linear equations we must now (in the worst case) compute the inverse of a Kv * Kv matrix and then solve a system of Kt linear equations.

Recalling that the complexity of the Gauss elimination solution method of systems of K linear equations is $O(K**3)$, the proposed approach reduces the complexity of the solution from $O((Kv+Kt)**3)$ to $O(Kv**3) + O(Kt**3)$.

Second, by decreasing the impact of the size of the vanishing marking set on the global complexity of the solution method, we are allowed greater freedom in the explicit specification of controls in the original PN net, which makes it easier to understand the related environment dynamics.

The reduced solution method has been used in the Dynamics Analyzer, a tool that supports the automatic derivation of the operation frequencies in the computer aided version of the DATAID methodology [1].

4. EXTENSION OF THE DATAID METHODOLOGY

In this Section we describe an extension of the DATAID methodology whose goal is the simplification of the process for deriving the function and operation frequencies.

The extension consists of a methodological phase covering the first steps of the dynamics analysis within the database design. Some primitives are given in order to identify systematically the organization functions within an environment and the mutual relationships among these functions.

The dynamics of the organization environments is modeled in the functions schema by using the PN formalism at an abstract level: transitions represent the environment functions and the places represent the conditions between them. In this model, an organization function has two only alternatives for communication with another function: the activation of the function and its disactivation with the production of the function post-conditions representing its results. Once the functions have been isolated, the design of the internal operations is carried out as in the DATAID methodology.

The development of an environment functions schema of the organization can be carried out by stepwise refinements starting from a gross abstract description of the organization environments and then substituting functions with well-formed elementary nets.

This approach to the function design gives a method for deriving the function frequencies which is based on the structure of the functions schema and not on the related marking space. As we will see this means a reduction of the complexity for computing the function frequency with respect to the general method applied to compute the operation frequencies. The operation frequency computation is still made according to the general method because the inner structure of a function is a general extended Petri Net. But, because of the isolation from the external world of the operations within a function, the marking space of the operations is limited with respect to the marking space of the whole organization environment (as it will be if the isolation condition should not hold). Thus, the operation frequency computation complexity is also reduced.

4.1 The function specification process.

The specification methodology described here is based on the work of Valette reported in [16]. In particular, Valette specifies a stepwise refinement methodology for the design of Petri Nets such that some remarkable properties of the net are maintained.

Given a places/transitions Petri Net, the methodology consists of substituting a transition t with a so called "block" which is again a Petri Net having an initial transition (that inherits the input places of t) and a final transition (that inherits the output places of t). Valette gives conditions under which the net resulting after a substitution is safe (i.e., the number of tokens in each place never exceed one) and live (i.e., each transition can be enabled) if the original net had these properties. The first property is the one required in the DATAID methodology. The second assures that every transition in the organization schemata is activable. If the liveness property does not hold we cannot consider the dynamics. design consistent.

Liveness and safeness properties automatically hold if the process of the net specification evolves with a top down way under certain restrictions that are:

a) the starting net is the one shown in Figure 6;

b) the blocks are only of the type shown in the same Figure.

We will use this methodology in the functions schemata design as follows. The G0 Petri Net is the initial functions schema, where the environment dynamics is represented as a single abstract function t. As the designer progressively understands the environment dynamics in grater detail, he modifies the current functions schema by substituting the functions in it with one of the elementary nets (blocks) shown in Figure 6.

Each substitution concerns one function t at a time. In particular, if the designer determines that t is a sequence of two functions ti and tf, related by a causal relationship, then t is substituted with the sequence net in Figure 6a . The while net in Figure 6b is used when a function t is an iteration of a function tk possibly preceeded and followed by other functions ti and tf; ti and tf can be control functions if no environment functions correspond to them. The exit-loop net in Figuree 6c is similar to the while net. It is used when a function t is the iteration of two functions tj and tk, with the exit condition between them. The fork-join net of Figure 6d is used when the function t can be considered as a set of functions tk1, tk2, ..., tkj which can be executed in any order before the execution of a function tf. The case net, Figure 6e, is used when the function t requires the execution of one and only one of the functions tk1,

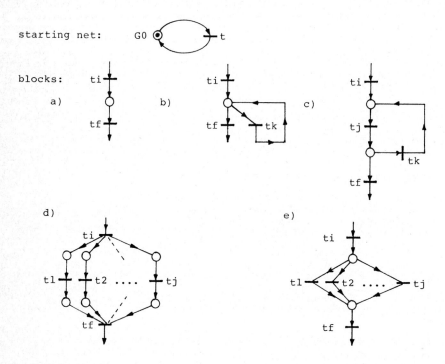

Fig. 6 : The starting net and the blocks for top-down refinement.

tk2,..., tkj. An <u>if-then-else</u> net can be easily derived from this
structure.

As an example of top-down design of a functions schema, in Figure 7
we show the design by refinement steps of the R net shown in Figure 1, interpreted as a functions schema.

4.2. Function frequency derivation.

Let us consider again the initial function schema G0. The single
function t appearing in it represents a whole organization environment and let us suppose that f is its frequency.

In Figure 8 we show the possible evolution of G0 into a set of functions schemata obtained by substituting t with any of the elementary
nets. In the Figure, the frequency of each function is shown beside
the function itself. For each elementary net, functions ti and tf
maintain the frequency f of the function t which has been substituted. In Figure 8b and 8c, n stands for the mean number of times
that the cyclic function is expected to be executed. In Figure 8d,
the functions within the fork-join structure are all executed after

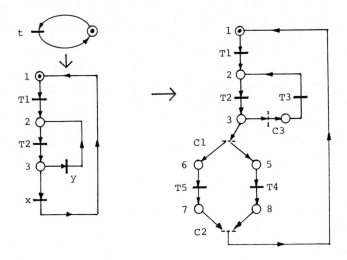

Fig. 7 : Top-down specification of the R net.

ti: hence, again, they inherit the same frequency f. In Figure 8e, p1, p2, ...,pj stand for the probability that, after function ti, function t1 or t2 or ... tj will be executed.

The direct derivation of the function frequencies shown in Figure 8 is very simple. For instance, if we use these rules to generate the net R of Figure 1, interpreted as a functions schema, we obtain the refinement process shown in Figure 9.

Frequencies in Figure 9 are equal to those computed in the previous section with the general method for operations frequency derivation (which is obviously also applicable in this case). Notice that the mean number n of executions of the cycle in Figure 9 is related to the probability p appearing in the solution vector F, shown in Section 3, as follows:

$$n = (1-p)/p$$

The top-down derivation of the function frequencies is applicable if the following conditions are satisfied:

a) the functions schema is obtained by using the refinement substitution rules of Figure 8, starting from the initial representation G0;

b) at each refinement step, the new functions that are introduced are completely independent from the existing functions, i.e. the execution of a new function does not depend on the state of the marking transition diagram related to the evolving net.

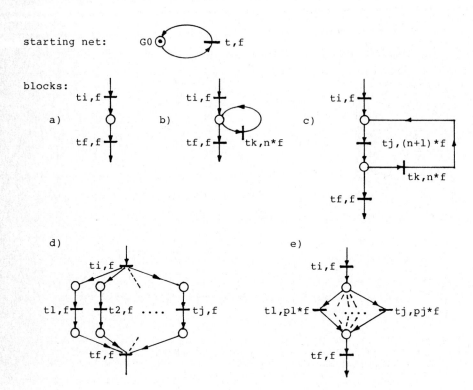

Fig. 8 : Frequency derivation for top-down refinement.

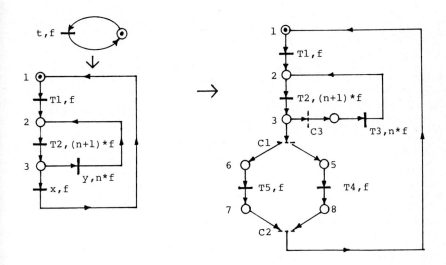

Fig. 9 : Function frequency derivation for the R net.

Conditions a) and b) are usually satisfied if the environment has a "simple" dynamics. However, in general:

a) not all possible functions schemata can be derived by using the above refinement substitution rules;

b) the execution of a function can influence the execution of another one in the same environment: in this case, the function execution frequencies must be evaluated by using the the general derivation method of Section 3.

5. CONCLUSIONS

We have shown that the analysis of functions and events schemata provides reliable estimates of operation frequencies which are the basis for an efficient logical and physical db design.

As regards the events schemata, a general frequency derivation method has been introduced. A first version of a tool which implements the derivation method (in its reduced form) has been developed.

Functions schemata can be defined by means of a refinement process which also gives the function frequencies, but this process can be applied under restricted conditions only. Current activities concern the implementation of the interactive tool which manages the refinement process and evaluates the function frequencies step by step. We are also investigating the extension of this method to take into account general conditions on the evolving net.

6. REFERENCES

[1]   Bert M., Ciardo G., Demo B.G., DiLeva A., Giolito P., Iacobelli
      C., Marrone V. "The Logical Design in the DATAID Project: the
      EASYMAP System" (in this volume).

[2]   Ajmone Marsan M., Balbo G., Conte G. "A Class of Generalized
      Stochastic Petri Nets for the Performance Evaluation of Mul-
      tiprocessor Systems" ACM Transactions on Computer Systems (1985)
      (to appear).

[3]   Balbo G., Demo B.G., DiLeva, A., Giolito P. "Dynamics Analysis
      in Database Design" Proc. IEEE Int. Conf. on Data Engineering
      (Los Angeles, 1984) 238-243.

[4]   Batini C., Lenzerini M., Moscarini M. "Views Integration" in:
      Ceri S. (Ed.) "Methodology and Tools for Data Base Design"
      (North-Holland, 1983) 57-84.

[5]   Bertaina P., Di Leva A., Giolito P. "Logical Design in CODASYL
      and Relational Environment" in: Ceri S. (Ed.) "Methodology and
      Tools for Data Base Design" (North-Holland, 1983) 85-118.

[6]   Bonfatti F., Maio D., Tiberio P. "A Separability Based Method
      for Secondary Index Selection in Physical Database Design" in:
      Ceri S. (Ed.) "Methodology and Tools for Data Base Design"
      (North-Holland, 1983) 149-160.

[7]   Bussolati U., Ceri S., De Antonellis V., Zonta B. "Views Con-
      ceptual Design" in: Ceri S. (Ed.) "Methodology and Tools for
      Data Base Design" (North-Holland, 1983) 25-56.

[8]   Ceri S. (Ed.) "Methodology and Tools for Data Base Design"
      (North-Holland, 1983).

[9]   DeAntonellis V., DiLeva A. "DATAID-1: A Database Design Metho-
      dology" Information Systems, vol.10, 1 (1985) (to appear).

[10] Demo B.G., DiLeva A., Giolito P. "Database Design Prototyping in
      a CODASYL Environment" in: Buddle R. et al. (eds.) "Approaches
      to Prototyping" (Springer-Verlag, 1984) 188-201.

[11] Denning P.G., Buzen J.P. "The Operation Analysis of Queing Net-
      work Models" ACM Comp. Surveys, vol.10 (1978).

[12] Olle T.W., Sol H.G., Verrijn-Stuart A.A. (eds.) "Information
      Systems design Methodologies: A Comparative Review" (North-
      Holland, 1982).

[13] Olle T.W., Sol H.G., Tully C.J. (eds.) "Information Systems
      Design Methodologies: A Feature Analysis" (North-Holland, 1983).

[14] Peterson J.L. "Petri Net Theory and the Modeling of Systems"
      (Prentice Hall, 1981).

[15] Staniszkis W., Sacca' D., Manfredi F., Mecchia A. "Physical
      Data Base Design for CODASYL DBMS" in: Ceri S. (ed.) "Methodol-
      ogy and Tools for Data Base Design" (North-Holland, 1983) 119-
      148.

[16] Valette R. "Analysis of Petri Nets by Stepwise Refinements" J.
      of Comp. and System Sciences, vol.18 (1979) 35-46.

AKNOWLEDGEMENTS

The authors would like to thank V. DeAntonellis for many helpful
comments during the preparation of this paper.

COMPUTER-AIDED DATABASE DESIGN: The DATAID Project
A. Albano, V. De Antonellis, and A. Di Leva (Editors)
© Elsevier Science Publishers B.V. (North-Holland), 1985

CHAPTER X

IMPORTANT ISSUES IN DATABASE DESIGN
METHODOLOGIES AND TOOLS (*)

Sham Navathe

Department of Computer and Information Science
University of Florida
512 Weil Hall Gainesville - Florida (U.S.A.)

1. INTRODUCTION

The purpose of this chapter is to provide an overview of the database design methodologies and design tools by focussing on several
important issues. It is not our intention to give a survey of the
existing work in this area. However, it is important to view the
database design problem, in its entirety and to see how it has been
approached with different scope, emphasis and solution procedure in
the past. This exercise will enable us to put the DATAID methodology in its proper perspective.
It was already mentioned in the introduction that DATAID is perhaps
one of the handful methodologies available today that encompasses
the total problem of database design. Now, the methodology has been
enriched by the development of the design tools mentioned in Part I
of this volume. This makes it almost essential for a researcher or
a practitioner to look at the present methodology and its supporting
tools as a very viable alternative for consideration. Readers
interested in understanding the basics of the DATAID methodology are
urged to read the first Six Chapters in the Part I of the companion
book [6] which preceded this volume. We shall discuss the database design problem in general terms first, followed by a brief sum-
mary of the approaches to this problem. Then we undertake a discussion of the "formal approaches" where the DATAID methodology
belongs. Design tools will be discussed next in a general way to
identify their common characteristics. Finally a critique of the
DATAID methodology and its tools will be presented in light of the
above framework.

2. THE DATABASE DESIGN PROBLEM.

The problem of database design can be simply stated as follows:
"Design the logical and physical structure of a database in a given
database management system to contain all the information required
by the users in an organization".

The implicit goals of the above activity are:

a) To meet all the information (content) requirements of the entire
   Spectrum of users in the organization.

(*) Work partly supported by NSF Grant No. INT. 8400216

b) To provide a "natural" and easy-to-understand structuring of the information content.

c) To support all the processing requirements and achieve a high degree of efficiency of processing.

It is obvious that the above problem is a complex problem due to the nature of the goals as well as the nature of the initial inputs to the design process. Specifically,

a) The initial input in terms of documents, reports, program listings tends to be scattered and somewhat disconnected.

b) The requirements collection activity mostly proceeds informally in the form of interviews, discussions etc. and a large amount of verbal/textual natural language material in spoken and written form is acquired.

c) While on one hand the inputs to the process are so informal, the final output of database design is a database definition with formal syntax and with quantitative decisions regarding physical placement, indexing and organization of data. This adds particular complexity to the database design process in that such a formal design must be turned out from, at times, extremely informal available information.

Raver and Hubbard [26] have given an example where in an environment dealing with hundreds of entities and relationships, if all possible combinations were to be used, several billions of valid designs would be possible.

The above inherent complexity of this problem makes it both interesting and difficult. To cope with this complexity, several ideas have been used in the work on database design:

a) Separating the wide gap between informal requirements and a formal operational database definition into several well defined steps. These steps are:

  1 - Requirements Collection and Analysis
  2 - Conceptual Design of User Views (Also referred to as View Modeling)
  3 - View Integration
  4 - Logical Design (Also referred to as Schema Mapping and Analysis)
  5 - Physical Design and Optimization.

  The above phases, which are also employed in the DATAID methodology, have been fairly well accepted as evidenced by some prominent workshops where academicians, consultants and large database users were brought together to discuss database design. These include the 1978 NYU Symposium on Database Design [30, 24], the 1978 New Orleans Workshop on database design [18], and the 1980 Database Directions III Workshop on Information Resource Management [20].

b) Separating the design problem into two areas: system-independent and system-dependent. It can be argued that the first three steps in the above list may be approached in a system-independent manner while the last two are inherently system-dependent. This separation allows one to concentrate on the conceptual design with the intangible and qualitative goals of naturalness, understandability etc. first. The resulting design is a "global information model" expressed in some "neutral" data model. The logical structuring constraints and the quantitative physical design parameters can be introduced afterwards. Again, DATAID has precisely followed this viewpoint.

c) Adopting different models to represent the design at different stages. For example, the results of requirements analysis may be expressed in natural language while those of view modeling may be in the form of a diagrammatic or a syntactic representation in a semantic data model.
The representations of the outcomes of steps 4 and 5 have to be in a system-specific data model at the logical and physical levels respectively. The use of models with higher abstraction capabilities and expressive power at the early stages often lends an easier solution procedure.

3. APPROACHES TO SOLVE THE DATABASE DESIGN PROBLEM.

The design problem has been faced by the database analysts/designers ever since database management systems came on the scene around mid 1960's. Obviously, thousands of databases have already been designed and are actually in operation. The feeling among the research community, however, is that complete systematic approaches which deserve to be called as "methodologies" are still not available in a truly useable form. The DATAID methodology deserves a special consideration since, in this author's opinion, it is by far the most comprehensive of the methodologies proposed so far. Although it is not available in a form where users at large can use the full methodology, the previous volume [6] has shown that the methodology has been fully developed as a manual approach to design. Moreover, the Part I of the present book also shows that the "computer-aided" aspect of this methodology is quite mature now in terms of the individual tools that have already been developed.

The major remaining challenges are twofold:

i) To integrate the current tools into a co-ordinated design tools system.
ii) To validate and evaluate the methodology as well as the tools against large complex design problems.

Let us consider the existing approaches to the problem and see how one may classify these into meaningful categories.

A. Approaches based on intuition and experience:

A majority of database professionals dealing with the design of databases have mostly relied on this method. Some of them have developed their own notations - e.g., the data structure diagrams of Curtice [9] or Palmer [25].
Approaches to integration such as the technique used in IBM's product DBDA [15] or in the product Data Designer, lend some formality to the design process. As in the above two commercial design tools, the integration approaches typically are based on the normalization of data as suggested in the relational data model. The

argument behind approaches such as Curtice´s or Palmer´s is that
having applied these ideas to design problems over and over again
they claim that the method "always works".

B. Practical methodologies or Cookbook approaches:

Some database practitioners have argued that the database design can
be reduced to a science rather than art. Specific methodologies have
been proposed which give step by step procedures for design. For
example, Sheppard [27] proposed a rather straighforward procedure
based on the information on existing data items and their use in
different processes (reports). After determining the affinity among
attributes, she provides heuristics for clustering, determination of
keys, composite keys and finally defines logical records and interconnections. Methodologies have also been proposed which are suppor-
tive of data base design but do not address data base design per se.
Examples are - data flow diagrams [13] or the design review methodology [16]. They serve as very good complements in terms of a
pre-design analysis in the former, or a post-design verification and
checkout in case of the latter. Some authors, e.g., Atre [2],
Howe [14], give checklists of design decisions and a step by step
procedure in certain situations, e.g. designing an IMS or CODASYL
database schema starting from certain given information.

The distinction between the (B) and (A) categories above is very
subtle and sometimes it is very difficult to assign an approach to
one or the other. If the practical step by step methodology starts
off with requirements in some form and leads up to a design in some
system, it should probably be placed under (B). Approaches in (A)
are in fact applied in day-to-day practice by thousands of designers
and practitioners but are rarely written up anywhere. Approaches in
(B) are documented but it is not clear to what extent they have been
successfully applied.

C. Formal Methodologies:

One can place in this category almost all the research literature in
the design area, although very little of it qualifies to be called
as design methodologies in a complete sense. It is not our intention
to survey the database design literature here; hence we will not
discuss the degree of completeness or the applicability of the various so-called design methodologies.

The formal nature of these methodologies stems from the formal techniques for modeling, analysis, transformations, synthesis, evaluation etc. adopted by them. The formalism varies widely. The following observations can be made about these methodologies.

The two camps

In this author´s opinion, there are basically two camps in this
approach. The first advocates a "synthesis approach" based on the
collection of elementary data and synthesizing it into a design.
Approaches based on the functional and other types of dependencies
(e.g. [5], [31]) are in this category. The other camp advocates
an "analysis and merging approach" based on objects or entities, and
relationships among them, including set-subset and generalization

relationships. Approaches which start off using views in the entity-relationship model or its variants and then integrating them fall in this classification. Approaches of Navathe and Elmasri [21, 11, 23, 12], or of Batini and Lenzerini [3, 4] exemplify this approach. The DATAID methodology follows the latter approach. In general, the advantages of this latter approach over the former are as follows:

i)   The analysis and merging approach is able to incorporate a lot more naming information as well as the detailed semantics about relationships. The synthesis approach is not geared for handling relationships among extensions of objects (see [11]), various types of attribute equivalences (e.g. see [19], generalizations etc.

ii) The synthesis approach works with the premise that minimal cover of a given set of dependencies produces the best design. This assumption is highly questionable since at the conceptual stage, a design is evaluated on the basis of more intangible factors stated earlier.

iii) The synthesis approach is a "one-shot" approach to design. It expects all the dependency information to be input at once in the beginning. This is both undesirable and impractical. The analysis and merging approach involves the designer in the design wop for a constant evaluation, modification and suggestions for conflict resolution.

iv) The basic philosophy behind the analysis and merging approach is to drive the integration by an analysis of the semantic properties of the input views. After identifying similarities and conflicts, the methodology tries to reach a global representation of data which is the "best compromise" among a given set of local views. The synthesis approach driven purely by dependencies cannot have this compromise notion.

Design guidelines vs. automated tools

The synthesis approach discussed above tends to be suitable for a fully automated design system. Since it requires little designer intervention, it can work by supplying all relevant information at the start and cranking out a design. The suitability of such a design in practice can be questioned.

The analysis and merging approach works more by providing design guidelines and design heuristics. As such, no claims can be made regarding its completeness or its guarantees of producing a workable design. The tools based on this approach can at best be semi-automated so that they deal with the large volume and complexity of the problem, yet leave the "design judgement" to the designer.

In an extreme situation, the formal approach may degenerate into the practical cookbook approach of classification (B) above, if the analysis is incomplete, in that it does not cover all possible cases in every situation. To be suitable for total automation, an approach must be algorithmic in nature. A non-algorithmic but heuristically, based approach is more suitable for an expert system.

4. FURTHER ELABORATION OF THE FORMAL APPROACH

Since the DATAID methodology falls in the category called the formal
approach, it is pertinent to discuss a few relevant issues here.

A. ISSUES RELATED TO INDIVIDUAL TOOLS:

When a methodology is as broad in its coverage as the DATAID, there
is a problem regarding what tools are the most appropriate tools and
how should they work together?

Design tools can generally be classified by the specific function(s)
which they perform or the part of design they automate. The usual
approach is to have the tools approach the five steps of design (see
2.) independently. This is possible because there is a fairly good
separation among these five steps so that the inputs and outputs of
each step can be **a priori** defined.

The above separation among tools also leads to the related problem
of their eventual integration or co-ordination. This integration can
best be accomplished by using a "common bus" through which design
data is transferred back and forth. It has been advocated (e.g. see
[20]) that a data dictionary system is the ideal vehicle for this
interchange of data.

The present tools mentioned in Part I of the book can also be attri-
buted to the different steps of design. See Table 1. As this table
demonstrates, the existing DATAID design tools cover the full Spectrum of design; the scope of tools is actually over-lapping.

	Tools	Phases of Design
	CATRA NLDA	1. Req.Collection and Analysis
	DIALOGO	2. Conceptual Design(View Modeling)
	GINCOD INCOD-DTE	3. View Integration
	EASYMAP	4. Logical Design (Schema Mapping)
ISIDE	IDEA EROS EOS	5. Physical Design and Optimization

Table 1 - Relationship of Design Tools and Design Steps.

B. ISSUES RELATED TO A COMPREHENSIVE/INTEGRATED METHODOLOGY.

Several issues are significant to the construction of a single,
comprehensive and formal approach to database design:

Role of the processing information:
The database design process can be either data driven, process

driven or both. Kahn [17] pointed out that it is necessary to consider both, the "the information structure perspective", and "the
usage perspective" in performing information systems analysis and
design. In general, it is very difficult to make use of the processing requirements to produce an efficient design from the early steps
during design. The obvious reason is that meaningful comparisons
among alternative structures cannot be drawn until the physical
design step. Approaches such as the logical record access approach
have been suggested [28] and utilized in some existing work [22,
7], but they should be looked upon as guidelines for selecting a
good initial feasible solution.

The DATAID methodology provides a detailed analysis of the processing information in the form of events and transactions [10] to be
utilized in the physical design.

Binary versus n-ary integration:
This is a basic design issue at the heart of the view integration
step. Binary integration proceeds by starting with a nucleus global
schema and incrementally incorporates an additional user view into
it each time. The DATAID methodology incorporates the work of Batini
et al. (e.g. [3, 4]) in view integration which is based on this
philosophy. This approach is easier to implement in that the complexity of each step is limited; however, it creates the problem of
ordering of schemas for integration. The number of iteration steps
is large and the outcome depends upon what schema transformations
are utilized during the integration process. It is also difficult to
predict the nature of conflicts that might arise when certain
choices are made early on during integration. Navathe and Gadgil
[21] proposed a variation of this approach by dividing user views
into classes based on some integration policy or other available
information. Integration could be first applied within classes and
then among classes.

El-Masri et al. [12] are pursuing a straight n-ary approach to
integration by supplying all the interobject and inter-relationship
information during an interactive data-collection or pre-integration
phase. This obviates several of the above difficulties; however, the
integration algorithm becomes more complex.

Role of Constraints:
Typically, the existing methodologies have done little to incorporate semantic constraints directly into the methodology. In the
DATAID methodology, constraints in the form of intraschema and
interschema properties are considered [4]; similarly the interdependencies among events are modeled in the form of Petri nets
[10], Navathe and Gadgil [21] pointed out that the designers
knowledge about the user views must be supplied in the form of
intra-views must be supplied in the form of intra-view and inter-
view assertions. They did not give a procedure for how these must be
internally processed.

The natural language component of DATAID, including the tool NLDA
has this difficult task of identifying such constraints and extracting them from the other extraneous details.

Constraints can be divided into two major categories. The first
includes structural and semantic constraints which refer to the
inherent properties of data and their relationships. These must be
included in the design.

The second category includes run-time or update constraints. They do not affect the design of the database per se unless the efficiency of database performance is included in design.

It is mandatory that run time constraints provided by the require-ments analysis phase be preserved and enforced to keep the database in a consistent state after it is designed and implemented.

C. ORTHOGONAL ISSUES

A database design methodology works with a certain philosophy by adopting a certain position against several of the above issues. For example, the DATAID methodology works with the processing informa-tion - its specification and utilization - in a certain way; it incorporates certain kinds of constraints and leaves out the update constraints etc.; the methodology is also based on a binary incre-mental integration strategy and incorporates a certain set of physi-cal design decisions.

Besides the above "stands" that a methodology must take on issues, it also works with certain other choices that must be made. In this author´s opinion, such choices are more or less orthogonal to the basic workings of the methodology. These choices include the selec-tion of a semantic data model, the choice of target database manage-ment systems or the type of physical design decisions incorporated. The broad philosophy behind the methodology remains unaffected by these choices. Thus, the fact that the DATAID methodology chooses a specific set of constructs in its extensions to the entity relation-ship model is not really constraining.
Assume that one needs to solve a specific database design problem in an organization using a semantic data model S and for a specific target database management system T. If a methodology such as DATAID is to be applied, the step-by-step approach still stays. What will have to change are the details of schema operations for comparison, merging and transformations, the mapping of semantic model con-structs from S into the specific constructs of T, as well as the specific physical design parameters for T. This must be kept in mind while considering the so-called general methodologies. To be attrac-tive, a methodology must be rich and complete in its analysis. The orthogonal issues are less significant.

D. EXPERT SYSTEMS APPROACH

The formal approaches in the analysis and merging category are ideally suited for developing an expert system for database design. Expert systems basically operate on the principle of combining the human judgement or selection with the expert guidance provided by a machine to achieve a high degree of performance. The database design methodologies such as DATAID lend themselves to this approach for the following reasons.

a) By the very nature of these methodologies, the database design is driven by a number of rules, heuristics or design guidelines.

b) Design is looked upon as a co-operative activity when the machine can sort out a very large number of alternative solutions and the designer/user can provide suggestions or make subjective deci-sions in choices of names, structures, etc.

c) Constant interaction and feedback is critical to producing an acceptable design. An expert system can provide explanations and analysis of tradeoffs to enable the designer/user understand the proposed solutions.

5. ISSUES OF DESIGN TOOL ARCHITECTURE

Earlier in this chapter we stated that the DATAID design tools are independent tools. Considering the complexity of the database design problem, it is safe to assume that this trend will continue. Even if a single design aid system is constructed, it will have to be modularly designed so that the separate problems corresponding to the steps of design mentioned in 2. are modularly addressed by separate tools.

Each design tool possesses most of the following common features:

a) Interfaces: These provide the interaction/dialog with the designer, communication with another tool or with a central repository of design information such as a data dictionary. The usefulness of a design methodology is critically dependent upon the quality of the interface of the particular tool which collects all the relevant information from the human user. Natural language interface such as the used in the NLDA tool is highly desirable, but has the disadvantage of a high amount of complex processing. It may allow incorrect, inconsistent, and ambiguous statements about the requirements unless some human screening of the input information is performed. Tools such as GINCOD are ideal for interacting with the designer since they like to work with diagrams and particularly so when they are laid out in an aesthetic way. In the DIALOGO tool the user interaction is performed by means of a single language (Galileo) to perform a variety of tasks including the specification of the structure and semantics of data as well as a process specification [1].

b) Analytical Component: Each design tool must provide some analysis capability to be of value. As shown in Table 2, the type of analysis performed varies depending upon the nature of the tool. The Analysis relates to consistency checking, naming analysis, conflicts detection among different representations etc. This aspect of tools mainly makes the tool worthwhile to use. It also enables the designer deal with realistically large sized problems, since manually such analyses are extremely tedious and error-prone. If the analysis can be performed using algorithms that produce results from the given information without user´s (designer´s) intervention, such a tool runs until it produces a valid solution or reports on errors (e.g. DIALOGO). On the other hand, if the analysis reveals conditions where user´s subjective choice or judgement is called upon from time to time, such a tool runs intermittently requiring constant user intervention, (e.g. INCOD-DTE).

c) Display of Results: Tools display their results in various forms - e.g. diagrammatic form (GINCOD), message form reporting on the specific results of analysis such as synonym-homonym problems, structural or semantic conflicts (e.g. INCOD-DTE, DIALOGO, etc.)

Some of the commercial tools such as DATA DESIGNER claim it as an advantageous feature to be able to show various reports by sorting and aggregating the collected design information in different formats.

d) Use of Design Heuristics: Whenever the design tool uses design guidelines or rules of thumb etc. in its analysis, one could say that the tool has built-in heuristic rules. For example the GIN-COD tool uses an expression based on the number of crossings among the lines to determine its aesthetic quality, and the EROS-EOS and IDEA tools find an implementation solution which has the minimal global response time on the basis of an heuristic algorithm.
Table 2 shows whether or not design heuristics are employed in the tools covered in this book.

e) Tradeoff Analysis: This is a desirable feature in any design system. When a designer is presented with a set of alternatives to choose from, he must be presented with adequate comparative information that will enable him to make the choice. This information is not always proved by the design tools surveyed in this book or available in general.

f) Design Verification: One other type of feature that will be desirable to have with the design tools is one of verification. There must be some mechanism by which the results of a tool are verified against the inputs presented to the tool. For example a conceptual schema design could be verified against all the processing specification supplied (e.g. DIALOGO) and the implementation design could be evaluated with respect to the expected transaction response time (e.g. IDEA, EOS).

6. GENERAL REMARKS ABOUT THE **DATAID** METHODOLOGY

Throughout this chapter we tried to relate the different issues to the DATAID methodology and the design tools covered in this volume. The purpose of this section is to highlight some of the strong points and weaknesses of this methodology.

Strengths of the DATAID methodology

Without doubt, DATAID can be considered as probably the most comprehensive piece of work to date which provides a unified methodological framework. It spans all steps of the design process; the steps are handled in a consistent way in that the output of one phase matches the inputs to the next phase. The analysis - qualitative as well as quantitative - performed in each step of design is quite elaborate and extensive.

The methodology, while being a formal methodology, is quite pragmatic in its perspective in that it uses design guidelines and heuristics that are derived from experience and appear reasonable. The methodology recognizes that a purely synthetic approach to design is not workable and hence gives constant scope to designer intervention and the use of designer's judgement during the selection of alternatives.

The data model used during conceptual schema design is the enhanced Entity-Relationship model. It has been reported [8] that the E-R model is by far the most widely known and used model in practice. Hence this choice appears to enhance the possibility that the DATAID

Tool Name	Phase of Design to which it is applied most	Type of Interface	Type of Analysis	Type of Display	Use of Design Heuristic
NLDA	Requirements Analysis	Natural Language (English or Italian)	Syntactic and Semantic Analysis of Requirements	Messages	Yes
CATRA	Requirements Analysis	Commands/ Forms	Intra and Inter Glossary Checks of Consistency and Completeness	Scenarios/ Messages	Yes
INCOD- DTE	Conceptual Design	Commands/ Forms	Consistency Checking Conflicts Analysis	Scenarios/ Messages	Yes
GINCOD	Conceptual Design	Commands/ Graphic sensors	Aesthetic Placement of E-R Diagrams	Diagrams	Yes
DIALOGO	Conceptual Design	Conceptual Language Galileo	Type Checking Execution Validation	Messages	No
EASYMAP	Logical Design	Commands	Performance Analysis	Messages	Yes
IDEA	Relational Physical Design	Commands	Performance Analysis and Evaluation	Messages	Yes
EROS+ EOS	Codasyl Physical Design	Commands	Performance Analysis and Evaluation	Messages	Yes

Table 2 - Features of Design Tools.

methodology would be actually used. The extension in terms of allowing generalization hierarchies, set-subset relationships, total-
partial relationships, cardinality constraints etc. seems very
important and lend semantic richness to the methodology. The
diagrammatic notation should make the communication of design
easier.

The methodology seems well suited to act as a basis for an expert
system environment. It provides a very good documentation of the
design decisions through various phases of design.

Shortcomings of the DATAID methodology

A few limitations and shortcomings of the methodology are worth noting:

There is a certain lack of preciseness and ad hoc nature to the
methodology in every phase. This is so because it is not a fully
automatic synthesis oriented methodology, and there is a lot of sub-
jectivity involved in the design decisions.

Although the methodology is complete in terms of covering all steps
of design, within each step the claim to completeness is again difficult to make. The analysis of natural language during requirements
analysis or the analysis of semantic conflicts during view integration cannot ever be proven to be complete because there is no limit
to how much and what type of analyses are relevant.

The methodology does not seem to possess a uniform degree of formalism - which is not necessarily a drawback. Concepts like filtering
of a natural language input are too informal, while those like event
analysis by using Petri nets are very sound and formal.

While it is shown in [6] with a large illustrative example as to
how a design activity proceeds from step-to-step, the co-ordination
among steps and the integration of design tools needs to be
addressed in more detail. It is clear that the input of a design
step is derived from the output of the previous step; what needs to
be researched is how all steps can share and update common design
information using a dictionary system.

The manual method has actually been tried in banking environments
and in governmental institutions. So far, there is no actual experience with using the semi-automated tools mentioned in this volume in
a cascaded fashion to perform a single large design. Such experience
will be valuable to debug the tools and enhance the methodology.

Application Development:
A database design methodology can only be considered successful if
the database is properly designed to support the intended applications. Typically, design methodologies and tools have overlooked the
problem of application development within the realm of database
design. Vetter [29] incorporates some application design toward
the end of his book on a database design methodology. Currently,
different commercial methodologies are being marketed for structured
analysis, top-down refinement, functional decomposition, etc. of
applications. It will be necessary in the future to combine these
two disciplines into a single discipline of database and applications design.

REFERENCES

[1]   Albano A., Cardelli L., and Orsini R., "Galileo: A Strongly Typed, Interactive Conceptual Language", ACM TODS, 1985 (to appear).

[2]   Atre S., "Data Base: Structured Techniques for Design, Performance and Management, Wiley Interscience, 1980.

[3]   Batini C., Lenzerini M., and Santucci G., "A Computer Aided Methodology for Conceptual Database Design" Information Systems, Vol. 7 Number 3, 1982.

[4]   Batini C., and Lenzerini M., "A Methodology for Data Schema Integration in the Entity Relationship Model, "IEEE Transactions on Software Engineering, Vol. SE-10, Number 6, November 1984.

[5]   Casanova M. A., and Vidal V.M.P., "Towards a Sound View Integration Methodology," Proceedings of the Second Symposium on Principles of Database Systems, ACM, New York, March 1983.

[6]   Ceri S. (Ed.), "Methodology and Tools for Data Base Design", North Holland, 1983.

[7]   Ceri S., Navathe S.B., and Wiederhold G., "Distribution Design of Logical Database Schemas", IEEE Transactions on Software Engineering", Vol. SE-9, Number 4, July 1983.

[8]   Childers, "Database Design: A Survey of Logical and Physical Design Techniques", Database, Vol. 15, Number 1, March 1983.

[9]   Curtice R.M., and Jones P.E., "Logical Data Base Design", Van Nostrand, 1982.

[10] De Antonellis V., Zonta B., "Modelling Events in Data Base Application Design", Proc. Int. Conf. on Very Large Data Bases, Cannes, 1981.

[11] Elmasri R., and Navathe S.B., "Object Integration in Database Design", Proceedings of the IEEE COMPDEC Conference, Los Angeles, April 1984.

[12] Elmasri R., Larson J., Navathe S.B., Sushidhar T., "A Comprehensive Methodology for Conceptual Design of Databases", in preparation.

[13] Gane C., and Sarson T., "Structured System Analysis: Tools and Techniques", Prentice Hall, 1979.

[14] Howe D.R., "Data Analysis for Database Design", Edward Arnold, 1983.

[15] I.B.M., "Database Design Aid: General Information Manual and Designer's Guide", Publication Number 5 GH20-1626-0 abd GH20-1627-0, 1975.

[16] Inmon W.H., and Friedman L.J., "Design Review Methodology for a Data Base Environment", Prentice Hall, 1982.

[17]   Kahn B.K., "A Method for Describing Information Required by the Database Design Process", Proceedings of the ACM-SIGMOD International Concerence on Management of Data, June 1976, ACM, New York.

[18]   Lum V.Y. et al., "1978 New Orleans Database Design Working Report", Proceedings of the 5th International Conference on Very Large Data Bases, Rio de Janeiro, Brazil, October 1979, pp. 328-339.

[19]   Mannino M.V., and Effelsberg W., "Matching Tecnicques in Global Schema Design", Proccedings of the IEEE COMPDEC Conference, Los Angeles, April 1984.

[20]   Navathe S.B. et al., "Logical Database Design", in Database Directions: Informations Resource Management - Strategies and Tools, NBS Special Publication Number 500-92 (Alan Goldfine, Ed.), U.S. Dpt. of Commerce, September 1982, pp. 73-140.

[21]   Navathe S.B., and Gadgil S., "A Methodology of View Integration in Logical Database Design", Proceedings of the Eight International Conference on Very Large Data Bases, Mexico City, September 1982.

[22]   Navathe S.B. and Cheng A., "Database Schema Mapping from an Extended Entity Relationship Model into the Hierarchical Model", Proceedings of the Third Entity Relationship Conference, Assaheim, CA, October 1983, North Holland.

[23]   Navathe S.B., Sashidhar T., Elmasri R., "Merging Relationships for Schema Integration", Proceedings of the Tenth Int. Conf. on Very Large Data Bases, Singapore, VLDB Foundation, August 1984.

[24]   Yao S.B., Navathe S.B., Kunii T., and Weldon J.I., eds, "Database Design Techniques I: Requirements and Logical Structures", Proceedings of the NYU Symposium on Logical Database Design, Published as Lecture Notes in Computer Science, Vol. 132, Springer Verlag, New York, 1982.

[25]   Palmer I.R., "Practicalities in Applying a Formal Methodology to Data Analysis", in [24].

[26]   Raver, N. and G.U. Hubbard, "Automated Logical Database Design: concepts and applications", IBM Systems Journal, Number 3, 1977.

[27]   Sheppard D., "Data Base Design Methodology - Parts I and II", Awerbach Data Base Management Series, Partfolios Number 5 23-01-01,02, 1977.

[28]   Teorey T.J., and Fry J.P., "The Logical Record Access Approach to Database Design", ACM Computing Surveys, Vol. 12, June 1980.

[29]   Vetter M., and Maddison R.N., "Database Design Methodology", Prentice Hall International, 1981.

[30]   Yao S., Navathe S.B., and Weldon J., "An Integrated Approach to Logical Database Design", in [24].

APPENDIX
THE DATAID PUBLICATION LIST

THE DATAID PUBLICATION LIST

[1]   Albano A., Occhiuto M.E., Orsini R. "A Uniform Management of
      Persistent and Complex Data in Programming Languages" in: Atkin-
      son M. (ed.) "INFOTECH State of the Art Report on Database"
      series 9, n.4 (Pergamon INFOTECH, 1981) 321-344.

[2]   Albano A., Orsini R. "An Interactive Integrated System to Design
      and Use Data Bases" in: Brodie M.L. and Zilles S.N. (eds.) ACM
      SIGMOD Special Issue 11, 2 (1981) 91-93.

[3]   Albano A. "Type Hierarchies and Semantic Data Models" ACM Sig-
      plan Systems (San Francisco, 1983) 178-186.

[4]   Albano A., Capaccioli M., Occhiuto M.E., Orsini R. "A Modulari-
      zation Mechanism for Conceptual Modeling" Proc. IX Int. Conf. on
      VLDB (Firenze, Italy, 1983) 232-240.

[5]   Albano A., Orsini R. "Dialogo: An interactive Environment for
      Conceptual Design in Galileo" in: Ceri S. (ed.) "Methodology and
      Tools for Database Design" (North-Holland, 1983) 229-253.

[6]   Albano A., Capaccioli M., Orsini R. "La Definizione del Galileo
      (Versione 83/6)" Rapp. Tech. Collana DATAID n.20 (Pisa, 1983).

[7]   Albano A., Giannotti F., Orsini R., Pedreschi D., "Data Types
      and Objects in Conceptual Modeling" First Int. Workshop on
      Expert Database Systems (Kiawah Island, 1984) 603-610.

[8]   Albano A., Orsini R. "A Prototyping Approach to Database Appli-
      cations Development" IEEE Database Engineering (1984) (to
      appear).

[9]   Albano A., Cardelli L., Orsini R. "Galileo: a Strongly Typed,
      Interactive Conceptual Language" ACM TODS (1985) (to appear).

[10] Atzeni P., Chen P.P. "Completeness of Query Languages for the
      Entity Relationship Model" in: Chen P.P. (ed.) "Entity Relation-
      ship Approach to Information Modeling and Analysis" (North-
      Holland, 1983) 111-124.

[11] Atzeni P., Batini C., Lenzerini M., Villanelli F. "INCOD: a Sys-
      tem for Conceptual Design of Data and Transactions in the Entity
      Relationship Model" in: Chen P.P. (ed.) "Entity Relationship
      Approach to Information Modeling and Analysis" (North-Holland,
      1983) 379-414.

[12] Atzeni P., Batini C., DeAntonellis V., Lenzerini M., Villanelli
      F., Zonta B. "A Computer Aided Tool for Conceptual Database
      Design" in: Schneider H.J., Wasserman A.I. (eds.) "Automated
      Tools for Information Systems Design" (North-Holland, 1982) 85-
      106.

[13] Atzeni P., Batini C., Carboni E., DeAntonellis V., Lenzerini M.,
      Villanelli F., Zonta B. "INCOD-DTE: a System for Interactive
      Conceptual Design of Data, Transactions and Events" in: Ceri S.
      (ed.) "Methodology and Tools for Database Design" (North-
      Holland, 1983) 205-228.

[14] Balbo G., DiLeva A., Sacco G.M. "Adaptive Query Optimizer in a
      point-to-point Networks" in: Schreiber F., Litwin W. (eds.)
      "Distributed Data Sharing Systems" (North-Holland, 1985) 119-
      129.

[15] Balbo G., Demo G.B., DiLeva A., Giolito P. "Dynamics Analysis in
      Database Design" Proc. IEEE Int. Conf. on Data Engineering (Los
      Angeles, 1984) 238-243.

[16] Batini C., Lenzerini M., Moscarini M. "Views Integration" in: Ceri S. (ed.) "Methodology and Tools for Database Design" (North-Holland, 1983) 57-84.

[17] Batini C., Nardelli E., Talamo M., Tamassia R. "A Graph Theoretic Approach to Aesthetic Layout of Information Systems Diagrams" Proc. 14-th Int. Workshop on Graphtheoretic Concepts in Computer Science (Berlin, 1984) (to appear).

[18] Batini C., Lenzerini M. "A System for Interactive Conceptual Database Design" Proc. 18-th ACM IEEE Design Automation Conf. (Nashville, 1981).

[19] Batini C., Lenzerini M. "A Methodology for Data Schema Integration in the Entity Relationship Model" IEEE Trans. on Software Engineering (1984) (to appear).

[20] Batini C., Lenzerini M., Santucci G. "Computer Aided Methodology for Conceptual Database Design" Information Systems, vol.7, 3 (1982).

[21] Batini C., Talamo M., Tamassia R. "Aesthetic Layout of Sparse Diagrams" Proc. IASTED 2-nd Int. Symp. on Applied Informatics (Innsbruck, 1984).

[22] Batini C., Talamo M., Tamassia R. "Computer Aided Layout of Conceptual Diagrams" J. of Systems and Software, 4.1 (1984) (to appear).

[23] Batini C., Demo B., DiLeva A. "A Methodology for Conceptual Design of Office Data Bases" Information Systems, Vol. 9, n.3 (1984) (to appear).

[24] Batini C., DeAntonellis V., DiLeva A. "Database Design Activities within the DATAID Project" IEEE Database Engineering (1984) (to appear).

[25] Bertaina P., DiLeva A., Giolito P. "Logical Design in Codasyl and Relational Environment" in: Ceri S. (ed.) "Methodology and Tools for Database Design" (North-Holland, 1983) 85-118.

[26] Bertaina P., DiLeva A., Giolito P., Iacobelli C., Marrone V. "An Automatic Tool for Logical Database Design" Proc. IEEE First Int. Conf. on Computers and Applications, (Peking, 1984) 385-391.

[27] Bertocchi R., DeAntonellis V., Zhang X.W. "An Interactive Events Handling System" Proc. IEEE First Int. Conf. on Computers and Applications, (Peking, 1984) 523-532.

[28] Bertocchi R., DeAntonellis V., Zonta B. "Concepts and Mechanisms for Handling Dynamics in Database Applications" Proc. ACM ICS (Teubner, Stuttgart 1983).

[29] Bonanno R., Maio D., Tiberio P. "An Approximation Algorithm for Secondary Index Selection in Relational Database Physical Design" The Computer Journal (1985) (to appear).

[30] Bonfatti F., Maio D., Tiberio P. "A Separability Based Method for Secondary Index Selection" in: Ceri S. (ed.) "Methodology and Tools for Database Design" (North-Holland, 1983) 149-160.

[31] Bonfatti F., Maio D., Spadoni M., Tiberio P. "An Indexing Tech-
     nique for Relational Databases" Proc. IEEE COMPSAC (Chicago,
     1980) 784-791.

[32] Bracchi G., Baldissera C., Ceri S., Pelagatti G. "Interactive
     Specification and Formal Verification of User's Views in Data-
     base Design" Proc. 5-th Int. Conf. on VLDB (Rio de Janeiro,
     1979).

[33] Bracchi G., Ceri S., Pelagatti G. "Structured Methodology for
     Designing Static and Dynamic Aspects of Database Applications"
     Information Systems, vol.6, n.1 (1981) 31-45.

[34] Bracchi G., Ceri S., Pelagatti G. "A Set of Integrated Tools for
     the Conceptual Design of Database Schemas and Transactions" in:
     Ceri S. (ed.) "Methodology and Tools for Database Design"
     (North-Holland, 1983) 181-204.

[35] Bracchi G., Ceri S., Pelagatti G. Integrated Specification of
     Static and Dynamic Requirements os Database Applications" Proc.
     IFIP80 World Cong. (North-Holland, 1980).

[36] Bussolati U., Ceri S., DeAntonellis V., Zonta B. "Views Concep-
     tual Design" in: Ceri S. (ed.) "Methodology and Tools for Data-
     base Design" (North-Holland, 1983) 25-56.

[37] Bucci G., Maio D., Sartori C. "Performance Modeling of a Distri-
     buted Information System" Proc. Int. AMSE Winter Symp. (Bermude,
     1983).

[38] Ceri S., Navathe S.B., Wiederhold G. "Distribution Design of
     Logical Database Schemas" IEEE Trans. Software Engineering, SE-
     9, n.4 (1983).

[39] Ceri S., Martella G., Pelagatti G. "Optimal File Allocation for
     for a Distributed Database on a Network of Minicomputers" in:
     Deen S.M. et al. (eds.) "Proc. 2-nd Int. Conf. on Databases"
     (Heyden, 1980).

[40] Ceri S., Martella G., Pelagatti G. "Optimal File Allocation in a
     Computer Network: a Solution Method Based on the Knapsack Prob-
     lem" Computer Networks, vol.6, n.5 (1982).

[41] Ceri S., Pelagatti G. "A Solution Method for the Non-additive
     Resource Allocation Problem in Distributed System Design" Infor-
     mation Processing Letters, vol.15, n.4 (1982).

[42] Ceri S., Navathe S., Wiederhold G., Dou J. "Vertical Partition-
     ing Algorithms for Database Design" ACM TODS, vol.9, n.4 (1984)
     (to appear).

[43] Ceri S., Negri M., Pelagatti G. "Horizontal Data Partitioning in
     Database Design" Proc. ACM SIGMOD Conf., (Orlando, 1982).

[44] Ceri S., Navathe S. "A Methodology for the Distribution Design
     of Databases" Proc. IEEE Spring Computer Conf. '83 (S.Francisco,
     1983).

[45] Colombetti M., Guida G., Somalvico M. "NLDA: a Natural Language
     Reasoning System for the Analysis of Database Requirements" in:
     Ceri S. (ed.) "Methodology and Tools for Database Design"
     (North-Holland, 1983) 163-180.

[46] Colombetti M., Guida G., Pernici B., Somalvico M. "The Use of Natural Language in the Design of Databases" Pocitace a Umela Inteligencia (Computers and Artificial Intelligence), vol.1, 2 (1982) 135-152.

[47] Colombetti M., Guida G., Pernici B., Somalvico M. "Reasoning in Natural Language Designing a Database" in: Elithorn A., Banerji R. (eds.) "Artificial and Human Intelligence" (North-Holland, 1984).

[48] D'Atri A., Sacca' D. "A Graph-Theoretical Approach to Database Mapping" Proc. AICA Conf. (Roma, 1984) 218-233.

[49] DeAntonellis V., DegliAntoni G., Mauri G., Zonta B. "Extending the Entity Relationship Approach to Take into Account Historical Aspects of Systems" in: Chen P.P. (ed.) "E-R Approach to Systems Analysis and Design" (North-Holland, 1980).

[50] DeAntonellis V., Zonta B. "Modeling Events in Database Applications Design" Proc. 7-th Int. Conf. VLDB (Cannes, 1981).

[51] DeAntonellis V., Demo G.B. "Requirements Collection and Analysis" in: Ceri S. (ed.) "Methodology and Tools for Database Design" (North-Holland, 1983) 9-24.

[52] DeAntonellis V., DiLeva A. "DATAID-1: a Database Design Methodology" Information Systems, 10, 1 (1985) (to appear).

[53] DeAntonellis V., Zonta B. "A Causal Approach to Dynamics Modeling" IEEE Database Engineering (1984) (to appear).

[54] Demo G.B., DiLeva A., Batini C. "A Tool for Automatic Design of Business form Database" in: N. Naffah (ed.) "Office Information Systems (North-Holland, 1982) 73-84.

[55] Demo G.B., DiLeva A., Giolito P. "Database design prototyping in a CODASYL environment" in: Budde R. et al. (eds.) "Approaches to Prototyping" (Springer-Verlag, 1984) 188-201.

[56] Demo G.B., Codrino A., Iacobelli C., Marrone V. "Use and extension of DATAID1 Methodology to Database Software Design" Proc. IEEE Int. Conf. MELECON, (Atene, 1983).

[57] Demo G.B. "Program Analysis for Conversion from a Navigation to a Specification Database Interface" Proc. Int. Conf. VLDB'83 (Firenze, 1983).

[58] Demo G.B., Kundu S. "A Basic System for Decompiling CODASYL DML into a Relational Database Interface" Proc. Int. Conf. ICS'84 (Taipei, 1984).

[59] Demo G.B., DiLeva A., Giolito P. "An Entity Relationship Query Language" in: Sernadas A., Bubenko J., Olive' A. (eds.) Proc. IFIP Conf. TFAIS-85, Spain, (North Holland, 1985) (to appear).

[60] DiLeva A., Giolito P. "Database Facilities for Decision Support Systems" Proc. IEEE Int. Conf. on Systems, Man and Cybernetics (Bombay and New Dehly, 1983) 845-849.

[61] DiLeva A., Giolito P. "Automatic Logical Database Design in a CODASYL Environment" Proc. ACM-IEEE 4th. Jerusalem Conf. on Information Technology (Jerusalem, 1984) 350-357.

[62] Gaudioso M., Grano A., Manfredi F., Staniszkis W. "An Automatic Tool for Physical Data Structures Design in a Codasyl DBMS Environment" Proc. AICA Conf. (Napoli, 1983) 59-68.

[63] Guida G., Somalvico M. "Interacting in Natural Language with Artificial Systems: the DONAU Project" Information Systems, vol.5, 4 (1980) 333-344.

[64] Guida G., Tasso C."NLI: a Robust Interface for Natural Language Person-Machine Communication" Int. Journal of Man-Machine Studies, vol.17, 2 (1982) 417-433.

[65] Guida G., Somalvico M. "Interactivity and Incrementality in Natural Language Understanding Systems" Cybernetics and Systems, vol.12 (1981) 363-383.

[66] Lenzerini M., Santucci G. "Cardinality Constraints in the Entity Relationship Model" in: Davis C. et al. (eds.) "Entity Relationship Approach to Software Engineering" (North-Holland, 1983) 529-550.

[67] Maio D., Sartori C. "Queueing network models - A Tool for Relational Database Design" Proc. 8-th Int. CODATA Conf. (North-Holland, 1982) 178-182.

[68] Maio D., Sartori C. "A Queueing Network Model Approach for Evaluating Relational Database Performances" Proc. 4-th IASTED Int. Symp. (Lugano, 1983).

[69] Maio D., Scalas M.R., Tiberio P. "A Note on Estimating Access Costs in Relational Databases" Information Processing Letters, 19 (1984) 157-161.

[70] Maio D., Scalas M.R., Tiberio P. "Dynamic Non-dense Indexes in Relational Databases" Information Systems, 9, 3 (1985) 201-211.

[71] Orlando S., Rullo P., Staniszikis W. "Transaction Workload Evaluation in the Codasyl Database Environment" Proc. IEEE Int. Conf. on Data Engineering (Los Angeles, 1984) 562-569.

[72] Sacca' D., Staniszkis W. "Physical Database Design in a Codasyl Environment" Proc. AICA Conf. (Pavia, 1981) 881-891.

[73] Sacco G.M. "Distributed Query Evaluation in Local Area Networks" Proc. IEEE Int. Conf. on Data Engineering (Los Angeles, 1984) 510-516.

[74] Sartori C., Scalas M.R. "An Access Method for Relational DBMSs adaptable to Irregular Data Distributions" Proc. 9-th CODATA Conf. (North-Holland, 1985) (to appear).

[75] Scalas M.R., Tiberio P. "The Use of the Nested Block Method for Computing Joins" Proc. IEEE COMPSAC (Chicago, 1983) 455-463.

[76] Schkolnick M., Tiberio P. "A Note on Estimating the Maintenance Costs in a Relational Database" ACM TODS (1985) (to appear).

[77] Spaccapietra S., Demo G.B., DiLeva A., Parent C., PerezDeCelis C., Belfar K. "An Approach to Effective Heterogeneous Database Cooperation" in: Van de Riet R.P., Litwin W. (eds.) "Distributed Data Sharing Systems" (North-Holland, 1982) 209-218.

[78] Spaccapietra S., Demo G.B., DiLeva A., Parent C. "SCOOP: a System for COOPeration between Existing Heterogeneous Distributed Databases and Programs" IEEE Database Engineering, vol.5, n.4 (1982) 52-57.

[79] Spaccapietra S., Demo G.B., Parent C., "SCOOP: a System for Integrating Existing Heterogeneous Distributed Databases and Application Programs" Proc. IEEE Int. Conf. INFOCOM (San Diego, 1983).

[80] Staniszkis W., Rullo P., Gaudioso M., Orlando S. "Probabilistic Approach to Evaluation of Data Manipulation Algorithms in a Codasyl Database Environment" Proc. Second Int. Conf. on Databases (Cambridge, 1983) 332-357.

[81] Staniszkis W., Rullo P., Orlando S. "Transaction Workload Analysis in the Codasyl Database Performance Predictor EOS" Proc. 7-th Int. Seminar on Database Management Systems (Budapest, 1983) 97-120.

[82] Staniszkis W., Rullo P., Orlando S. "Performance Oriented Database Design Laboratory" in: Bell D.A. (ed.) Infotech State-of-the-art Report: Database Performance (Pergamon Press, 1984) 132-160.

[83] Staniszkis W., Sacca' D., Manfredi F., Meccia A. "Physical Database Design for Codasyl DBMS" in: Ceri S. (ed.) "Methodology and Tools for Database Design" (North-Holland, 1983) 119-148.

[84] Tamassia R., Batini C., Talamo M. "An Algorithm for Automatic Layout of Entity Relationship Diagrams" in: Davis C. et al. (eds.) "Entity Relationship Approach to Software Engineering" (North-Holland, 1983) 421-440.

AUTHOR INDEX